Advanced ENGLISH Communication Skills Lab

Advanced ENGLISH Communication Skills Lab

Prof.K.R.Lakshminarayanan
Former Head
Department of Humanities and Social Sciences
Sri Venkateswara College of Engineering
Pennalur - Sriperumbudur
Tamizhnadu, India

SCITECH PUBLICATIONS (INDIA) PVT. LTD.
CHENNAI ❖ HYDERABAD ❖ KOLKATA ❖ PUNE ❖ BHUBANESWAR ❖ NEW DELHI

SCITECH PUBLICATIONS (INDIA) PVT. LTD.

Corp. Office: No.4, Anna Street, Chitlapakkam, CHENNAI – 600 064
E-mail: scitechcorp@yahoo.co.in

Reg. Office: 7/3c, Madley Road, T.Nagar, CHENNAI-600 017
E-mail: scitech@md5.vsnl.net.in
Visit us at: www.scitechbooks.in

Branches:

BHUBANESWAR: scitech_bbsr@yahoo.co.in

CHENNAI: scitech@md5.vsnl.net.in

HYDERABAD: scitech_hyd@yahoo.co.in

KOLKATA: scitech_kol@yahoo.co.in

PUNE: scitech_pune@yahoo.co.in

NEW DELHI: scitech_del@yahoo.co.in

Second Reprint – October 2010

978 81 8371 187 6

Production Co-ordinator: K. Madhu Sudhan

Published by: M. R. Purushothaman for Scitech Publications (India) Pvt. Ltd.
3-4-249/1, Beside Venkataramana Theatre Lane, Street No.2, Lingampally,
Kachiguda, Hyderabad -500 027. Printed at: Sathya Bharath Printers, Hyderabad.

PREFACE

Dear Student

This Coursebook—**Advanced English Communications Skills Lab**—is based on the Syllabus for second semester of the third year B.Tech. Course of Jawaharlal Nehru Technological University.

This Coursebook fulfils the expectation of the Syllabus by *integrating theory and lab course* to enable you to use 'good' English. Besides treating the Syllabus content in depth, it provides additional information, which I know will be helpful to you.

Part *One* covers Functional English (lots of 'formal', 'semi-formal' and 'informal' dialogues), Vocabulary building (lots of exercises, including those on 'analogy'), Group discussion, Interview skills, Resume writing (with how to get an electronic resume ready), Reading comprehension (how to improve comprehension and reading speed), Technical report writing. It **includes** guidance and exercises on (1) 'Listening' which is a vital component of communication skills (and helps you with TOEFL preparation), and (2) 'Sounds of the English Language' (to help you become an *educated* user of English). It also treats '**essay writing**' in depth, which will help you with the 'writing section' of TOEFL.

Part *Two* helps you comprehend, appreciate and develop *soft skills* that are essential for your personality growth and professional competence. It provides **additional** information on '***Creativity***', an essential skill for thinkers and researchers, which is what you will turn into in your professional career.

Parts *Three* and *Four* are added *attractions*. Part Three, entitled 'retaining the job', provides additional information on pair communication, brainstorming, oral presentation. It foresees the roles you will have to play as employees, and helps with discussion and tips. Part Four, entitled 'use of English', treats, with plenty of examples and exercises, formation of sentences and questions, concord, and reported speech, which you will find handy in answering 'structure section' of TOEFL and writing essays.

A CD goes with this Book. It guides and helps you to (1) **read** with appropriate pauses for and with comprehension, (2) **listen** to short and long passages and dialogues, (3) **pronounce** monophthongs, diphthongs, consonants in words and sentences, (4) **place accent** appropriately, (5) **utter** statements, questions, exclamations **with appropriate 'tones'**.

Enjoy learning!

K. R. Lakshminarayanan

CD Content—List

Practice (1) dialoguing/ role-play (2) reading for and with comprehension
(3) listening for and with comprehension (4) learning to pronounce sounds
(5) learning to use 'accent' (6) learning to use 'intonation' patterns

Track one -- **Introduction**

Functional English

Track two -- **Telephone conversations (10)**
Track three -- **Conversations in context (9)**

Reading Comprehension

Track four -- **Reading with appropriate pauses**
Track five -- **further practice (3 extracts from reading passages)**

Listening Comprehension

Track six -- **passages 1-10**
Track seven -- **passages 11, 12**
Track eight -- **passages 13, 14, 15**
Track nine -- **Ex. 47**
Track ten -- **Conversations (10), passages (4), lectures (2)**

Pronunciation, Accent and Intonation

Track eleven, twelve --}
thirteen --} **12 pure vowels**
Track fourteen -- **distinguishing vowels with minimal pairs**
Track fifteen -- **8 diphthongs**
-- **inappropriate pronunciation of some vowels and diphthongs**
Track sixteen -- **Commonly mispronounced words—1** (138 words)
Track seventeen -- **Commonly mispronounced words—2** (meaning change)
Track eighteen -- **difficulty with some consonant sounds**
Track nineteen -- **saying words with accent** (138 words)
Track twenty -- **'Rhythm' of the English language**
Track twenty-one -- **'Stress' for meaning change**
Track twenty-two -- **Three 'tones'**

Contents

Part I

Part II

This Part deals with the topics in the Syllabus listed under 'train2success.com'.

Part IV : Use of English 301 - 358

PART ONE

1. Functional English

1.1 Have a problem?

You may have problems using English to speak and listen. Or you may be really good at using English. If you have problems, try the help given below. If you have no problems, help your classmates who have, using the 32 dialogues in the next few pages. You can also go one step further. You and your friends who are as good as you are can spend time with those who hesitate to approach you for help because they cannot use English like you do; you can help these with a 50-50 mix of English and Thelugu initially, a 60-40 mix, a 70-30 mix, a 80-20 mix and finally using only English. This will be a great service on your part! And don't be condescending, please.

1.2 Aim for accuracy

You may have had your school education through a medium other than English. As a result, you experience difficulty using English to make friends, to share your thoughts, to listen to others'. Your difficulty increases when you fear you might be laughed at or you might be looked down upon.

It's this fear that has made you tongue-tied. And you allow this fear to control you. You allow this fear to make you underestimate yourself and your capabilities. Remove that fear, don't let it take control of your future! Believe in yourself for you're as good as anybody else, you have the God-given ability to learn to use any language. How do you do this? You have to speak in English. You **have to make mistakes**. You have to *learn from your mistakes*. This is how you learnt Thelugu. This is how you'll learn English. There is no other way. So, speak, use every opportunity to speak, don't bother about what others think of you; to you, your goal is important. So speak, make mistakes, continue to speak, make mistakes, speak and suddenly you'll find, to your surprise, you're as good as everyone else.

To help you experience this, below are 32 pair dialogues. Each pair has 'a' and 'b' dialogues—short and long. The 'fluency dialogues' reflect how you'd be using English initially, and the 'accuracy dialogues' show you how you should be expressing the 'a' thoughts. The dialogues have one or two participants speaking English accurately.

Practise the 32 'b' dialogues in class and elsewhere. You can switch roles so that you also get to say 'accurate' part of these dialogues.

1.3 Dialogues for practice

All dialogues with numbers and letter 'a' are how you are likely to say what you want to say. There are errors here. Continue to speak with errors. In time, you'll speak like you see in dialogues under 'accuracy'.

All dialogues with numbers + letter 'b' are how you should be saying what you want to say.

fluency
1a

accuracy
1b

1. self-introduction

1a (fluency)

Shakti : My name is Shakti. Your name?

Gopal : Gopal. Your subject?

Shakti : Mechanical. Your?

Gopal : ECE. 'B' batch. You?

Shakti : 'C' batch. I, you friends?

Gopal : Yes.

Shakti : Thanks, Gopal. Bye.

Gopal : Bye.

1b (accuracy)

Shakti : My name is Shakti. [extends his hand]

Gopal : [shakes his hand] I'm Gopal. Mine is ECE branch. 'B' batch. What is yours?

Shakti : I got Mechanical, the branch I wanted. Mine is 'C'. Can we be friends?

Gopal : I got my choice, too. Yes, we'll be friends.

Shakti : Thanks, Gopal.

Gopal : Glad to know you. Bye.

Shakti : Glad to know you, too. Bye.

The underlined expressions in *1a* are not wrong for a beginner like you. You are clear in what you want to say. And that is very important when you're beginning to speak.

1b helps you to save time by giving you the right expressions when 'introduction' takes place. In fact, all dialogues in 'b' help save time. They contain the right expressions.

---

fluency
2a

accuracy
2b

2. helping someone

2a (fluency)

Shakti : Hello! Your pen?

Monica: Thanks.

Shakti : My name is Shakti.

Monica: Monica. Bye.

Shakti : Bye.

2b (accuracy)

Shakti : Hello, is this your pen?

Monica: [looks back] Oh yes, it is. Thanks.

Shakti : My name is Shakti.

Monica: I'm Monica. Bye.

Shakti : Bye.

2a contains no errors. But it is 'informal' which we use when we speak to friends. College students don't behave formally.

2b uses appropriate expressions because Shakti and Monica are meeting for the first time.

---

fluency	accuracy
3a	3b

3. asking to clear a doubt

3a	3b
Gopal : Sir, one doubt, sir. Mr Sriram: In today's lecture? Gopal : Yes, sir. Mr Sriram: Come to my room, okay?	Gopal: Excuse me, sir. I have a doubt. Mr Sriram: In today's lecture? Gopal: Yes, sir. Mr Sriram: Come to my room, okay?
The error is underlined.	Gopal is a student and is talking to a faculty, so, he has to use 'formal' language.

---

fluency	accuracy
4a	4b

4. locating a staff's room

4a	4b
Shakti : Gopal! Gopal : What Shakti? Shakti : Mr Sriram you know? Gopal : Who is he? Shakti : He teach Physics. Gopal : Okay. What you want to know? Shakti : I have doubt. Come to my room he say. Where is his room? Gopal : No idea. Ask Physics Dept. Shakti : Where it is? Gopal : Sorry, Shakti. I also don't know.	Shakti : Gopal! Gopal : Hello, Shakti. What's the matter? Shakti : Do you know Mr Sriram? Gopal : A lecturer? Shakti : Yes, he teach*es* us Physics. Gopal : I see. Mr Verma is our Physics lecturer. Why do you ask? Shakti : Got a doubt. He asked me to meet him in his room. Do you know where his room is? Gopal : No idea. Why don't you go to the Physics Dept.? Shakti : I have no idea where it is. Gopal : Sorry, Shakti. I don't know either.

- Questions are not asked like in *4a*. Questions are asked like in *4b*.
- The next error is 'reported' speech: "Come to my room he say" The correct 'reported' speech is: He asked me to meet him in his room.
  'Reported' speech is very common in conversations. So learn to report correctly.
- The next error is the use of 'also'. When you agree 'affirmatively', use 'also'; when you agree negatively, use 'either' like in 4b.
- "I see" is a statement that says you understand something or you come to know about something only at that moment.

fluency	accuracy
5a	5b

5. borrowing

5a		5b	
Selvi :	Ramya, give pen. My pen not write.	Selvi :	Ramya, you have a pen to spare? My pen is not writing.
Ramyaa :	Ink finished?	Ramyaa :	Is there no ink?
Selvi :	No.	Selvi :	There is.
Ramyaa :	Give me. Oh, ink is blocking. I repair in lunch *time*. Use this *upto that*.	Ramyaa :	Let me take a look. I think the ink is dry at the neck. I'll try to make it work during lunch break. Use this *for now*.
Selvi :	Thank you.	Selvi :	Thanks, Ramyaa.

- Say 'give me a pen' for 'give pen'. But it's better to say: you have a pen to spare?
- 'is there no ink' is better than 'ink finished'. *4b* contains better expressions. Learn them.
- It's not definite that Ramyaa can help Selvi. So, instead of 'repair' ''ll try to make it work' is better. 'during' is better than 'in'.

fluency

6a

accuracy

6b

6. clearing a doubt

Shanmugam : Mohan!

Mohan : Yes, Shanmugam.

Shanmugam : I no understand sum.

Mohan : Which one?
Sit down, Shanmugam.
Now listen carefully,
okay?

Shanmugam : Thank you, Mohan.

Mohan : You're welcome.

Shanmugam : Welcome? What it mean?

Mohan[laughing]: It's a polite reply.

Shanmugam : Another way to say?

Mohan : Yes. I can say
" Don't mention it."

Shanmugam : Thanks. In Thelugu I say
"no matter."

Mohan : Instead you can say 'no
problem.'

Shanmugam : Mohan!

Mohan : Yes, Shanmugam.

Shanmugam : I don't understand a sum.

Mohan : Which one?
Sit down, Shanmugam.
Now listen carefully,
okay?

Shanmugam : Thank you, Mohan.

Mohan : You're welcome.

Shanmugam : Welcome? What does it
mean?

Mohan[laughing]: It's a polite reply.

Shanmugam : Is there any other way of
saying this?

Mohan : Yes. I can say
"Don't mention it."

Shanmugam : Thanks. In Thelugu we
say "It doesn't matter."

Mohan : Instead you can say 'no
problem.'

1. 'no' is used only as a reply to a question. In sentences, we generally use 'not', and 'do' should come before it.
2. 'sum' is countable and in the singular and so article 'a' should come before it.

fluency 7a	accuracy 7b

7. a friendly enquiry

7a		7b	
Mohan	: Hello, Shanmugam!	Mohan	: Hello, Shanmugam!
Shanmugam	: Hello, Mohan!	Shanmugam	: Hello, Mohan!
Mohan	: How are you?	Mohan	: How are you?
Shanmugam	: I am good. How are you?	Shanmugam	: I am fine. How are you?
Mohan	: Fine. How was the weekend?	Mohan	: Fine. How was the weekend?
Shanmugam	: I go my village. It taked half hour by bus from Nellore.	Shanmugam	: I went to my village. It takes half an hour by bus from Nellore.
Mohan	: Okay, see you.	Mohan	: Okay, see you.
Shanmugam	: Okay, bye.	Shanmugam	: See you.

"Fine" without "thank you" is informal and common between friends and even between young people who may not know each other. Please avoid using 'good' in place of 'fine'.

---

fluency 8a	accuracy 8b

8. asking for notes

8a		8b	
Sekhar	: Robin, one minute.	Sekhar	: Robin, Just a moment/minute.
Robin	: Yes, Sekhar.	Robin	: Yes, Sekhar.
Sekhar	: Borrow me your Physics notes. I copy and give you.	Sekhar	: Lend me your Physics notes. I need to copy Monday's.
Robin	: Okay.	Robin	: Okay.
	[the next day]		[the next day]
Sekhar	: Hi, Robin!	Sekhar	: Hi, Robin!
Robin	: Hi, Sekhar! Have you finished copying?	Robin	: Hi, Sekhar! Have you finished copying?
Sekhar	: Yes, but some remain. Writing not clear.	Sekhar	: not completely. In some places your handwriting is not clear.
Robin	: Let me see.	Robin	: Let me see.

"borrow me" is a very common mistake. Say 'lend me' or 'I want to borrow….'

You can also say: "Are you done with copying?" instead of 'Have you finished copying?'

---

fluency 9a	accuracy 9b

9. asking for a loan

9a	9b
Shakti : Gopal! Gopal : What Shakti? Shakti : I…I want….. Gopal : Tell. Shakti : I want…..some…. money. Gopal : Money? How much? Shakti : hun….hundred. Gopal : For what? Shakti : Buy gift for my sister son birthday. Gopal : When? Shakti : tomorrow next day. Gopal : Will give. Will I Come? Shakti : Definitely.	Shakti : Gopal! Gopal : What Shakti? Shakti : I…I want….. Gopal : What? Shakti : I want…..some…. money. Gopal : Money? How much? Shakti : One hun….hundred. Gopal : What for? Shakti : To buy a gift for my nephew. I want to attend his birthday. Gopal : When? Shakti : The day after tomorrow. Gopal : I'll lend you the money. Can I join you? Shakti : Sure.

'I lend you the money'= 'I give you the money' but 'I borrow money from you'= 'I receive money from you'. Note the other improvements.

10a	10b

10. asking a student to answer a question

10a	10b
Mr Kasi : You with the blue shirt in the last row! Answer the question. Shakti : ………. Mr Kasi : What's your name? Shakti : Shakti, sir. Mr Kasi : Answer the question. Shakti : ….Thelugu medium,sir. Mr Kasi : OK, answer in Thelugu. Shakti : No understand, sir. But tomorrow I say, sir. Mr Kasi : [smiling] Okay, sit down	Mr Kasi : You with the blue shirt in the last row! Answer the question. Shakti : ………. Mr Kasi : What's your name? Shakti : Shakti, sir. Mr Kasi : Answer the question. Shakti : I am from Thelugu medium school, sir. Mr Kasi : OK, answer in Thelugu. Shakti : I did not understand, sir. Can I give the answer tomorrow, sir? Mr Kasi : [smiling] Okay, sit down.

11a | 11b

11. introducing one person to another

11a

Mohan : Shakti, come, I introduce you to my friend.

Mohan : Rajesh! This is Shakti. Shakti, this is Rajesh.

Shakti : [shakes hand] Hello!

Rajesh : [shakes hand] Hello!

Mohan : Rajesh, you're from Thelugu Medium, Shakti, you're from Thamizh medium. You have to speak to each other in English. Of course, I'll help you, too.

Shakti : Rajesh, what's your father doing?

Rajesh : My father is farmer. What's your father doing?

Shakti : My father also farmer.

[The bell rings.]

Mohan : We'll meet again. Let's go to our classes.

11b

Mohan : Shakti, come, I'll introduce you to my friend.

Mohan : Rajesh! This is Shakti. Shakti, this is Rajesh.

Shakti : [shakes hand] Hello!

Rajesh : [shakes hand] Hello!

Mohan : Rajesh, you're from Thelugu Medium, Shakti, you're from Thamizh medium. You have to speak to each other in English. Of course, I'll help you, too.

Shakti : Rajesh, what's your father?

Rajesh : He is a farmer. What's your father?

Shakti : He is also a farmer.

[The bell rings.]

Mohan : We'll meet again. Let's go to our classes.

- When you want to know the job that somebody does, you ask: What's your father/mother/sister/brother?
- Don't say: Also I help you. Say: I will help you, too.

fluency 12a | accuracy 12b

12. meeting a staff

12a (fluency)

Shakti : [knocks on the door] Sir!

Mr Sriram : Yes, come in.

Shakti : Thank you, sir. Good morning, sir.

Mr Sriram : Sit down, Shakti. Say 'good afternoon'.

Shakti : I see you first time, sir.

Mr Sriram : That's right. But now, it's afternoon, isn't it?

Shakti : Good afternoon, sir. you say come to my room. Doubts in physics.

Mr Sriram : Doubts?

Shakti : Yes, sir, I not understand many words.

Mr Sriram : Did you study in a Thamizh medium school?

Shakti : Thelugu, sir.

Mr Sriram : Oh, if it was Thamizh, I could help. Mm.. Mr Rao of ECE Dept. can help. See him. And feel free with me, okay?

Shakti : Very very thank you, sir. But I don't know him.

Mr Sriram : I'll inform him. Meet him tomorrow.

12b (accuracy)

Shakti : [knocks on the door] Sir!

Mr Sriram : Yes, come in.

Shakti : Thank you, sir. Good morning, sir.

Mr Sriram : Sit down, Shakti. Say 'good afternoon'.

Shakti : I'm meeting you first time today, sir.

Mr Sriram : That's right. But now, it's afternoon, isn't it?

Shakti : Good afternoon, sir. You asked me to come to your room. I have several doubts in Physics.

Mr Sriram : Doubts?

Shakti : Yes, sir, I don't understand many words.

Mr Sriram : Did you study in a Thamizh medium school?

Shakti : Thelugu medium, sir.

Mr Sriram : Oh, if it was Thamizh, I could help. Mm.. Mr Rao of ECE Dept. can help. See him. And feel free with me, okay?

Shakti : Thank you very much, sir. But I don't know Mr Rao.

Mr Sriram : I'll inform him. Meet him tomorrow.

fluency 13a | accuracy 13b

13. meeting another faculty for help

13a (fluency)

Shakti : [knocks] I come in, sir?

Mr Rao : Yes, come in.

Shakti : Thank you, sir. Good afternoon, Sir.

Mr Rao : Good afternoon. You are…..

Shakti : My name is Shakti, sir. Mr Sriram, Physics Lecturer, said to meet you, sir.

Mr Rao : Oh yes, I remember now. Sit down.

Shakti : Thank you, sir. I am Thelugu medium, sir. Very difficult for understanding lectures. Please help, sir.

Mr Rao : I can understand. Make a list of words you don't understand in maths, physics, chemistry, electronics. Several words you already know in Thelugu. I'll help you with the new words. Meet

me every Monday at 4.15. Do you have your plus one and plus two books with you? [No, sir] Okay, get them from home.

Shakti : Thank you very much, sir. You are God, sir.

13b gives you the corrections. Note the last correction carefully. Godsend=something that happens suddenly and helps

13b (accuracy)

Shakti : [knocks] May I come in, sir?

Mr Rao : Yes, come in.

Shakti : Thank you, sir. Good afternoon, sir.

Mr Rao : Good afternoon. You are….

Shakti : My name is Shakti, sir. Mr Sriram, Physics Lecturer, told me to meet you, sir.

Mr Rao : Oh yes, I remember now. Sit down.

Shakti : Thank you, sir. I studied in Thelugu medium, sir. I find it difficult to understand lectures. I need your help, sir.

Mr Rao : I can understand. Make a list of words you don't understand in maths, physics, chemistry, electronics. Several words you already know in Thelugu. I'll help you with the new words. Meet me every Monday at 4.15. Do you have your plus one and plus two books with you? [No, sir] Okay, get them from home.

Shakti : Thank you very much, sir. You are a godsend, sir.

14. planning to spend a weekend

fluency 14a	accuracy 14b
Shakti : Gopal! We go somewhere coming Sunday, okay?	Shakti : Gopal! Shall we go for an outing this Sunday?
Gopal : Where? Cinema?	Gopal : How about seeing a film?
Shakti : No cinema. Queensland?	Shakti : No film. Queensland?
Gopal : For that lot of money we need.	Gopal : The idea is good. But you need a lot of money.
Shakti : How much? Five hundred?	Shakti : How much? Five hundred?
Gopal : Something like that.	Gopal : Something like that.
Shakti : Is it too much for you?	Shakti : You can't afford it?
Gopal : No. I have to ask my father.	Gopal : I have to ask my father.
Shakti : I already ask my father. He agree. Hey, we ask Mohan. He'll come, no?	Shakti : I've already asked my father. He's agreed. Shall we ask Mohan? He'll come, won't he?
Gopal : We ask Govind also?	Gopal : Shall we ask Govind, too?
Shakti : Okay. Also call Ram?	Shakti : Okay. Shall we find out if Ram will join us?
Gopal : We'll decide tomorrow.	Gopal : No harm in asking. Let's meet and decide tomorrow.
[next day]	[next day]
Shakti : Hi, everybody!	Shakti : Hi, everybody!
All : Hi, Shakti!	All : Hi, Shakti!
Shakti : So? What you all decided?	Shakti : So? What have you decided?
Mohan: We can each save Rs.50/-. I've managed to get two of the Queensland's ads. Let's use the money for our refreshments.	Mohan: We can each save Rs.50/-. I've managed to get two of the Queensland's ads. Let's use the money for our refreshments.
Gopal : Refreshments?	Gopal : Refreshments?
Mohan: Cool drinks, kurkure, Lay's etc.	Mohan: Cool drinks, kurkure, Lay's etc.
Govind: Hey, that's good.	Govind: Hey, that's good.
Mohan: We meet at Queensland this Sunday at 9.30. One more thing. Don't forget to wear helmets, pillion-passengers included.	Mohan: We meet at Queensland this Sunday at 9.30. One more thing. Don't forget to wear helmets, pillion-passengers included.
Ram : What is 'pillion'?	Ram : What is 'pillion'?
Govind: a seat for a passenger behind the driver of a motorcycle.	Govind: a seat for a passenger behind the driver of a motorcycle.

Note the corrections and use them.

'You' in 'you need a lot of money' is used in a general sense, not addressing the person you're talking to. It means 'anybody'. 'cinema'=building where films/movies are shown.

fluency

15a

accuracy

15b

15. explaining absence of a friend

Mr Rao : [takes attendance] Gopal!
………..: ………………..
Mr Rao : Gopal!
Jagan : He went to village, sir.
Mr Rao : Why?
Jagan : His mother died yesterday.
Mr Rao : cause of death?
Jagan : sugar, sir.
Mr Rao : May her soul rest in peace!

Mr Rao : [takes attendance] Gopal!
………..: ………………..
Mr Rao : Gopal!
Jagan : He's gone to his village, sir.
Mr Rao : Why?
Jagan : His mother passed away yesterday.
Mr Rao : cause of death?
Jagar : sugar, sir.
Mr Rao : May her soul rest in peace!

People say 'pass away' to avoid saying 'die'.

16a

16b

16. enquiry about health

Mr Ramesh : Govind!
Govind : Good afternoon, sir.
Mr Ramesh : How are you?
Govind : Fine, sir.
Mr Ramesh : You're limping!
Govind : Ankle pain, sir.
Mr Ramesh : Any fracture?
Govind : No, sir. Ankle twist, sir.
Mr Ramesh : Did you fall off a motorcycle?
Govind : No, sir. I fell from steps.
Mr Ramesh : Take care. Bye!
Govind : Thank you, sir. Goodbye, sir.

Mr Ramesh : Govind!
Govind : Good afternoon, sir.
Mr Ramesh : How are you?
Govind : Fine, thank you, sir.
Mr Ramesh : You're limping!
Govind : pain in the ankle, sir.
Mr Ramesh : Any fracture?
Govind : No, sir. I twisted my ankle.
Mr Ramesh : Did you fall off a motorcycle?
Govind : No, sir. I slipped from the staircase and the ankle got twisted.
Mr Ramesh : Take care. Bye!
Govind : Thank you and goodbye, sir.

Add 'thank you, sir/mam/uncle' to 'fine' when you respond to an elder's 'how are you?'

fluency 17a | accuracy 17b

17. consoling a student

17a

Mr Ramesh : Gopal !
Gopal : Sir?
Mr Ramesh : I heard your mother passed away.
Gopal : [weeps] ……..
Mr Ramesh : I know how shocking it must be to you. How old was she?
Gopal : She was…..fif…fifty years old.
Mr Ramesh : Oh, so young. Any health problem?
Gopal : Yes, sir. Sugar problem.
Mr Ramesh : Was the count very high?
Gopal : Sir?
Mr Ramesh : I mean, what was the amount of sugar?
Gopal : Doctor said 500.
Mr Ramesh : Oh, God! Gopal! Your mother wanted you to become an engineer, right?
Gopal : [unable to speak, nods]
Mr Ramesh : Good. Study well and get top grades. Your mother will be happy, won't she?
Gopal : Yes, sir.

17b

Mr Ramesh : Gopal !
Gopal : Sir?
Mr Ramesh : I heard your mother passed away.
Gopal : [weeps] ……..
Mr Ramesh : I know how shocking it must be to you. How old was she?
Gopal : …..fif…fifty
Mr Ramesh : Oh, so young. Any health problem?
Gopal : Yes, sir. Blood sugar level was quite high.
Mr Ramesh : Was the count very high?
Gopal : Sir?
Mr Ramesh : I mean, what was the amount of sugar?
Gopal : Almost 500.
Mr Ramesh : Oh, God! Gopal! Your mother wanted you to become an engineer, right?
Gopal : [unable to speak, nods]
Mr Ramesh : Good. Study well and get top grades. Your mother will be happy, won't she?
Gopal : Yes, sir. Thank you very much, sir.

There are no errors in 17a because Gopal utters very few words. But note how the teacher uses English to get information and to console Gopal.

18. consoling a friend

fluency 18a

Shakti, Mohan,
Govind,

Jagan : Gopal!
Gopal : [opens the door, all enter].......
Shakti : [puts his arm around Gopal's shoulder.] I shocked to hear your mother's death.
Gopal : [starts crying]........
Mohan : So was I. Please don't cry.
Govind : Sorry ra*, don't cry.
Jagan : No, let him cry. It'll ease the pressure on his mind.
Shakti : What happened?
Gopal : Her sugar count high. [continues to weep] Why she leave me alone? I want to die.
Mohan : Now, now, calm down.
Shakti : Gopal! Your mother wish you to become engineer, isn't it?
Jagan : This is the time to be brave. study hard, and we are with you.
Govind : Yes, we'll help you. Shakti, on the TV.
Gopal : Please, no.
Mohan : Okay, shall we go to temple, Gopal?
Gopal : [nods]
Shakti : Wash face, put another dress.
[after sometime]
Govind : [locks the door] Let's us to go.

accuracy 18b

Shakti, Mohan,
Govind,

Jagan : Gopal!
Gopal : [opens the door, all enter].......
Shakti : [puts his arm around Gopal's shoulder.] I was shocked to hear about your mother's death.
Gopal : [starts crying]........
Mohan : So was I. Please don't cry.
Govind : Sorry ra*, don't cry.
Jagan : No, let him cry. It'll ease the pressure on his mind.
Shakti : Was she bed-ridden?
Gopal : Her sugar count was very high. [continues to weep] Why did she leave me alone? I want to die.
Mohan : Now, now, calm down.
Shakti : Gopal! Your mother wanted you to become an engineer, didn't she?
Jagan : This is the time to be brave. study hard, and we are with you.
Govind : Yes, we'll help you. Shakti, switch on the TV.
Gopal : Please, no.
Mohan : Okay, shall we go to temple, Gopal?
Gopal : [nods]
Shakti : Have a wash, put on another dress.
[after sometime]
Govind : [locks the door] Let's us go.

- ra* is a suffix commonly used in Thelugu, 'da' in Thamizh, 'yaar' in Hindi between friends in conversation.
- 'isn't it?' or 'no?' at the end of a sentence is common in Indian languages. But in English, it should be an appropriate tag question.
- Another common mistake is to use 'on' and 'off' as verbs when speaking in English.
- 'Let+object+to+verb' is another common mistake we make. 'Let+object+verb' is the right structure. See what Jagan says in 18a and 18b: Let him cry.

fluency

19a

accuracy

19b

19. encouraging a friend to join a team

Shakti : [bends, picks up a pen]
Gopal! Look this. Your pen?
Gopal : No.
Shakti : Now I remember. It is Monan pen. I will give it.
Gopal : Shakti! There is selection for football team tomorrow. You take part?
Shakti : I will get selection?
Gopal : Sure. Try.
Shakti : Next year I will see.
Gopal : Go tomorrow. Don't leave.
Shakti : Thanksra.

Shakti : [bends, picks up a pen]
Gopal! Is this yours?
Gopal : No.
Shakti : I know it's Mohan's. I'll give it to him.
Gopal : Shakti! There is selection for football team tomorrow. Why don't you register?
Shakti : You think I stand a chance?
Gopal : I know.
Shakti : I think I'll try next year.
Gopal : No, Shakti. You're going tomorrow.
Shakti : Thanks for the confidence.

20a

20b

20. requesting staff to help start a bank account

Shanmugam : [knocks at the door]
May I come in, sir?
Prof. AG : Yes, come in. Sit down.
Shanmugam : It's okay, sir.
Prof. AG : No formalities. Sit down.
[Shanmugam sits.]
Tell me now.
Shanmugam : Want help, sir.
Prof. AG : What help?
Shanmugam : [shows the form for opening a bank account]
Bank Manager tell to me to get sign from you.
Prof. AG : [sees the form] Oh, you mean I should introduce you?
Shanmugam : Yes, sir, that is what I mean, sir.
Prof AG : Okay. [fills and signs]
Shanmugam : Thank you, sir.

Shanmugam : [knocks at the door]
May I come in, sir?
Prof. AG : Yes, come in. Sit down.
Shanmugam : Thank you.sir, but…
Prof. AG : No formalities. Sit down.
[Shanmugam sits.]
Tell me now.
Shanmugam : I need a favour, sir.
Prof. AG : Yes?
Shanmugam : [shows the form for opening a bank account]
Bank Manager told me to get your signature.
Prof. AG : [sees the form] Oh, you mean I should introduce you?
Shanmugam : That's what I meant, sir.
Prof AG : Okay. [fills and signs]
Shanmugam : Thank you, sir.

21. registering for team selection

fluency

21a

Shakti : Want to see PD.
Raghu : Go to second room on the right hand side.
Shakti : OK. Good afternoon, sir.
PD : Yes?
Shakti : A notice came yesterday for football selection, sir.
PD : You're a first year student?
Shakti : Yes, sir.
PD : Sports quota?
Shakti : I don't know, sir.
PD : What is your position?
Shakti : Goalkeeper, sir.
PD : I see. You've got certificates?
Shakti : Yes, sir. Brought xerox.
PD : Good. Be at the stadium tomorrow at nine sharp.
Shakti : Sir, there is lab……
PD : Don't worry. You'll get attendance.

accuracy

21b

Shakti : I want to meet the PD.
Raghu : you'll find him in the second room to your right.
Shakti : Thank you.
....
Shakti : Good afternoon, sir.
PD : Yes?
Shakti : There was a notice yesterday about football selection, sir.
PD : You're a first year student?
Shakti : Yes, sir.
PD : Sports quota?
Shakti : No, sir.
PD : What is your position?
Shakti : Goalkeeper, sir.
PD : I see. You've got certificates?
Shakti : Yes, sir. I've brought copies.
PD : Good. Be at the stadium tomorrow at nine sharp.
Shakti : Sir, I have a lab……
PD : Don't worry. You'll get attendance.

fluency 22a	accuracy 22b

22. talk between a senior and a junior

22a	22b
Somu : Shakti! Wait!	Somu : Shakti! Wait!
Shakti : Who are you?	Shakti : You're…….
Somu : I'm Somu. Vice-Captain, football team.	Somu : I'm Somu. Vice-Captain, football team.
Shakti : Oh, very happy. [shakes hands]	Shakti : Oh, glad to meet you. [shakes hands]
Somu : You catch ball nicely?	Somu : Are you good at keeping goal?
Shakti : That is what I am thinking.	Shakti : I think so.
Somu : For how many years you are representing your school?	Somu : For how long did you represent your school?
Shakti : From class nine.	Shakti : Four years.
Somu : Good. But college matches are sometime dangerous. They hurt you.	Somu : Good. But keeping goal can be risky. You can get hurt.
Shakti : O God! Really?	Shakti : You aren't scaring me, are you?
Somu : No worry. If selected, I'll help you. Okay?	Somu : Don't you worry. If you get selected, I'll help you. Okay?
Shakti : How to thank you I don't know.	Shakti : I can't thank you enough.

- When a stranger calls you by name, your response generally is one of these: 1. Yes? 2. You're….. 3.You called me? [with stress on 'you'] 4. turn round to see who called you. But don't ask: who are you? You pose this question to a stranger only when you feel he or she is a threat to you.
- "How to thank you I don't know" is acceptable only when you get very emotional. In normal circumstances, it should be: 'I don't know how to thank you.' "I can't thank you enough" is a polite expression.
- Matches can never be 'dangerous'.

23. discussion between two friends

fluency

23a

Jagan : Congrats, Shakti!

Shakti : Thanks, Jagan.

Jagan : I watched you keep goal. You were fantastic, I tell you.

Shakti : You are telling the truth?

Jagan : Of course, I am. Even our PD was impressed. He was captain of his College team, you know.

Shakti : Really? But he no speak to me.

Jagan : I saw him smile every time you saved a goal. But he never praises.

Shakti : If he no speak, how I know I play well or not.

Jagan : If he lets you play three games in a row, it means he likes your game.

Shakti : Is it?

accuracy

23b

Jagan : Congrats, Shakti!

Shakti : Thanks, Jagan.

Jagan : I watched you keep goal. You were fantastic, I tell you.

Shakti : You aren't serious, are you?

Jagan : Of course, I am. Even our PD was impressed. He was captain of his College team, you know.

Shakti : Really? But he did not speak to me.

Jagan : I saw him smile every time you saved a goal. But he never praises.

Shakti : If he doesn't speak, how do I know I played well or not?

Jagan : If he lets you play three games in a row, it means he likes your game.

Shakti : Oh, I see.

- 'congrats' is informal and 'congratulations' is formal. 'thanks' is informal and 'thank you' is formal. Adults make these distinctions but not college or school students, who generally don't follow formalities.

fluency
24a

accuracy
24b

24. asking for leave

24a

Deepika	: Excuse me, madam, may I come in?
Mrs Gomathi	: Yes, come in.
Deepika	: I want two days leave, madam.
Mrs Gomathi	: When?
Deepika	: Next Monday and Tuesday.
Mrs Gomathi	: Why?
Deepika	: My bigger sister engagement, madam.
Mrs Gomathi	: Is it necessary for you to be there?
Deepika	: Yes, madam. I am no there, is insult to boy family.
Mrs Gomathi	: I see. Fill in this Leave Permission Form.
Deepika	: Thank you very much, madam.

24b

Deepika	: Excuse me, madam, may I come in?
Mrs Gomathi	: Yes, come in.
Deepika	: I need leave for two days, madam.
Mrs Gomathi	: When?
Deepika	: Next Monday and Tuesday.
Mrs Gomathi	: Why?
Deepika	: My elder sister is getting engaged, madam.
Mrs Gomathi	: Is it necessary for you to be there?
Deepika	: Yes, madam. The groom's family will consider my absence an insult.
Mrs Gomathi	: I see. Fill in this Leave Permission Form.
Deepika	: Thank you very much, madam.

We have two expressions in English to show that someone is more in age than another: 'older' and 'elder'. We use 'elder' with a noun like '*elder+brother/sister*'. We use 'older' in 'comparative structure': Kamini is older than me/I am.

We can also say: Kamini is my elder by five years. But this is not a comparison.

25. registering for a competition

fluency 25a

Jyothi	: Excuse me, madam, may I come in?
Mrs Gomathi	: Yes, come in.
Jyothi	: A notice came for singing competition. I want to register, madam.
Mrs Gomathi	: Carnatic or light music?
Jyothi	: Light music.
Mrs Gomathi	: Do you sing well?
Jyothi	: Yes, madam.
Mrs Gomathi	: Have you got certificates?
Jyothi	: Yes, madam. I win in several competitions, mam.
Mrs Gomathi	: Good. Fill in your particulars on this sheet.
Jyohi	: Thank you very much, madam.

accuracy 25b

Jyothi	: Excuse me, madam, may I come in?
Mrs Gomathi	: Yes, come in.
Jyothi	: I would like to register for the singing competition, madam.
Mrs Gomathi	: Carnatic or light music?
Jyothi	: Light music.
Mrs Gomathi	: Do you sing well?
Jyothi	: Yes, madam.
Mrs Gomathi	: Have you got certificates?
Jyothi	: Yes, madam. I've won in several competitions.
Mrs Gomathi	: Good. Fill in your particulars on this sheet.
Jyothi	: Thank you very much, madam.

26. praising performance

fluency 26a

Suchithra	: Excuse me, madam, may I come in?
Mrs Gomathi	: Ah, Suchi, come in.
Suchithra	: Good morning, mam.
Mrs Gomathi	: Congratulations, Suchii!
Suchithra	: Thank you, mam.
Mrs Gomathi	: Honestly, I didn't expect you to win the competition.
Suchithra	: I also didn't expect. So many good singers.
Mrs Gomathi	: Anyway, I'm happy for the College. You'll be part of the College team.
Suchithra	: Really madam? I'll be so lucky.

accuracy 26b

Suchithra	: Excuse me, mam, may I come in?
Mrs Gomathi	: Ah, Suchi, come in.
Suchithra	: Good morning, mam.
Mrs Gomathi	: Congratulations, Suchi!
Suchithra	: Thank you, mam.
Mrs Gomathi	: Honestly, I didn't expect you to win the competition.
Suchithra	: Neither did I, mam. There were so many good singers.
Mrs Gomathi	: Anyway, I'm happy for the College. You'll be part of the College team.
Suchithra	: Really madam? I'm very lucky. You've been very encouraging. Thank you, mam.

In this dialogue, Suchithra speaks very little. But you can also learn to speak good English without making mistakes all the time [!] by reading and listening to good conversations.

fluency
27a

accuracy
27b

27. praising performance

27a (fluency)

Shakti : Suchi! Stop!
Suchi : Hi, Shakti!
Shakti : You sing so well in the Competition. Congrats!
Suchi : Thanks. You seen me singing?
Shakti : Yes, yes. All enjoyed. I also enjoyed. You have good voice.
Shanmugam : Hi,Shakti! Hi, Suchi! I don't know what to say. I'm happy for you.
Mohan : Hi, Suchi! What a voice you've got!
Jagan : Oh, You are all here! Suchi! You're just great! You're going to be the talk of the town, I tell you, once you take part in an intercollegiate competition.
Suchi : I….I don't…..
Mohan : When you came on stage many seniors were mocking at you and there was a lot of noise. I really admired your courage.
Suchi : My all classmates clapped and encouraged. I don't know how to thank.

27b (accuracy)

Shakti : Suchi! Stop!
Suchi : Hi, Shakti!
Shakti : You sang so well in the Competition. Congrats!
Suchi : Thanks. You heard me sing?
Shakti : Yes. All the students enjoyed the way you sang. So did I. You have a good voice.
Shanmugam : Hi,Shakti! Hi, Suchi! I'm at a loss for words. I'm happy for you.
Mohan : Hi, Suchi! What a voice you've got!
Jagan : Oh, You are all here! Suchi! You were just great! You're going to be the talk of the town, I tell you, once you take part in an intercollegiate competition.
Suchi : I….I don't…..
Mohan : When you came on stage many seniors were mocking at you and there was a lot of noise. I really admired your courage.
Suchi : All my classmates clapped and encouraged me. I don't know how to thank them.

fluency	accuracy
28a	28b

28. Strangers at a bus stop

28a (fluency)	28b (accuracy)
Mala : Excuse me! Where Sai Baba temple is?	Mala : Excuse me! Can you tell me the way to Sai Baba temple?
Sheela : Go straight, take first left, there you'll see.	Sheela : Go straight, take the first left turn, you'll see it on your right.
Mala : First left?	Mala : First left?
Sheela : Yes.	Sheela : Yes.
Mala : Okay.	Mala : Thanks.

fluency	accuracy
29a	29b

29. Strangers at a bus stop

29a (fluency)	29b (accuracy)
Kumar : Which bus goes to MIOT Hospital?	Kumar : Which bus goes to MIOT Hospital?
David : 115, 127, 154.	David : You can take 115, 127 or 154.
Kumar : Bus stops in MIOT?	Kumar : Do they stop at MIOT?
David : No.	David : No.
Kumar : where should I get down?	Kumar : Which is the nearest bus stop I should get down at?
David : Hallmark Plaza.	David : Hallmark Plaza.
Kumar : Then?	Kumar : And?
David : You should walk forward, cross the zebra crossing, turn to right.	David : You should walk forward, cross the zebra crossing, turn right.
Kumar : Thank you.	Kumar : Thank you.
David : Welcome.	David : You're welcome.

fluency	accuracy
30a	30b

30. Friends

30a (fluency)

Sita : Bag is very nice.
Shaheena : Sure?
Sita : Gift?
Shaheena : Bought.
Sita : Where you bought?
Shaheena : Spencer Plaza.
Sita : how much?
Shaheena : 300 bucks.
Sita : Is it?
Shaheena : Cheap?
Sita : I think.

30b (accuracy)

Sita : Your handbag is very nice.
Shaheena : Really?
Sita : Yes. Is it a gift?
Shaheena : No. Bought it.
Sita : Where?
Shaheena : Spencer Plaza.
Sita : how much?
Shaheena : 300 bucks.
Sita : You're not serious!
Shaheena : I'm. Isn't it a bargain?
Sita : It is.

---

fluency	accuracy
31a	31b

31. A girl in a restaurant

31a (fluency)

Girl : Hello! Menu card please.
Waiter : Menu card, mam.
Girl : I want 1 plate cheese pizza.
Waiter : That's all, mam?
Girl : First I'll eat pizza, then I'll order.
Waiter : O.K., mam.
Girl : Hot water, please.

31b (accuracy)

Girl : Hello! Can I have a menu card?
Waiter : Here you are, mam.
Girl : Thank you. Mmm, I'll have a plate of cheese pizza.
Waiter : Anything else, mam?
Girl : I may order later.
Waiter : Yes, mam.
Girl : Ah, can I have a glass of hot water?

fluency — 32a

accuracy — 32b

32. Nanda with a Customer Care Executive over the phone

32a (fluency)

CCE : Good morning, Airo Customer Care.

Nanda : From morning I can't able to send sms

CCE : Is this first time you're facing this problem, sir?

Nanda : Yes.

CCE : I'll take this as a complaint and within 24 hrs I'll solve this problem.

Nanda : Okay.

CCE : Sorry for the inconvenience. Thank you for calling Airtel

Nanda : O.K.

32b (accuracy)

CCE : Good morning, Airo Customer Care.

Nanda : Today is no public holiday; yet I'm having problems with sending SMS.

CCE : I'm sorry to hear that, but is it the first time, sir?

Nanda : Yes.

CCE : Please bear with us, but rest assured, sir, we'll have your problem sorted out within the hour.

Nanda : That's fine, thank you.

CCE : You're welcome and thank you for calling Airo.

1.4 Relationships

Another aspect of Functional English is **the choices we make** in our words and sentence structures to convey messages. Let's see what decides these choices.

Language helps us communicate messages. We put a group of words in a particular way. This way indicates, among other things, relationships. You are by necessity polite to a stranger, you are respectful to elders, you are very free with some friends, you keep distance with some others. Know more about this.

formal

You don't live in isolation, do you? Because you have people who are *officials* in public or private sector, who are your *superiors* at college or workplace. Then you have *strangers* (whom you don't know at all). Your relationship with them is *formal*. So your choice of words and sentences will be formal.

semiformal

You don't live in isolation, do you? Because you also have some people whom you met at a party, at a marriage reception, on a journey, at a cafe. They are your *acquaintances*. If you meet them only occasionally, your relationship with them will be ***semiformal***. You have *elders* in your community, you know several *public figures* because of their service to society. You may meet them often but you need to be respectful to them because of their status. Your relationship with them will be semiformal. You also have *relatives*, *neighbours* whom you may meet only infrequently. So your relationship with them is semiformal. And your choice of words and sentences will be semiformal.

informal

You don't live in isolation, do you? Because you have friends, relatives, neighbours. You are very close to some of your friends and not so close to some others. You are very close to some of your relatives and not so close to some others. You are very close to some of your neighbours and not so close to some others. When you are very close to a friend, a relative or a neighbour, your intimacy level is very high. Now your relationship with them is ***informal***. So your choice of words and sentences will be informal. When you are not close to a friend, a relative or a neighbour, your intimacy level is low. Now your relationship with them is not as informal as with the previous group.

Exercise 1

Instruction one:

You'll find several dialogues in the next few pages. Read them carefully and write down the category to which each belongs. The categories are: formal, semi - formal, informal. The expressions (the language) will help you. Decide the relationship and discuss what made you choose one relationship over the others.

1.

A: I wonder if you could make these trousers a little wider at the ankle. I find them rather tight.

B: Well, Sir, it's the fashion. All my customers are asking for very narrow trousers.

A: Oh, I see. I'm afraid I'm rather ignorant of the fashions.

2.

A. Can you come and see us this evening?

B. I don't think I can. I have to give a talk. If it's important, can I suggest tomorrow evening?

3.

A: Meet me this evening.

B: No.

A: Why?

B: Don't you remember? I have a a talk to give.

A: How about tomorrow morning, then?

B: Okay.

4.

A: Let's meet this evening, shall we ?

B: Sorry Raj. I have a talk to give.

A: I see. Shall we meet tomorrow morning ?

B: Mm, Agreed.

5.

A: If you aren't too busy, could we meet this evening ?

B: I should love to, but I have an appointment.

A: Could we possibly meet tomorrow morning, then?

B: That would be fine.

6

A: Excuse me. I wonder if you could tell me how to reach the post office.

B: I'm so sorry. I'm also new around here. If I may suggest ...

A: Yes, please.

B: You might try the Chemist across the street.

7.

A: Excuse me. Which is the way to the post office ?

B: I'm also a stranger. You can try the Chemist across the street.

A: Thank you.

8.

A: I'd like to meet Mr. Kadir.

B: Oh, you must be Mr. Raman. I am Kadir, please come in. I've been expecting you.

A: I got lost coming here.

B: I'm awfully sorry. I ought to have told you how to get here. Would you care for a drink?

A: No, thank you. I must hurry back. Here's the package I've been asked to deliver.

B: Thank you so much.

9.

A: How are you, Mrs. Sadhana ?

B: Very well, thank you. I've come about Siddharth.

A: Yes.

B: You see, he's always complaining of stomachache.

10.

A: Nasty accident that !

B: Yes. Subhash's lost four of his fingers.

A: It's going to be tough for him. Don't you think ?

B: It'll be, I guess.

11.

A: I don't like going to the cinema.*1

B: I'm surprised. All people enjoy films.

A: The trouble is that most of the films are Westerns *2 which bore me.

*1 the cinema = a place where films are shown. We use this to mean a film. And we use 'the theatre' as a synonym for 'the cinema'. But 'the theatre' actually refers to a place where dramas are staged or shown.

*2 westerns are cowboy films.

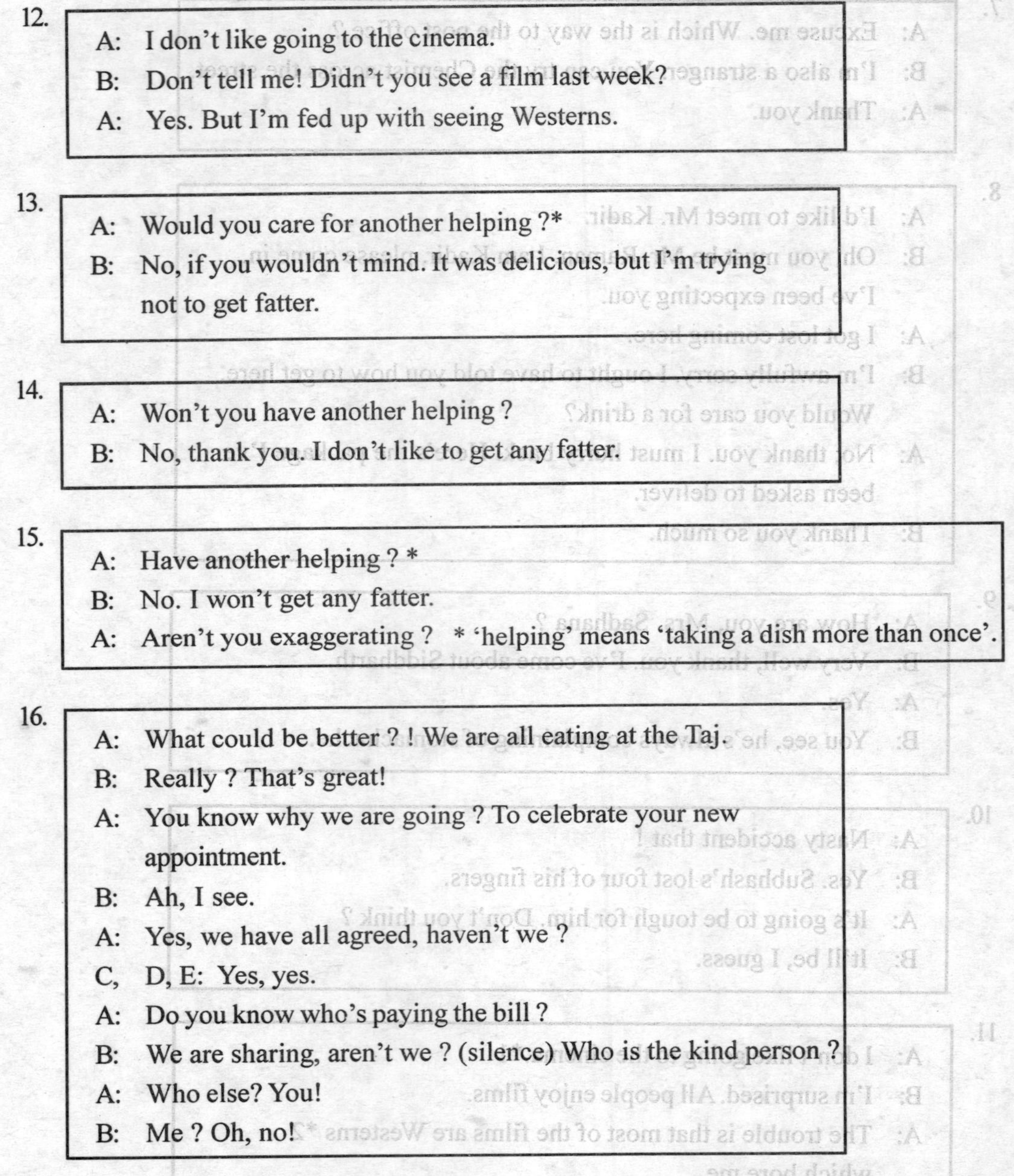

12.

A: I don't like going to the cinema.

B: Don't tell me! Didn't you see a film last week?

A: Yes. But I'm fed up with seeing Westerns.

13.

A: Would you care for another helping ?*

B: No, if you wouldn't mind. It was delicious, but I'm trying not to get fatter.

14.

A: Won't you have another helping ?

B: No, thank you. I don't like to get any fatter.

15.

A: Have another helping ? *

B: No. I won't get any fatter.

A: Aren't you exaggerating ? * 'helping' means 'taking a dish more than once'.

16.

A: What could be better ? ! We are all eating at the Taj.

B: Really ? That's great!

A: You know why we are going ? To celebrate your new appointment.

B: Ah, I see.

A: Yes, we have all agreed, haven't we ?

C, D, E: Yes, yes.

A: Do you know who's paying the bill ?

B: We are sharing, aren't we ? (silence) Who is the kind person ?

A: Who else? You!

B: Me ? Oh, no!

Note : Check your answers with your neighbours and then with your lecturer. It's important you understand the three relationships very clearly. I hope these dialogues have helped. Don't hesitate to ask for explanation to clear your doubts.

Instruction two: I don't think you had any problem identifying the relationships. Now, with the help of your lecturer/professor, play the roles in these 16 dialogues.

Telephone conversations. Listen to these on Track two on your CD. Practise them.

1. The telephone rings
"Hello!"
"Is Sundar there?"
"Which Sundar?"
"What do you mean?"
"There's no Sundar here."
"How come? Oh, isn't that 2627 5533?"
"Wrong number!" (idiot!)

2. Hello!
Isn't that 2627 5335?
No.
Sorry I bothered you!
No problem. (That's okay.)

3. Hello!
Can I speak to Sundar?
Which number do you want?
Isn't that 2627 5335?
No.
I'm sorry to have troubled you.
It's OK.

4. "Hello!"
"Is that 2627 5533?"
"Yes."
"Can I speak to Sundar?"
"Who do I say is calling?"
"Kapil, a friend of Sundar's."
"Please hold on. Sundar, a call for you."

5. "Hello!"
"Is that 2627 5533?"
"Yes."
"Can I speak to Sundar? I'm Kapil, a friend of Sundar's."
"Please hold on. Sundar, a call for you."

6. "Good morning, TVS."
"You see I'm a businessman.
I'm a retailer. I've a shop at Pondy Bazaar….."
"Excuse me. Could you please tell me……"
"I was coming to that, wasn't I? Yes, I've a shop at Pondy Bazaar……"

7. "Mr Kumar's residence."
"Could I speak to Mr Kumar?"
"May I know who is speaking?"
"I'm Raghavan, a friend of Mr Kumar's."
"Will you please hold on?"
"Yes, thank you."

8.

"This is double two three six seven nine O." [2236790]

"Good morning. Is Mr Narasimhan in?"

"I'm his mother. He's gone to keep an appointment."

"Oh. Is he likely to be back soon?"

"Are you by any chance Mr Murugan,?"

"Yes, Mam."

"He said he had already put in a word to Mrs Savitha and you could meet her the day after tomorrow at 3.30 p.m."

"Thank you, mam."

"You're welcome."

"Please convey my regards to Narasimhan."

9.

"This is double two three six seven nine O." [2236790]

"Good morning. Is Mr Narasimhan in?"

"I'm his mother. He's gone to keep an appointment."

"Oh. Is he likely to be back soon?"

"….I don't really know. May I know your name so I can inform my son.?"

"Rajan, a colleague of his."

"I see. I can take a message."

" I'll give a call around five. If he comes earlier, ask him to give a call,"

"I'll do that."

"Thank you, mam."

"Not at all."

10.

"Good afternoon, TVS."

" I'd like to speak to the service engineer."

"Just a moment, please….. Excuse me, the service engineer is unavailable. Will anyone else do?"

"Yes, thank you………..Am I speaking to the deputy service engineer?"

"Yes, sir. What can we do for you?"[How can we help?/Can I be of help?]

"I'm Gopalarathinam, Professor at IIT. My car was supposed to be ready last evening. Its registration number is TN—01 Y3254."

"Just a moment, sir……I'm afraid it's not ready yet. You may collect it tomorrow at 10 a.m."

"But……"

"Sorry to interrupt you, Prof. We ran out of stock of one spare part. In fact, yours is one of the cars being attended to right now."

"Couldn't I have it later in the day?"

"Much as we are eager to oblige you, it's being driven out for the last leg of servicing."

"Last leg of servicing?"

"Yes, Dr Gopalarathinam. It'll be driven through the streets to check its fitness state. Should there be any problem, we'll need time to attend to it. Hence the delivery tomorrow."

"You've made me happy. Thank you for your time and explanation."

"The pleasure is ours, Prof."

"Good night, Mr……"

"Thomson, Joe Thomson."

"Thank you very much, Mr Thomson."

Exercise 2 Conversation samples

Listen to these on Track three on your CD and practise them.

A party where strangers, acquaintances and friends are together. Depending on who meets who, the situation may be formal / semi formal/ informal.

[A]

Suman : Raj, come, I'll introduce you to Dr. Raghu.

Dr Raghu, this is Prof. Raj.

Raj : (extending his hand) How d'you do ?

Raghu : (shaking hands) How d'you do ?

(the conversation continues . . .)

note: 'How d' you do?' is the response to 'How d' you do?' This expression has no meaning of its own.

[B]

Suresh : Hello, Shyam!

Shyam : Hello! How come you are here ?

I thought you were ......

Suresh : Supposed to be at Kolkata. Had to cancel it.*

Shyam : Anything wrong with Raji ?

(anxiously)

Suresh : No, no. She is of course recovering.

It's the storm. Didn't want to risk.........*

Shyam : Risk ? What risk ?

Suresh : I meant the mess at Kolkata.

[C]

Mr Guha : Good evening, Mr. Prabhu!

Mr. Prabhu : Oh good evening, Mr Guha! What a pleasant surprise!

Mr. Guha : But I had expected you, here.

---

* Incomplete sentences (especially without subject) are common in informal conversations.

A is formal, B informal and C semiformal.

A train journey is one where people stay together. Where people talk to each other without getting introduced, from where they leave without a word said or without getting introduced

A

Passenger A	:	Excuse me, is the Sports Star the latest ?
Passenger B	:	Yes. (extending it)
Passenger A	:	Thank you.
Passenger B	:	Not at all.
Passenger A (returning the magazine)	:	Thank you. I'm Karthik.* Works Manager, HCL
Passenger B	:	I'm Chandran *, Sales Manager, GCIM.
Passenger A	:	Then you must be knowing Mr. Kanthan, your Works Manager.
Passenger B	:	I do. In fact, we're very close. How do you....
Passenger A	:	We were classmates at SIM, Bengaluru.

* We are generally known by our own names (Christian names) not our fathers' (Surnames). But Westerners use their *surnames* in formal / official situations (Not their Christian names) ; they use their Christian names only when there is a degree of intimacy or where intimacy exists or is permitted.

When you introduce yourself, don't use any title with your name (Mr/ /Dr) But see below.

B

In a conference (during lunch)

Participant A	:	Congratulations! You raised a few very disturbing questions. I'm Mrs Deepika Chandran, Editor, Science Section, SCITECH, Chennai.
Participant B	:	Thank you, Mrs. Deepika. I wondered if any one listened at all. I'm Ms.Chandrika, lecturer in Economics, SIET, Mayiladuthurai.

As a woman, introduce yourself as Mrs if you wish to be addressed so. Otherwise, use Ms (pronounced as Miz) or simply your name [I'm Chandrika].

C

In a debate competition

Karthik : Congrats, Mr. Sekhar for winning the Cup.

You were faultless.

I'm Karthik, third year student of Mech. NEC, Thanjavur.

Sekhar : Experience, I guess. Is it your first in Chennai? (Karthik nods)

Well, for a novice, you spoke extremely well but poor time management was your problem.

Karthik : You are quite right. I had so much to say. Mr Sekhar, you are a. . . . .

Sekhar : Sorry to interrupt. But no Mr. I'm just Sekhar.

Final year Law, Madras Law college.

Glad to know you, and see you soon. Bye.

Karthik : Glad to know you, too. Before I leave, will your College participate if my College invites?

Sekhar : Honestly, we don't go to the districts but now that I know you, I'll see to it.

Karthik : I'm so glad. That'll be another opportunity to listen to you. Bye, Sekhar.

A is formal, B is semiformal, C is informal though in all of them the speakers are strangers to begin with. But in B and C the speakers have something in common and this makes them avoid being formal though they are meeting for the first time.

On the Phone

.... : Hello!

Sankar : Is that 8253763? [eight two five three seven six three]

.... : Yes.

Sankar : Could I speak to Suresh ?

Suresh's mother : Suresh is not in. I'm Suresh's mother. And you are ......

Sankar : Sankar. Suresh's classmate.

I'm calling to know if he has decided to go with me for the field trip.

Suresh's mother : You have a phone?

Sankar : Yes, he has my number.

Suresh's mother : That's fine. You can also reserve for him.

Sankar : Thank you, Madam. Bye.

…………	:	Hello! This is 6328107. [six three two eight one 0 seven]
Sharanath	:	I'd like to speak to Mr Pande.
Mr. Pande	:	Speaking.
Sharath	;	Good morning, Mr. Pande. I'm Sharath, Student President, GEC. Your PA told me you'd be available at your house today. She gave me your residence number.
Mr. Pande	:	Good morning, Mr Sharath. What's the urgency ?
Sharath	:	Sorry to disturb you, sir. I had to ring you because she said you were going on a tour and I wanted to know if you would be free to give a lecture.....
Mr. Pande	:	Sorry to interrupt you, Mr. Sharath. When do you want me for the lecture ?
Sharath	:	Any day between the 20th and the 25th, sir.
Mr. Pande	:	I see. Will 22nd be all right ?
Sharath	:	That would be fine, sir. We'd like you to speak on journalism in India.
Mr. Pande	:	Mm. Am I free to choose - anything close to this ?
Sharath	:	Of course, yes, sir.
Mr Pande	:	Please meet me on 19th at my office at 10 am.
Sharath	:	Yes. And thank you, sir. Good bye.

Krishnan	:	Hello ! Krishnan, here.
Kuruvilla	:	Guess who's speaking.
Krishnan	:	Is that Abey kuruvilla ?
Kuruvilla	:	Who else could it be? How ARE* you, Krish?
Krishnan	:	How are YOU*, Abey? Is this an STD call?
Kuruvilla	:	Yes, I'm coming to Chennai next week. Let's have a chat.
Krishnan	:	Sure. How long are you staying?
Kuruvilla	:	Five days.
Krishnan	:	When are you arriving? I'll receive you.

When you meet a friend after a long gap, if you are asking first, you stress 'ARE' and your friend 'YOU'. This emphasis indicates affection.

A complaint

Mr Narayanan	:	Yes, come in.
Sundar	:	Mr Narayanan? I'm Sundar.
Mr. Narayanan	:	Please be seated, Mr. Sundar. How can I help you?
Sundar	:	Our phone is not working.
Mr. Narayanan	:	Are you the owner of the phone?
Sundar	:	No. It's my father, Prof. Raghavan.
Mr. Narayanan	:	Is the sound coming garbled? Is it cross talk? Or Is the phone dead?
Sundar	:	Our problem is we are always getting wrong numbers.
Mr. Narayanan	:	Did you have trouble before?
Sundar	:	Not as far as I know.
Mr. Narayanan	:	I see. On your way out, please fill particulars on a form at the reception. We'll send down someone tomorrow.
Sundar	:	Tomorrow?
Mr. Narayanan	:	We are short of personnel. Latest tomorrow, we'll have your phone working. Bye, Mr. Sundar.
Sundar	:	Thank you. Bye, Mr. Narayanan.

A visitor to home

Somu's dad	:	Somu, see who is at the door.
Somu	:	Yes, dad. (opens the door, sees a stranger) Yes?
Visitor	:	Is Mr. Sugumaran at home?
Somu	:	Yes. May I. . . .
Visitor	:	I'm Gnanasekaran. A friend of Mr. Sugumaran.
Somu	:	I'm Somu, his son. Please come in. (Mr. Gnanasekaran enters) Please be seated. (Switches on the fan.)
Visitor	:	No, thank you. It doesn't agree with me.
Somu	:	(Switching it off) I'm sorry! I didn't know.
Visitor	:	It's okay. How could you?
Somu	:	I'll inform father. In the meantime, would you like to read today's Hindu?
Visitor (receiving it)	:	Thank you, Somu.
Somu	:	Dad! A Mr Gnanasekaran has come to see you. (comes back) He'll be here in a moment. What would you like for a drink?
Visitor	:	Nothing for the moment. Thank you, anyway.

---

2. Vocabulary Building

2.1 Synonyms and Antonyms

In this Section, we will see how we could build our vocabulary using different words in a given context; we'll learn that there is relationship between words in terms of meaning, which could be similar or dissimilar. Similar meaning words are termed **synonyms**, and dissimilar meaning words termed **antonyms**. *Cheap* and *inexpensive* are synonyms. *Basic* and *fundamental* are synonymous. *Rude* and *polite* are antonyms. *Hold* and *release* are antonymous.

The exercises that follow will help confirm your vocabulary range or add new words to your vocabulary bank. Do these exercises.

synonyms

Exercise 3

match these synonyms:

1. seal	a. close
2. seek	b. ask
3. argue	c. disagree
4. shut	d. close
5. speculative	e. imaginative
6. sweep	f. clean
7. strangle	g. kill
8. jolly	h. happy
9. split	i. divide
10. discover	j. find

Exercise 4

Match these synonyms.

11. mysterious	a. risky
12. accelerating	b. punishment
13. dangerous	c. remove
14. peep	d. plan
15. chalk	e. improving
16. junk	f. look
17. revel	g. overspend
18. extravagant	h. enjoy
19. repeal	i. waste
20. sentence	j. unknown

Exercise 5

Match these synonyms.

21. malady	a. evident
22. unmoved	b. link
23. witless	c. shake
24. seldom	d. mad
25. construct	e. gather
26. throng	f. build
27. senile	g. occasionally
28. jerk	h. stupid
29. relate	i. unaffected
30. conspicuous	j. ailment

Exercise 6

Match these synonyms.

31. souvenir	a. remembrance
32. lofty	b. extendable
33. exorbitant	c. sullen
34. elastic	d. dishonest
35. engaging	e. interesting
36. morose	f. costly
37. morbid	g. supervise
38. corrupt	h. rebellion
39. monitor	i. high
40. mutiny	j. abnormal

Exercise 7

Match these synonyms.

41. confused	a. unclear
42. opaque	b. close
43. evaluation	c. speak
44. rejoice	d. grumble
45. slam	e. invisible
46. mutter	f. search
47. utter	g. judgement
48. rummage	h. enjoy
49. murmur	i. noise
50. rumpled	j. dishevelled

Exercise 8

Match these synonyms:

51. ploy	a. bet
52. encircle	b. pain
53. glory	c. trick
54. meddle	d. interfere
55. agony	e. device
56. gamble	f. blunder
57. gadget	g. increase
58. gaff	h. merry-making
59. gaiety	i. fame
60. gain	j. embrace

Exercise 9

Match these synonyms:

61. gale	a. decorate
62. gall	b. collect
63. gallant	c. wind
64. gape	d. talkative
65. garb	e. dress
66. garner	f. annoy
67. garnish	g. stare
68. garrulous	h. produce
69. generate	i. kind
70. generous	j. brave

Exercise 10

Match these synonyms:

71. genial	a. food
72. glad	b. depression
73. glee	c. provoke
74. gloom	d. bribery
75. goad	e. credulous
76. graft	f. friendly
77. grief	g. sorrow
78. gross	h. delighted
79. grub	i. vulgar
80. gullible	j. delight

Exercise 11

Choose from the expressions labelled a, b, c, d, e the ones that are nearest in meaning to the expressions that are in bold in the sentences below:

1. "Have you had your grub?" he **queried**.
   a. said b. told c. inquired d. requested e. ordered
2. The serenity of the ashram **soothed** my nerves.
   a. calmed b. excited c. strengthened d. spoiled e. distorted
3. The **serenity** of the ashram soothed my nerves.
   a. tranquility b. busy-ness c. stormy d. excellence e. noise
4. His frugality is **commendable**.
   a. despicable b. praiseworthy c. disgusting e. criticisable e. welcome
5. His **frugality** is commendable.
   a. frolic b. careful spending c. extravagance d. carefulness e. scarcity
6. She is known for her **largesse**.
   a. frugality b. miserliness c. generosity d. thoughtfulness e. intelligence
7. The **leverage** he has in political circles is well-known.
   a. strength b. fame c. popularity d. influence e. unpopularity
8. A PR job entails **liasing** between the public and the employer.
   a. disputes b. conferences c. conflicting d. presentations e. linking
9. Unless you stop **vacillating,** you'll achieve very little.
   a. wavering b. contemplating c. quarrelling d. delegating e. blinking
10. His booming voice **reverberated** around the hall.
    a. heard too loudly b. filled c. echoed d. was too feeble e. moved
11. The child was **rebuked** for his behaviour in the party.
    a. punished b. praised c. reprimanded d. slapped e. thanked
12. The judge called for a short **recess**.
    a. rest b. break c. witness d. discussion e. presentation
13. She was too **stubborn** to admit her guilt.
    a. complacent b. angry c. obstinate d. unwilling e. confused
14. He was so lost in thought that he was **oblivious** to his surroundings.
    a. unaware b. deprecating c. endorsing d. pedantic e. prejudiced
15. He was **hampered** by a hamstring.
    a. helped b. debilitated c. earmarked d. hindered e. humiliated
16. He was **ridiculed** for his petty behaviour.
    a. humbled b. mocked c. praised d. called names e. beaten

17. **Incredible**! You mean you're in love?
   a. Congrats! b. enjoyable c. unbelievable d. interesting e. wonderful
18. The government is bent upon **equitable** distribution of wealth.
   a. profitable b. fair c. unreasonable d. thoughtful e. simple
19. His **abrupt** remark displeased everyone present.
   a. sudden b. intentional c. unintentional d. pleasing e. critical
20. "I heard Tilak was jailed for a day." "It's **hearsay**."
   a. true b. a rumour c. impossible d. a fact e. doubtful

Exercise 12

Fill in each blank with an appropriate synonym for the word given in brackets:

1. This ——————[craziness] did win him some of the most —————— [good-looking] women in the industry, but was it also what made him more ——————[loving] to the people, one wonders.
2. To receive this special ——————[group] of Indian film songs along with your Toiletry Case, simply ——————[affix] below seal in the space —————— [shown] on your Rupees 5 million Sweepstake Certificate.
3. If ——————[not possible to deliver], please return to sender. To be opened by ——————[receiver] only.
4. Ideally, communicating is a ——————[non-stop] process of cause and effect.
5. In Ayurvedic philosophy everything in the universe is ——————[made up] of five elements, the panchamahabhutas. These ——————[group] into three doshas[the tridoshas] or bioenergetic force that ——————[rule] our health and ——————[decide] our prakriti, or physical constitution. The three gunas—or psychic forces—determine our ——————[mind] and spiritual health. Ayurveda is a ——————[comprehensive] system of health care that teaches us to balance these energies in order to achieve —————— [maximum] heath and well-being and to —————— [maintain] life.
6. I was ——————[amaze] to see the —————— [grit] of the ——————[workers] who, —————— [in spite of] the premature winding up of their ——————[previous] projects, were —————— [desirous] to —————— —————— [proceed].
7. Scientists are ——————[fundamentally] —————— [feeling] people. Once they stumble, it is ——————[not easy] for them to —————— themselves —————— [take control of feelings].
8. On-site processing of solid wastes is used to ——————[get back] the ——————[use again] materials from the solid wastes.

9. Today almost all nations are ——————————[trying] their —————— [maximum] to bring into the lives of their people the —————— [wonders] of science and technology. ——————[In truth], human life on this planet has been greatly ——————————[made rich] with the —————— —————— [unbelievable] technological ——————————[progress].
10. What ——————————[attracted] her most at her College was the sight of two decommissioned ——————————[planes] —————— ——[exhibited]. She felt a ——————————[unusual] attraction towards them. After —————— [completing] her first year when she had to —————— [choose] for a ——————————[particular] branch, I almost —————— —————— [without thinking] chose aeronautical engineering.

Antonyms

Exercise 13

Match these antonyms:

1.	relax	a.	occasional
2.	strengthen	b.	wet
3.	disable	c.	enable
4.	accept	d.	tense
5.	sensible	e.	weaken
6.	genuine	f.	miser
7.	frequent	g.	remember
8.	forget	h.	reject
9.	dry	i.	senseless
10.	spendthrift	j.	fake

Exercise 14

Match these antonyms:

11.	extravagance	a.	mean
12.	simple	b.	ignore
13.	elastic	c.	full
14.	lofty	d.	miserliness
15.	generous	e.	divided
16.	blank	f.	complex
17.	straight	g.	zigzag
18.	excited	h.	dull
19.	united	i.	low
20.	attend	j.	stiff

Exercise 15

Match these antonyms:

21. gentle	a. relaxed
22. jocular	b. epilogue
23. sharp	c. harsh
24. obsolete	d. current
25. relieved	e. vague
26. precise	f. serious
27. tense	g. dull
28. prologue	h. worried
29. defunct	i. existing
30. defuse	j. inflame

Exercise 16

31. worsen	a. arrive
32. adverse	b. favourable
33. slacken	c. firm
34. leave	d. purposeful
35. accidentally	e. traditional
36. derelict	f. tighten
37. despicable	g. destitute
38. trendy	h. lovable
39. weak	i. intentionally
40. desultory	j. improve

Exercise 17

Match these antonyms:

41. critical	a. angelic
42. release	b. trust
43. speculative	c. safe
44. seldom	d. joy
45. split	e. hold
46. save	f. factual
47. diabolic	g. affected
48. deceit	h. frequent
49. melancholy	i. fritter
50. impervious	j. join

Exercise 18

51. centre	a. periphery
52. feisty	b. quiet
53. perpetual	c. occasional
54. greed	d. contentment
55. perky	e. dull
56. sink	f. surface
57. passable	g. unacceptable
58. quell	h. encourage
59. simplistic	i. serious
60. jittery	j. calm

Exercise 19

61. dogged	a. docile
62. sustain	b. enslave
63. resist	c. perfunctory
64. tranquil	d. disturbed
65. discreet	e. reckless
66. sanguine	f. righteous
67. rebellious	g. disheartened
68. nefarious	h. pessimistic
69. emancipate	i. impede
70. rigorous	j. comply

Exercise 20

Choose from the expressions labelled a, b, c, d, e the ones that are opposite in meaning to the expressions that are in bold in the sentences below:

1. She is known for her **largesse**.
   a. miserliness b. fame c. perfection d. simplicity e. ego
2. The child was **rebuked** for her conduct.
   a. punished b. lauded c. ignored d. adopted e. ranked
3. The government is bent upon **equitable** distribution of wealth.
   a. stern b. fair c. unreasonable d. acceptable e. lawful
4. He promised he would **reveal** the truth at any cost.
   a. tell b. disclose c. hide d. print e. expose
5. Was he pretending or was he really **oblivious** to the surroundings?
   a. unaware b. conscious c. thinking of d. unhappy e. unmindful

6. The proposal originally **emanated** from the opposite camp.
   a. was brought from   b. did not come from
   c. wasn't welcome to   d. was challenged by
7. The government are **concerned** about the increasing number of the unemployed.
   a. worried about   b. excited by   c. bothered   d. uninhibited   e. unmindful of
8. I **accidentally** gave her the wrong change.
   a. eventually   b. knowingly   c. wilfully   d. illegally   e. unsmilingly
9. You can applaud the government for its **bias** in this matter.
   a. reliability   b. accountability   c. hostility   d. impartiality   e. prejudice
10. The enquiry had completely **exonerated** the minister.
    a. cleared   b. implicated   c. impersonated   d. unaccounted   e. praised
11. I had broken the vase **inadvertently**.
    a. maliciously   b. intermittently   c. deliberately   d. spiritedly   e. carelessly
12. My boss is very **strict** in his application of rules.
    a. confused   b. flexible   c. straightforward   d. radical   e. precise
13. Bechkam's performance in today's match was **dismal**.
    a. ordinary   b. excellent   c. gloomy   d. awful   e. spooky
14. He's always **denigrated** my achievements.
    a. insulted   b. commended   c. criticise   d. despised   e. deplored
15. She **implored** him to put up with her intemperance.
    a. ordered   b. begged   c. advised   d. suggested to   e. demanded
16. Those are **compelling** arguments, aren't they?
    a. revealing   b. forceful   c. weak   d. unbelievable   e. deceitful
17. Whenever he is about to lose an argument he **throws a tantrum**.
    a. throws his weight around   b. uses a weapon   c. accepts defeat gracefully
    d. pretends to be frustrated   e. exhibits controlled anger
18. He's very **negligent** about his health.
    a. understanding   b. watchful   c. careless   d. boastful   e. casual
19. He is an **eminent** writer.
    a. obscure   b. famous   c. careful   d. careless   e. liberal
20. He's known for his **sagacity**.
    a. wisdom   b. intemperance   c. outbursts   d. coolness   e. inefficiency

Exercise 21

Fill in each blank with an appropriate antonym for the word given in brackets:

1. His ____________[legal] business is ____________ [sinking].
2. ____________[surely] I rose and responded. My speech was followed by a thunderous ____________[criticism].
3. The ____________[last] thing that struck me when I met Prof. Deshpande was his ____________[artificial] ____________[sorrow] at meeting me. There was ____________[dullness] in his talk, an ____________[delayed] sympathetic ____________[enmity], accompanied by ____________ [slow] ____________[ugly] movements.
4. By the time we ____________[began] our work, it was already ____________[evening].
5. While I was forming teams and organising activities, I ____________[lost] the space available at Hyderabad was ____________[somewhat] ____________ [sufficient] to meet the ____________[worsened] requirements of our factory.
6. He was an intellectual ____________[dwarf] with a ____________ [strong] constitution. He had a ____________[childish] innocence and I always considered him a ____________[sinner] among scientists.
7. The ____________[first] time he was here he had been ____________[sober] and now he struggled to ____________[forget] ____________[vaguely] where jazz club was.
8. "Obviously." Tilde's tone was ____________[polite], and he ____________ [knew] she was ____________[pleased] by what she had just witnessed.
9. However, human activities are ____________[then] ____________[deducting] to the ____________[artificial] green house effect and ____________ [cooling] up the planet at an ____________[known upto now] rate.
10. In the ____________[absence] of witness or ____________ [contradicting] evidence, that isn't going to be an ____________[difficult] ____________ [fact] to ____________[buy] to a jury.

Exercise 22

You have below numbered pairs of sentences. In each numbered pair, the second sentence has one or two blanks. Fill in these blanks with expressions that are **antonymous** of those words underlined in the first sentence:

e.g. Keep him at arm's length. keep him beside you

Speak and be followed. Be silent and be one of the crowd

Pregnant words earn appreciation. Empty/Hollow words earn criticism

Lead by example. Follow by dictate.

1. He's treacherous by intent. He's ________ by ________.
2. Mind the opportunity and succeed. ________ the opportunity and ________.
3. It's a thankless job but I'm ________ I've got a job.
4. Life is full of imperatives. Life is ________ of ________.
5. Where there is less hope, there is ________ ________.
6. Seal the cracks, save the marriage. ________ the cracks, ________ the marriage.
7. One false step, you can be ruined. One ________ step, you can be ________.
8. Too much ego is harmful. Too ________ ego is ________.
9. Sensible approach will solve problems. ________ approach will ________ problems.
10. patience is a blessing. ________ is a ________.
11. Sink your differences, earn friendship. ________ your differences, earn ________.
12. Work hard, success will result. Work ________, ________ will result.
13. Be mirthful, you'll sparkle. Be ________, you'll ________.
14. Sensationalism leads to false security. ________ leads to ________ security.
15. Bloat your ego, be foolish. ________ your ego, be ________.
16. Education is only something. ________ is ________.

17. Favour the brave, ______________ the ______________.
18. Ambition is healthy, ______________ is ______________.
19. Emote and cheat, ______________ and ______________.
20. Save words and earn peace. ______________ words and earn ______________.
21. Busy keeps you breezy, ______________ keeps you ______________.
22. Promptness keeps you brisk, ______________ keeps you ______________.
23. Please and be pleased, ______________ and be ______________.
24. Sensing she was in danger, he grabbed her by the arm, dashed through the door, banged it shut, danced down the steps, rushed her into an approaching taxi.

    ______________ she was ______________, he ______________ her by the arm, ______________ the door, ______________ it ______________, ______________ the steps,

    ______________ her into a waiting taxi.
25. Seeing the man closing in, he looked frantically for a hiding place.

    Seeing the man ______________ ______________, he looked ______________ for a hotel.

2.2 One-Word Substitution

Learn these:

1. a person not available at a given place = absentee
2. act of a substance being taken in = absorption
3. a paragraph with the main ideas of a document = abstract
4. performance of difficult acts and movements = acrobatics
5. a word formed from first letters of certain words = acronym
6. short form of a word = abbreviation
7. selling through print or visual media = advertisement
8. exciting movements done in aircraft = aerobatics
9. science of building and flying aircraft = aeronautics
10. science describing relationship between crops and and environment = agronomy
11. list of items for discussion at a meeting = agenda
12. Chinese method of treating pain and illness = acupuncture
13. one who believes it is not possible to know if God exists = agnostic
14. one who cannot stop drinking = alcoholic
15. money paid to ex-husband or ex-wife = alimony
16. character and atmosphere of a place = ambience

17. study of human/animal body = anatomy
18. relative who lived long ago = ancestor
19. collection of poems, stories, essays = anthology
20. study of human race = anthropology
21. professional giving beauty treatment = beautician
22. something used as a standard for comparison = benchmark
23. loss of relative or friend = bereavement
24. agreement to marry somebody = betrothal/ engagement
25. the year something happened 200 years ago = bicentenary
26. divide into two parts = bifurcate
27. study of plants and animals = biology
28. about living cells and bacteria in industrial processes = biotechnology
29. stupid and careless mistake = blunder
30. become red in the face because of embarrassment = blush
31. skilled and qualified people leaving the country = brain drain
32. the way a group of people think to solve or come up with good useful ideas = brainstorming
33. person supporting a family = bread winner
34. important development leading to agreement = breakthrough
35. flat container for keeping paper and documents = briefcase
36. meeting where instructions or information given = briefing
37. meal not served at table = buffet
38. a system of following official rules strictly = bureaucracy
39. one killing animals and sells their meat = butcher
40. a group of government ministers = cabinet
41. electronic device for dealing with numbers = calculator
42. talking to people supporting a party = canvass
43. person having wealth and producing more wealth = capitalist
44. people crossing a desert with people, vehicles, animals = caravan
45. a dead animal's body for meat = carcass
46. of sky or heaven = celestial
47. a famous person = celebrity
48. liquid to make people unconscious for operation = chloroform
49. disease lasting for a long time = chronic
50. extreme fear of being in a small enclosed place = claustrophobia

51. most exciting event or part in a story/film = climax
52. a regular traveller to city for work from far away = commuter
53. money given for hurt or damage = compensation
54. act of discussing before deciding = consultation
55. study of the universe and its origin = cosmology
56. people from different countries and cultures = cosmopolitan
57. looks like genuine but in reality is not = counterfeit
58. one accused of a crime = defendant/the accused
59. one making a formal complaint in court = plaintiff
60. loss of too much water from body = dehydration
61. study of changes in births, deaths in a community =demography
62. device helping bomb explode = detonator
63. very religious person = devotee
64. unable to decide between two things = dilemma
65. place where one lives [official or legal] = domicile
66. moon or sun cannot be seen clearly = eclipse
67. relation between man and environment = ecology
68. chemicals as waste from industries = effluent
69. person leaving country to live another = emigrant
70. person of one country living in another = immigrant
71. include a large number of things = encompass
72. set of books giving complete information = encyclopaedia
73. study of insects = entomology
74. a disease occurring at the same time in a community = epidemic
75. great academic knowledge = erudition
76. formal rules of correct behaviour = etiquette
77. study of words = etymology
78. getting secret information about rivals [spying] = espionage
79. killing without pain one suffering from incurable disease = euthanasia
80. user's information about how something works = feedback
81. diagram showing connection in a process or system = flow chart
82. say about future based on present = forecast
83. say about future using magic powers = foretell
84. remains of animals or plants = fossil
85. goods sent through transport system = freight

86. one running away to avoid being caught = fugitive
87. study of family history = genealogy
88. study of earth and its features = geography
89. study of earth's origin and history[rocks and soil] = geology
90. one who eats too much = glutton
91. place with equipment for doing exercises =gym[nasium]
92. behaviour peculiar to an individual = idiosyncrasy
93. judging your own thoughts, reasons = introspection
94. one who avoids spending time with others = introvert
95. one who spends time with others = extrovert
96. a handle to move images in computer games = joystick
97. group of common people hearing a case and deciding guilt = jury
98. edge of raised sides of a road [pavement or sidewalk] = kerb
99. money paid illegally for work done = kickback/bribe
100. a small shop selling newspapers, drinks = kiosk
101. a body of people with power to make and change laws = legislature
102. most important person of an organisation or plan = linchpin
103. scientific study of language = linguistics
104. one who is making or defending a case in court = litigant
105. disease producing too many blood cells causing weakness = leukaemia
106. a great performer[especially a musician] = maestro
107. animal giving birth to babies = mammal
108. one who behaves differently from others with his own opinions =maverick
109. soldier fighting for any country for money = mercenary
110. being married to only one person at a time = monogamy
111. having more than one wife at the same time = polygamy
112. study of coins and medals = numismatics
113. brief information as news about one who has died = obituary
114. having total power = omnipotent
115. being present everywhere = omnipresent
116. knowing everything = omniscient
117. having a pleasant taste = palatable
118. one living on others = parasite
119. permission to a prisoner to leave before due time = parole
120. branch of medicine concerned with children = paediatrics

121. a person walking in the street = pedestrian
122. people working for an organisation = personnel
123. specialist in medicine = physician
124. a person studying physics = physicist
125. study of normal functions of living things = physiology
126. having developed certain abilities earlier than usual = precocious
127. existing from the earliest of human history = primeval/primordial
128. information document about education in an institution = prospectus
129. a name other than the real one = pseudonym
130. scientific study of mind = psychology
131. separation of a person with a disease from others = quarantine
132. give up physical pleasure for religious purposes = renounce
133. one leaving country for lack of security [during war] = refugee
134. enjoyment from others' suffering = sadism
135. criticism with humour on faults and weaknesses = satire
136. message requesting for urgent help from ship or plane = SOS
137. opinions or behaviour typical of a person, attitude, social problem = syndrome
138. connected with saying goodbye = valedictory
139. observing positions of stars as influencing human beings = astrology
140. study of heart functions and diseases = cardiology
141. study of human skin = dermatology
142. dictionary compilation = lexicography
143. science of weather = meteorology
144. study of birds = ornithology
145. study of earthquakes = seismology
146. without name = anonymous
147. a list of books related to a particular topic or subject = bibliography
148. belonging to the same period = contemporary
149. a person with negative attitude/outlook = cynic
150. speaking extremely well = elocution
151. one who runs own business = entrepreneur
152. no longer in existence = extinct
153. a large group of stars = galaxy
154. a list of important words with meanings = glossary
155. important printed government communications/news = gazette

156. of same kind = homogeneous
157. of different kind = heterogeneous
158. without preparation = impromptu
159. that can easily catch fire = inflammable
160. something given for remembrance = memento
161. last but one = penultimate
162. one with exceptional talents far beyond age = prodigy
163. an unmarried woman = spinster
164. an unmarried man = bachelor
165. commonly used, present everywhere = ubiquitous
166. in complete agreement = unanimous

2.3 Prefixes and Suffixes

2.3.1 Introduction

A language derives or forms more words from words. Nouns can be formed from verbs, adjectives can be derived from nouns and verbs, verbs can be formed from nouns and adjectives. Such word derivatives or formations are got with the help of 'affixes'.

When we add a **letter** or a **syllable** to a word, affixing occurs and we get another word.

The word '**a**moral' has 'a' as a letter affix; The word 'shad**y**' has 'y' as a letter affix; The word '**de**merit' has a syllable affix; The word 'damp**en**' has a syllable affix. The affixes are printed in bold.

The letter affix 'a' is fixed before the word 'moral'; the letter affix 'de' is also fixed before the word 'merit'. Such affixes preceding [coming before] words [or roots or stems] are known as **prefixes**.

The letter affix 'y' is fixed at the end of the word 'shade'; the letter affix 'en' is also fixed at the end of the word 'damp'. Such affixing following [coming at the end of] words [or roots or stems] are known as **suffixes**.

Exercise 23

In the following sentences or paragraphs, you'll find blanks followed by words in brackets. Fill in each blank with the word formed by adding an appropriate prefix, suffix or both to the word given in brackets:

1. Don't depend on him; he's very ______________ . [rely]
2. He's been ______________ [special] interested in the welfare of Tamil medium students.
3. Did you read the ______________[editor] in yesterday's Hindu?

4. There's been a ________________[consider] ________________ [reduce] in the ________________[deploy] of the army in the Kargil area.

5. I respect your ________________[friend].

6. Our ________________[reduce] sales are on from tomorrow.

7. We provide quality ________________[treat] to our patients.

8. That's a ________________[sense] ________________[suggest] from you. Thank you.

9. I've ________________[place] my wallet; I can't find it.

10. When you place a heavy object in a bucket full of water, the water gets ________________ [place].

11. To everyone's ________________[amaze] the ________________[magic] changed himself into a bird.

12. If you give me a ________________[recommend] letter, it'll ________________ [able] me to get a job.

13. Questionnaires are used as part of research for ________________[collect] of data.

14. The ________________[defend] ________________[law] objected to certain expressions used by the public ________________[prosecute] .

15. Customers are warned that on ________________[pay] of ________________ [electric] bills within stipulated time, power will be ________________[connect].

16. Even today, ________________[literacy] is very high in villages.

17. I could see ________________[satisfy] in her face.

18. I shouted at you, yes, but that's no ________________[justify] for having me beaten up.

19. The mobile and the internet have ________________[revolution] our ________________ [communicate] channels.

20. We won't accept your ________________ [deny].

21. Your ________________[accuse] is totally false.

22. I'm afraid that our ________________[develop] programmes are ________________ [adequate]

23. He's always ——————————[treat] me. I hate him.

24. Though these ——————————[refuge] are in need of —————— [rehabilitate], the ——————————[govern] is ——————————[ignore] this problem.

25. You can't fight alone against ——————————[corrupt]. If you persist, your life will be ————[misery].

26. In most ——————————[organise], newsletters are —————— [circulate] to pass on local news to their ————[employ].

27. Is the diameter of the ——————————[wood] posts of the main structure 100 mm?

28. Next, several ——————————[suggest] or —————— [recommend] are made to ——————[sure] ——————————[correct] action. For instance, ——————————[work] may undergo —————— [retrain]. ——————————[supervise] may need to be stepped up. New —————— ——————[equip] may benecessary. Or the —————— [operation] processes may need ——————[revise]. Further, it may be necessary or — ——————————[desire] to take another look at standards set for output or quality. Even ——————————[manage] goals may require —————— ————[modify] or ——————————[transform].

29. It is imperative that we ——————[careful] utilise our —————— —————— [renew] resources of soil, plant and animal life to sustain our economic —————— —————— [develop]. Over- ——————————[exploit] of these is reflected in soil —————— [erode], ——————————[silt], floods and rapid —————— ——————[destroy] of forest, floral and wild life resources. The —————— [deplete] of these resourcesoften tends to be ——————————[reversible] and since the bulk of our ——————[populate] depends on these natural resources to meet their basic needs, ——————[particular] of fuel, fodder and —————— [house] material, it has meant a ——————————[deteriorate] in their quality of life.

30. The following are some of the common methods of ——————————[assess]. ——————————[usual], an ——————————[evaluate] uses all three components to gather ——————[inform] about a child.

Now let's take a look at some frequently used **prefixes**:

2.3.2 Negative Prefixes:

'a' = without

amoral	=	not caring about right or wrong
apolitical	=	[person] not interested in politics
	=	[organisation] not connected with any political party
asexual	=	without sex or sexual organs
asocial	=	avoiding or inconsiderate of others
asymmetry	=	lack of symmetry
atheism	=	lack of belief in the existence of God
atheist	=	one who does not believe in the existence of God
atypical	=	not typical

'anti' = opposed to antisocial[harmful to society], antiseptic

= opposite of antithesis, anticlockwise

= preventing antifreeze, anticoagulant, antibiotic

'counter' = against, opposite

counter-argument, counter-attack, counterbalance, counterclaim

countermeasure, counterproductive, counter-terrorism

= corresponding, substitution

counterpart, countersign

'de' = opposite of

debrief, debug, decamp, decentralise, declassify, decode, decompose, decom press, decontaminate, decontrol, decriminalise, deflate, deforest, deform, defrock, defrost, dehumanise, dehydrate, demerit, demoralise, demystify, denationalise, deplane, depopulate, deregulate, destabilise

---

'dis' = not, opposite of

disability, disable, disabled, disadvantage, disaffected, disafforest[deforest], disagree, disallow, disappear, disappoint, disapprove, disarm, disarrange, disband, disbar, disbelieve, disclaim, disclose, discomfort, disconnect, discontent, discontinuation, discourage, discover, discredit, disease, disengage, disfigure, disillusion, disincentive, disinfect, disintegrate, dislike, dislocate, disloyal, disorder, disobey, disorganised, distrust, disunity, disuse

---

'dys' = bad, difficult [used in medical terms]
dysfunctional, dyslexia, dyspepsia, dyspnoea

'il', 'im', 'in', 'ir' = not, opposite of
illegal, illegible, illiterate, illogical
imbalance, immaterial, immature, immobile, immodest, immoral, impatient, imperfect, impermanent, impersonal, impossible, impracticable, imprecise, improbable, improper, impure inability, inaction, inactive, inadequate, inapplicable, inappropriate, inattentive, inaudible, incapable, incoherent, incompatible, incompetent, incomplete, incomprehensible, indescribable, indigestible, indirect, indiscretion, indispensable, indistinct, ineffective, inefficient, inexpensive, inexperience, inexplicable, insane, insecure, insensible, inseparable, insincere, insufficient,
intransitive, invalid, invariably, invisible

'mal' = bad, not correct
maladjusted, malfunction, malnutrition, maltreat

'mis' = bad, wrong
misapply, misappropriate, misbehave, misconception, misconduct, misdeed, misdirect, mishandle, mishear, misinform, misinterpret, misjudge, mislay, mislead, mismatch, misplace, mispronounce, misrepresent, misrule, mistrust, misunderstand, misuse
= hate
misanthrope, misogynist

'non' = not
non-aggression, non-alcoholic, non-aligned, non-appêarance, non-committal, non-controversial, non-cooperation, non-existent, non-fiction, non-refundable, non-renewable, non-resident, nonsense, non-smoker, non-standard, non-stop, non-violent, non-white

---

'sub' = below, less

subhuman: subeditor, subnormal, subordinate, substandard, substructure subzero, subtropical

= under

subconscious, sublet, submarine, submerge, subplot, subsection, subtitle, subway

= smaller part

subatomic, subcommittee, subgroup, subdivide, subset, subtotal

---

'un' = not, opposite of [in adjectives, adverbs, nouns]

unable, unabridged, unacceptable, unaffected, unafraid, unaided, unambiguously, unarmed, unattractive, unavailable, unbearable, unbeatable, unbelief [n], unbeliever [n], unbreakable, uncensored, uncertain, uncertainly, unclaimed, uncommon, unconditional, unconscious, unconvincing, uncooked, undecided, undefeated, unfair, unfit, unfortunate, unhappy, unhealthy, unimaginable, unlawful, unmoved, unnatural, unpopular, unsafe,unsold, untiring,

= opposite of [in verbs of process]

unbend, uncork, uncover, undo, unfold, unlock, untangle

'under' = below

undercover, undergrowth, under age, underclothes, underfloor underground, underline,

= lower

underbid, undercharge, undercut, undergraduate, underestimate underprivileged, underrate, undersell, understate, underweight

= not enough

underachieve, undercooked, underdeveloped, underfed, undernourished, underpaid, understaffed

---

2.3.3 Negative Suffix

'less' = without

breathless, careless, clueless, deathless, friendless, goalless, luckless, meaningless, speechless, tactless, treeless, wireless

= not affected by: tireless, selfless

2.3.4 Other Prefixes

prefixes

'ambi' = referring to both of two : ambidextrous, ambivalent

'ante' = before, in front of : antedate, antenatal, ante-room

'auto' = of or by yourself : autobiography, autosuggestion

'bi' = two, twice, double : biannual [twice a year], bicentenary [200 years ago] bicycle[two wheels], biennial [once in two years]. bilabial[using two lips], bilateral [two groups], bilingual [two languages]

'demi' = half, partly : demigod

'en/em' = put into condition mentioned : enable, enact, encamp, encase, encash, endanger, empower, entrap, embalm,

= cause to be : encourage, endear, enlarge, enliven, embolden entrust, embed, embitter

'ex' = former : ex-minister, ex-president, ex-husband, ex-wife

'extra' = outside, beyond : extracurricular, extramarital, extraterrestrial,

= very : extraordinary, extra-thin, extra-special

'hemi' = half : hemicylindrical, hemisphere

'homo' = same : homocentric, homogeneous, homomorphic, homophone, homosexual

'inter' = between, among : international, interaction, interactive, interchange, interdepartmental, interdependent, nterdisciplinary interlingual, interlink, intermediate, interpersonal, interview

'intra' = within : intranational, intravenous, intramural

'multi' = more than one : multicoloured, multilingual, multimedia, multinational, multiparty, multiple-choice, multipurpose, multitasking

'out' = go beyond [exceed] : outperform, outwit, outgrow, outnumber, outlive outlast, outrank, outweigh

= outside : outhouse, outflow, outdoor, outsider, outward

'over' = too much : overload, overproduction, over-optimistic, overconfident, overanxious, overbalance, overcharge, overcrowded, overdraft, overeat, overspend

= completely : overjoyed

= upper, outer : overcoat, overtime, overestimate, overflow, oversell

= above : overhang, overcast,

'post' = after : postgraduate, post-mortem, postnatal, postscript postpone

‘pre’ = before : preamble, preconceived, precondition, predestined, preface, prefix, prejudge, premarital, premature, premeditated, prepaid, preposition
‘pro’ = in favour of : proactive, pro-democracy, promotion,
‘pseudo’= false, not genuine : pseudonym, pseudo-intellectual, pseudo-science
‘re’ = again : readmit, reappear, reapply, rearrange, reassess, reassure, rebirth, rebuild, recall, recharge, reconsider, reconstruct, recount, recycle, redefine, reintroduce, relocate, reproduce, resell, retell, review
‘semi’ = half, partly : semicircle, semicolon, semi-final, semivowel
‘super’ = more than : superhero, superhuman, superman, supermarket, supernatural, supersonic, superstar
= above : superimpose, superstructure
‘tele’ = over a long distance : telegraph, telephone, teleprinter, television, telescope, telecast
= done using a telephone : telemarketing, telesales
‘ultra’ = beyond a particular limit : ultrasonic, ultrasound, ultraviolet
‘infra’ = below : infrared, infrasonic
‘uni’ = one : uniform, unilateral
‘vice’ = next in rank : vice chairman, vice chancellor, vice president vice admiral

---

2.3.5 Other Suffixes

1. to form nouns

‘acy’/cy : accurate—accuracy , infant—infancy, delicate—delicacy, bankrupt—bankruptcy, democrat—democracy, celibate—celibacy autocrat—autocracy, primary—primacy, supreme—supremacy sufficient—sufficiency, urgent—urgency

‘age’ : carry—carriage, drain—drainage, teen—teenage, marry—marriage, break—breakage, coin—coinage,

‘al’ : recite—recital, retrieve—retrieval, approve—approval, betray—betrayal, deny—denial, bury—burial, survive—survival

‘ance’ : maintain—maintenance, remember—remembrance, deliver—deliverance, rely—reliance, relevant—relevance, reluctant—reluctance, vigil—vigilance, defy—defiance, remit—remittance, acquaint—acquaintance

‘ant’ : attend—attendant, defend—defendant, depend—dependant, account—accountant, occupy—occupant, inhabit—inhabitant, militate—militant, combat—combatant, apply—applicant

‘ence’ : revere—reverence, emerge—emergence, permanent—permanence, impertinent—impertinence

'ation'	:	aspire—aspiration, inspire—inspiration, realise—realisation, simplify—simplification, adapt—adaptation, regularize—regularization,
'ion'	:	regulate—regulation, negate—negation, simulate—simulation, relate—relation, suggest—suggestion, digest—digestion, suspect—suspicion, articulate—articulation, abort—abortion, distinct—distinction
'tion'	:	intend—intention, introduce—introduction abolish—abolition, redeem—redemption, repeat—repetition, compose—composition,
'sion'	:	decide—decision, divide—division, divert—diversion, expel—expulsion, repel—repulsion, extend—extension, intrude—intrusion, collide—collision, compel—compulsion
'hood'	:	baby—babyhood, child—childhood, man—manhood, woman—womanhood, brother—brotherhood, preiest—priesthood, false—falsehood
'ism'	:	real—realism, social—socialism, national—nationalism, opportune—opportunism,
'ity'	:	able—ability, active—activity, real—reality, timid—timidity, rapid—rapidity, relative—relativity, regular—regularity, intense—intensity, civil—civility, spontaneous—spontaneity, clear—clarity, polar—polarity
'ment'	:	arrange—arrangement, engage—engagement, govern—government, manage—management, measure—measurement, equip—equipment, accomplish—accomplishment
'ness'	:	blind—blindness, bright—brightness, calm—calmness, dry—dryness, fit—fitness, good—goodness, kind—kindness, lively—liveliness,
'ship'	:	companion—companionship, friend—friendship, citizen—citizenship,
'ure'	:	close—closure, legislate—legislature, fail—failure
'y'	:	discover—discovery, victor—victory, jealous—jealousy deliver—delivery, recover—recovery,
'let'	:	book—booklet, ankle—anklet, river—rivulet
'ing' [gerund]	:	be—being, earn—earning, live—[the] living, walk—walking, greet—greeting, dance—dancing, race—racing, swim—swimming

persons

'an'/ 'ian' : India—Indian, Ethiopia—Ethiopian, republic—republican, America—American, Brazil—Brazilian, mathematics—mathematician, Indonesia—Indonesian, Sri Lanka—Sri Lankan, Europe—European, magic—magician, academic—academician, statistic—statistician, Canada—Canadian, Russia—Russian, Africa—African

'er' : abstain—abstainer, absorb—absorber, adopt—adopter, admire—admirer, announce—announcer, bake—baker, consume—consumer, decide—decider, employ—employer New Zealand—New Zealander

'ee' : absent—absentee, devotion—devotee, employ—employee, pay—payee, appoint—appointee, address—addressee, divorce—divorcee,

'eer' : mountain—mountaineer, auction—auctioneer, voluntary—volunteer

'ese' : Japan—Japanese, China—Chinese

'ist' : abortion—abortionist, active—activist, apology—apologist, analyse—analyst, copy—copyist, ideal—idealist, rape—rapist, geology—geologist, economics—economist, physics—physicist, chemistry—chemist

'or' : abduct—abductor, act—actor, debt—debtor, aggression—aggressor, audit—auditor, arbitrate—arbitrator, administrate—administrator, credit—creditor, guarantee—guarantor, council—councillor, dictate—dictator, coordinate—coordinator, counsel—counsellor

---

2. to form **verbs**

'ed' : talk—talked, walk—walked, like—liked, act—acted, bake—baked

'ing' : talk—talking, walk—walking, like—liking, act—acting, bake—baking

'en' : sharp—sharpen, red—redden, damp—dampen, wide—widen, strength—strengthen, black—blacken,

'[i]fy' : simple—simplify, ample—amplify, false—falsify, speech—speechify, pure—purify, solid—solidify, horror—horrify

'ise'/'ize' : regular—regularise, standard—standardise, critic—criticise, hospital—hospitalise, theory—theorise, private—privatise, national—nationalise, rational—rationalise, capital—capitalise

---

3. to form **adjectives**

'al' : music—musical, logic—logical, magic—magical, verb—verbal,

'able' : rely—reliable, capacity—capable, tax—taxable, fashion—fashionable, comfort—comfortable, change—changeable, agree—agreeable, read—readable, suit—suitable 'ar' : molecule—molecular, circle—circular

'ary' : budget—budgetary, money—monetary,

'fic' : terror—terrific, majesty—majestic, specify—specific

'ful' : colour—colourful, cheer—cheerful, law—lawful, sorrow—sorrowful, forget—forgetful, force—forceful

'ible' : digest—digestible, force—forcible, defence—defensible, horror—horrible, terror—terrible, reverse—reversible

'ical' : farce—farcical, geology—geological, geography—geographical

'ious' : religion—religious, vice—vicious, ferocity—ferocious, space—spacious, caution—cautious

'ish' : child—childish, girl—girlish, Sweden—Swedish, Dane—Danish, yellow—yellowish, blue—bluish

'ish' [approximate time] : threeish, sixish etc

'ive' : collect—collective, mass—massive, disrupt—disruptive operate—operative regulate—regulative

'like' : child—childlike

'ous' : courage—courageous, religion—religious, mountain—mountainous, gas—gaseous, poison—poisonous, glory—glorious

'ed' : talent—talented, educate—educated, bad-temper—bad-tempered, depart—departed

'en' : earth—earthen, lead—leaden, mistake—mistaken, wood—wooden gold—golden

'ly' : brother—brotherly, sister—sisterly, mother—motherly, father—fatherly, hour—hourly

4. to form **adverbs**

'ly' : [with adjectives] great—greatly, skilful—skilfully, real—really severe—severely, secret—secretly

---

Shall we do a few exercises?

Exercise 24

From the following words, write down those that have been formed or derived with the help of prefixes, suffixes or both and underline the affixes:

e.g. unreliable, bureaucracy, immeasurable, joyous, demotivate, disengage

abnormal, ably, absolutely, accessible, accuracy, adage, package, amoral, afoot, alacrity, enormity, dictionary, military, endure, endanger, enemy, enable, mission, permission, misplace, discussion, disappear, generous, uniform, immature, immaculate, emblem, empower, illicit, illegible, declare, decompose, mistrust, distrust, ill-treat, mistreat, mistake, mistime, irreversible, inappropriate, misappropriate, incredulous, incredible, visible, spacious, circular, regular, religion, digestion, counsellor, speechless, reproduction, deepen, demerit, anticipate, antibacterial, counterpose, countersign, dismissal, deactivation, creator, motor, rebellion, creamy, barmy, shaky

____

____

____

____

____

____

____

____

____

Exercise 25

From the prefixes given below attach the right one for each of the following words:

non, dis, de, mis, ir/im/in/il, un, counter, mal, sub, under

[For some words, more than one prefix can be attached.]

____regulate ____unity ____appear ____ convincing ____measure

____classify ____ability ____responsible ____nutrition ____human

____editor ____able ____efficient ____stop ____Whites ____considerate

____populate ____cover ____material ____logical ____cooked

____member ____weight ____religious ____marine ____pleased

Exercise 26

Rewrite the following words using appropriate suffixes given below:

less, acy/cy, age, al, ity, ness, y, [i]fy, ise/ize, ment, hood, able, ful, ive, ly, en, ous, ation, er, or, ic

[For some words, more than one suffix can be attached.]

brother, speech, admire, bear, reflect, nation, rely, silk, colour, happy, neighbour, despot, dictate, announce, audit, design, secret, mile, malaria, regular, specific,

____

rest, examine, hard, intense, count, amplify, deny, read, success, soft

____

____

Exercise 27

Correct the spelling of the following words where necessary:

budgetery captor reportor arguement judgment repeatition advertisment

____

republican rebellian calculater regulator unforgetable covertion attackor advisor

____

administeration perfarmance revealation indicater invension revision jugglar

____

compelsion eradication sensasion probationor perversion prevension sensation

____

dependant dependent defendant capter catchible saleable removable reversible

____

educater distributer miner racer racist teacher sprintor decorator admissible

____

Exercise 28

From each of the following passages, write down the words formed with affixes:

1.

The key to effective communication
This is the essential practical guide for anyone who wants to improve their written and spoken language skills. It provides advice, tips, and ideas to help you communicate better in a wide range of everyday situations. Real-life examples, an invaluable glossary, and *You Try* boxes provide clear and accessible guidance.[" blurb" of Oxford guide to writing and speaking]

....

______________________ ______________________

2.

> Using good English
> Use the extensive coverage of the technicalities of the English language to improve your understanding of grammar, vocabulary, spelling, punctuation, and speech.

3.

> **The first paragraph is about using the overdraft facility and the second concerns overdraft protection, an insurance protecting the user against being unable to repay the overdraft in the event of illness or unemployment**

2. ____________________ ____________________ 3. ____________________ ____________________

____________________ ____________________ ____________________ ____________________

____________________ ____________________ ____________________

4.

> **These principles underpinning effective performance appraisal have wider relevance than simply improvements in individual performance. They are also concerned with the development of a participative organizational culture.**

____________________ ____________________ ____________________ ____________________

____________________ ____________________ ____________________ ____________________

5.

> **Ayurveda is the most ancient form of medicine in the world, and the forerunner of all other great systems of medicine. It literally means 'knowledge of life'; its guiding principles are believed to have been handed down from the Hindu gods to the great seers. The written texts of Ayurveda date back 3,500 years and the incredibly complex and advanced concepts that embody them still form the basis of much Indian medicine today.**

____________________ ____________________

____________________ ____________________

6.

Brinkerhoff looked up. It was Midge Milken, Fontaine's internal security analyst. She was sixty, slightly heavy, and much to the puzzlement of Brinkerhoff, quite appealing. An ex-wife three times over, Midge prowled the six-room directorial suite with a saucy authority. She was sharp, intuitive, worked ungodly hours, and was rumoured to know more about the NSA's inner workings than God himself. "D.Brown's Digital Fortress"

7.

It was a Saturday night, and Mahogany Row was all but deserted, its executives long gone——off enjoying whatever pastimes influential men enjoyed in their leisure. Although Brinkerhoff had always dreamed of a 'real' post with the agency, he had somehow ended up as a 'personal aide'—the official cul de sac of the political rat race. The fact that he worked side by side with the single most powerful man in American intelligence was little consolation.

8.

[i] Also to learn about several unknown factors of space travel such as physiological effects of prolonged weightlessness and of possible radiation in space.

[ii] As system engineers they defined the technical requirements of the parts that constitute a system……

[iii] A text is organized description or narration or information. It is usually split or divided into paragraphs.

7.

8. i.

8.ii

8.iii

9.

Staring intently at the barren pocket of land, Langdon sensed that it was plenty large enough. Excitement surged through him. This was obviously where the camerlengo planned to take the antimatter! The chopper was pointing directly toward it! ["D. Brown's Angels and Demons"]

10.

In the distance to the west, Langdon could see the twinkling delineation of the Mediterranean coast—a jagged border of luminescence beyond which spread an endless dark expanse of nothingness. [Angels and Demons]

9. ________ ________

________ ________

10. ________ ________

________ ________

11.

World-renowned Harvard symbologist Robert Langdon is summoned to a Swiss research facility to analyse a cryptic symbol seared into the chest of a murdered physicist. What he discovers is unimaginable: a deadly vendetta against the Catholic Church by a centuries-old underground organisation—the illuminati. Desperate to save the Vatican from a powerful time bomb, Langdon joins forces in Rome with the beautiful and mysterious scientist Vittoria Vetra. Together they embark on a frantic hunt through sealed crypts, dangerous catacombs, deserted cathedrals, and the most secretive vault on earth... The long-forgotten illuminati

11.

________ ________ ________

________ ________ ________

________ ________ ________

________ ________ ________

________ ________ ________

________ ________ ________

12. When the NSA's invincible code-breaking machine encounters a mysterious code it cannot break, the agency calls its head cryptographer, Susan Fletcher, a brilliant and beautiful mathematician. What she uncovers sends shock waves through the corridors of power. The NSA is being held hostage....not by guns or bombs, but by a code so ingeniously complex that if released it would cripple U.S. intelligence. Caught in an accelerating tempest of secrecy and lies, Susan Fletcher battles to save the agency she believes in. Betrayed on all sides, she finds herself fighting not only for her country.....
"Blurb of D. Brown"s Digital Fortress"

12.

________________-- ________________ ________________

________________-- ________________ ________________

________________-- ________________ ________________

13.

A lot of guidance in this book concerns written expression. This is because people seek advice and information about written English far more often than they do about spoken English. We all use speech apparently fairly naturally and usually without any obvious problems. Also, most of the time, spoken words disappear as soon as they have been uttered, so it is difficult for them to come back to haunt us.

13.

________________-- ________________ ________________

________________-- ________________

________________-- ________________ ________________

Exercise 29

Complete each word given below using appropriate prefix, suffix or both:

1. conduct——— = one who conducts
2. competit——— = one who competes
3. select——— = one who selects
4. regulat——— = one that regulates
5. sprint——— = one who sprints
6. employ——— = one who works for another
7. employ——— = one who provides jobs
8. transmit——— = one that transmits
9. judge——— = sentence given by a judge
10. product——— = act of producing
11. swim——— = act of moving in water
12. prosecut——— = one who prosecutes
13. record——— = one that records
14. senat——— = member of upper assembly in US.
15. tract——— = motor vehicle used on farms
16. sens——— = device that detects
17. decorat——— = one who decorates
18. refer——— = one who sees to the adherence of rules in a game
19. examin——— = one who sits for an examination
20. absorb——— = one that absorbs
21. ———timely = not suitable
22. ———administer = administer dishonestly
23. ———allow = not allow
24. ———hydrate = lose a large amount of water
25. ———united = lacking unity
26. ———trust = lack of trust
27. ———value = reduce the value
28. ———moved = unaffected
29. ———sell = sell for a lower price
30. wit——— = stupid

2.4 Idioms and Phrases

2.4.1 Verb phrases (1)

Phrasal verbs are combinations of

verbs + particles (= adverb and for preposition).

1. He went into the room.
   V P
2. She turned down the offer.
   V P
3. Everyone looks down upon me.
   V P P
4. They called the deal off.
   V P
5. The terrorists blew up the bridge.
   V P

Very often, **phrasal verbs express meanings different from the literal meanings of the words in combination**. For instance, 'turn down' means 'reject' and 'look down upon' means 'have a poor opinion of', esp, as being below one's social level'.

It's impossible, in a book of this nature, to list **all** the phrasal verbs. There are several dictionaries available. Longman's Dictionary of phrasal verbs is one which contains 12,000 phrasal verbs.

However, you'll be acquainted with a few common ones.

(I) Below you'll find a very few common ones with examples:

account for : *explain/give a reason*

6. How do you **account for** your strange behaviour in the party?

accustom to +ing : (*passive*)

7. **I'm** not **accustomed to listening** to drivel.

admit to : *confess*

8. The thief **admitted his guilt to** the police.
9. The stranger **admitted to stealing** the jewels.

allow for : *take* (*something*) *into consideration*

10. **Allowing for** traffic jam on the way, we set off in the wee hours.

answer back : *reply rudely*

11. Raghu said : "Raj, don't talk like that!"
    Raj **answered back**, "Who are you to interfere?"

back out : *fail to do what is expected*

12. you said you' stand by me, why do
    you **back out** now?

bargain for : *(usually in the negative)*

(not) expect something to happen and so (not) be prepared for it

13. I did not **bargain for** a 'yes' from her when I proposed to her!

bleed white : *cheat (someone) of all money*

14. Money lenders **bleed** borrowers **white** with their high rate of interest.

blow over : *stop / cease*

15. Don't worry. His anger will **blow over**.

break even : *show neither profit nor loss*

16. I've been doing business for years now.

But I've only managed to **break even**.

buoy up : *keep (something) high*

17. When there was no promotion letter forth coming, I **buoyed my spirits up** by telling myself that no one was getting promotions this year.

catch flat footed : *catch someone by surprise as in doing something wrong*

18. We were trying to jump through the classroom window but **were caught flatfooted**.

cave in : *yield*

19. I didn't expect you to **cave in** and lose the argument so easily ?

clamour for : *demand (something) loudly*

20. Chennaites **are clamouring for** only one thing: water.

cook up : *invert / think of (usually something wrong)*

21. He's always **cooking up** stories for his absence from duty.

cotton on : *understand*

22. It took me sometime to **cotton on** to why my boss was angry with me.

count in : *include someone by choice*

23. I hear you're asking for volunteers.

Count me **in**.

crack down on : *deal firmly with (something / someone negative)*

24. The government has promised to **crack down on** seminal activities.

dawn on/upon : *become known by (someone) or obvious to*

25. As I came to the cash counter, it suddenly **dawned on** me that I'd left my credit card at home.

deal in : *buy and sell*

26. I **deal in** leather goods.

divorce from : (*passive*) *completely different / separate from*

27. Your expectations are **divorced from** reality.

drive home to : *convince / make someone understand/believe something*

28. Please **drive home** to **your friend** that he'll lose more from the marriage than gain.

figure out : understand

29. I can't **figure** my wife **out**.

hanker after/for : *have a strong drive for something, esp. if you cannot or should not have it*

30. Eventhough she's gone, he still **hankers after her.**

hush up : *keep (information) secret by enforcing silence about it.*

31. These days, it's difficult to **hush up** murders for political causes.

phase out : *stop / remove in stages*

32. The MSc computer science will be **phased out** with the present batch.

rifle through : *search quickly with dishonest intentions*

33. Someone's been **rifling through** my drawers, some important papers are missing.

trim down : *reduce*

34. We'll have to **trim down** our spending to fit our income.

2.4.2 Verb phrases (2)

There are several **verbs** that derive **as many meanings as the particles** that are **used with them**. A few of them are:

get, give, go, keep, look, make, put, run, see, take.

You can learn several of them from the following exercise. Use a dictionary if necessary to make the correct choices.

Exercise 30

1. Don't fall ________ his arguments; he's trying to take advantage of you.
   (a) for (b) behind (c) in (d) to
2. You promised to help me. Why do you back ________ now?
   (a) out (b) up (c) down (d) away
3. I don't think I'm cut ________ teaching; I don't have the necessary patience.
   (a) up about (b) out for (c) down to (d) down on

4. They've patched up their differences and are getting ___________ nicely.
   (a) about (b) along (c) away (d) back
5. What are you getting ___________ ? speak plainly!
   (a) at (b) across (c) about (d) after
6. Students have no way of getting ___________ their teachers who mark their work unfairly.
   (a) away with (b) back at (c) back to (d) away from
7. Few teachers can get ___________ students who don't want to learn.
   (a) through with (b) out of (c) through to (d) up with
8. A good teacher's patience never gives ___________.
   (a) in (b) out (c) up (d) off
9. How did your speech go ___________ the crowd?
   (a) back on (b) away with (c) along with (d) down with
10. There are whispers going ___________ the place that our GM is being retired early.
    (a) by (b) after (c) about (d) off
11. As I was in the middle of my explanation, she hung ___________.
    (a) up (b) on (c) over
12. I was able to hold ___________ my anger and avoid a fight.
    (a) in (b) back (c) down (d) on
13. I don't hold ___________ some of the strange ideas you believe in.
    (a) with (b) up (c) to (d) out
14. As an engineer, you need to keep ___________ new developments in your field.
    (a) after (b) abreast of (c) at (d) up
15. I depended on you for support. But you let me ___________.
    (a) off (b) out (c) in (d) down
16. Will the old man live ___________ the day ?
    (a) by (b) for (c) out (d) through
17. The college looks ___________ such behaviour.
    (a) about (b) after (c) down on (d) for
18. I was passing this way; so I though I would look ___________.
    (a) forward to (b) in (c) upon (d) out
19. We chased them for long but the thieves made ___________ the jewels.
    (a) off (b) over (c) out (d) off with
20. When he heard the shocking news, he passed ___________.
    (a) out (b) by (c) up (d) through
21. Your strategy ultimately paid ___________ and we are reaping the benefits.
    (a) back (b) for (c) off (d) over

22. I don't know where my children have picked ________ those rude words.
    (a) up (b) out (c) on (d) at
23. Don't play ________ me. I'm serious about marriage. What do you say ?
    (a) along (b) at (c) on (d) with
24. The firm pulled ________ from its agreement.
    (a) back (b) down (c) in (d) off
25. You're feeling low, I know. But a good holiday, I'm sure, will pull you ________.
    (a) out (b) round (c) up (d) over
26. Even if you're justified, put ________ your anger and listen to me.
    (a) about (b) across (c) aside (d) forward
27. Thank you for your offer. But I have a little money put ________.
    (a) away (b) by (c) down (d) forward
28. She puts ________ two hours on her English studies every day.
    (a) in (b) into (c) off (d) out
29. My temper ran ________ me and I hit the stranger.
    (a) across (b) away from (c) away with (d) back over
30. The poor boy has been run ________ by a lorry.
    (a) behind (b) down (c) for (d) off
31. Who's going to see ________ the visitors when they arrive ?
    (a) about (b) after (c) in (d) into
32. This is all I have. Hope this amount will see you ________ till your loan cheque is cleared.
    (a) through (b) to (c) over (d) off
33. The terrible communal clash has set neighbour ________ neighbour.
    (a) against (b) about (c) aside (d) back
34. Teachers should stand ________ and let their students run the activities their own way.
    (a) by (b) back (c) behind (d) between
35. How can you stand ________ and watch your friends fighting ?
    (a) by (b) down (c) for (d) out
36. When you believe injustice is being done, stand ________ authority.
    (a) up for (b) up to (c) out against (d) out for
37. I'm sorry he disobeyed instructions. I'll take him ________ when he gets back.
    (a) after (b) amiss (c) apart (d) back
38. I'm sorry I took you ________ your brother, you're so much alike.
    (a) down (b) for (c) from (d) in
39. She regrets her marriage; she was taken ________ by her husband's good looks.
    (a) in (b) into (c) off (d) on

40. Only Ramu has the initiative to take this project ______ to completion.
 (a) out (b) over (c) through (d) to

2.4.3 Idioms

1. My brother is considered as the black sheep of the family.
2. You should never put all eggs in one basket.
3. It is always good to have the ball at one's feet.
4. There is no use beating a dead horse.
5. Why does he keep beating about the bush?
6. The suggestion was considered as the best of both worlds.
7. Why do you always blow hot and cold?
8. There's no use jogging once in a blue moon.
9. The snake appeared out of the blue.
10. It's always good to be in your boss's good books.
11. It took some time for her to break the ice.
12. You should avoid burning the candle at both ends.
13. Present day students rarely burn the midnight oil.
14. It's no use burying one's head in the sand during a crisis.
15. By and large, the question paper wasn't difficult to answer.
16. When will you stop building castles in the air?
17. She is thought to be a chip of the old block.
18. Kumar came off with flying colours in the GRE.
19. Don't shed crocodile tears. No one believes you.
20. Watching cricket is not my cup of tea.
21. He's been working sincerely day in and day out.
22. He hates doing the same job day after day.
23. If you don't mend your evil ways, you'll have to face the day of reckoning very soon.
24. My advice to you is when in Rome do as Romans do.
25. I'm caught between the devil and the deep sea.
26. You can have peace of mind if you let sleeping dogs lie.
27. He's been in the doldrums ever since his wife deserted him.
28. If company affairs are run in this fashion, the company will go to dogs.
29. The writing is on the wall; he'll be dismissed soon.

30. He's earning just enough to keep the wolf from the door.
31. He drinks like a fish; he'll soon be sorry for it.
32. If you do anything at the eleventh hour, you many not succeed.
33. With his meagre income, he's finding it dlfficult to make both ends meet.
34. If a couple don't see eye to eye, there'll be trouble in the family.
35. A self-made man stands on his own feet.
36. "We're going to have a party?" "Who's footing the bill?"
37. I had to run from pillar to post to get my eligibility certificate from the university.
38. When you called him a coward, you hit the nail on the head.
39. When I was told to resign, I was given a Hobson's choice.
40. The letter is a plain one; there's nothing in it to read between the lines.
41. You have a long way to go; don't rest on your laurels.
42. The rangers have to go through fire and water to save wild life.
43. What is done is done; you can't put the clock back.
44. "Do what I say. Remember he who pays the piper calls the tune."
45. I don't like to play second fiddle to anyone; I like to keep my individuality.
46. We may close down your department; it has become a white elephant.
47. Though the last year's champion threw down the gauntlet, he lost in the first round.
48. "I don't believe you; I'll get it straight from the horse's mouth."
49. Please don't let the cat out of the bag until it is officially announced.
50. He's such a kind man; he wouldn't hurt a fly.
51. Never lend an ear to gossip.
52. I sympathise with you; I wouldn't like to be in your shoes.
53. Thank you for the suggestion; I'll sleep on it for a day or two.
54. I always take any news from my brother with a pinch/grain of salt.
55. He's ready to go to any lengths to win.
56. I'm safe; I hope Sam is out of the woods, too.
57. Some people are in the habit of setting the cat among the pigeons.
58. He keeps his room neat as a pin.
59. I don't understand why you have to fly off the handle all the time?
60. He's been a slow coach all his life.
61. Don't waste my time; I have other fish to fry.
62. With his excellent presentation, he carried the day.

63. Don't spend all your earnings; save some for a rainy day.
64. Who said getting loans is easy. I had to move heaven and earth to get one.
65. He deals with people in a high-handed fashion.
66. His business has been in the red for quite some time.
67. We have no raincoats. So we must make do with this umbrella.
68. A gentleman keeps his word.
69. There's no love lost between me and my family.
70. I advised her not to live in an ivory tower.
71. I've always believed that fortune favours the brave.
72. He is a superb speaker; he can make speeches off the cuff/ impromptu.
73. The weather in Ooty is a far cry from Chennai's.
74. He took his time to respond to the question from the journalist.
75. My boss praised me but I wondered if the praise was not back-handed compliment.
[in American English it is 'left-handed compliment']
76. She didn't bat an eyelid when I told her the good news.
77. I'll get to the bottom of this accusation.
78. If you let the grass grow under your feet, the opportunity may slip through your fingers.
79. He's really in his element when he cracks jokes.
80. I don't like him; he's too clever by half.
81. He has the gift of the gab; he can convince anyone.
82. It's not manners to look a gift horse in the mouth.
83. "Is Suresh getting married?" "Your guess is as good as mine."
84. I don't believe you; you must be kidding!
85. I've been in this town for a month, I still feel like a square peg in a round hole.

2.5 Analogy (GRE Type)

This Anology section does not reflect GRE analogy items typically. To be able to answer GRE analogy accurately you need to

i. learn several words not in high frequency of use*, not part of day to day vocabulary* and their meanings and
ii. see the intricate relationship between pairs of such words. You'll have plenty of guidance in books meant to prepare you for success in the GRE.

However, in this Section, you are **trained to see the direction your mind should take** to be able to tackle GRE analogy test items.

Look at a few of typical GRE analogy items:

1. *hypothesis* : *Proof*
a. statement : expression
b. promise : fulfilment
c. urging : need
d. execution : intention

hypothesis is at concept level, proof is at the concrete level. so (b) is the choice.

2. *vigilant* : *danger*
a. thrifty : indigence*
b. compulsive : thoroughness
c. arbitrary : justice
d. persevering : innocence

If you are vigilant you can avoid danger. (a) if you are thrifty (= economical) you can avoid indigence = (being poor)

3. *incline* : *precipice*
a. alteration : mutation
b. selfishness : greed
c. wilderness : jungle
d. partisan : zealot

vertical is the common factor in the head pair. Only (a) has a common factor: change.

4. perspicacious* : insight
a. authority : despotism
b. audacious : hearing
c. torpid* : activity
d. zealous : enthusiasm

A despot has authority
a. but all who have authority are not despots.
b. There is no connection between 'recklessly bold' and hearing
c. contains antonyms (torpid = inactive)
d. contains synonyms and is the choice because the head pair is synonymous.

5. *chevron** : *badge*
a. caisson* : cart
b. calcium : bone
c. wax : candle
d. oration : euology

'The answer is (a). chevron badge with V shape cassion = ammunition wagon

6. *hack* : *carve*
a. grind : polish
b. snip* : mince
c. hew : fell
d. gouge* : engrave
c. is the answer.

Exercise 31

In each of the following items, a pair of words is followed by four pairs. Choose the pair which is an analogy to the head pair and write its letter.

1. *Edison* : *Electric bulb*
a. Pencillin : Alexander Fleming
b. Rontgen : X-ray
c. Durayodhana : Mahabharta
d. Mahatma Gandhi : India

2. *Miniature* : *enlargement*
a. commence : begin
b. zenith : apex
c. alpha : omega
d. praise : flatter

3. *ingenious* : *skillful*
a. ferocious : kind
b. loquacious : dumb
c. ingenuous : frank
d. extravagant : miserly

4. *witness* : *courtroom*
a. inspector : jail
b. teacher : education
c. doctor : operation
d. guard : train

5. *fruit* : *orange*
a. house : kitchen
b college : playground
c. table : furniture
d. crime : murder

6. *nose* : *smell*
a. tongue : taste
b. stomach : digest
c. bed : sleep
d. leg : crawl

7. *train* : *coal*
a. car : wheels
b. teacher : chalk
c. man : brain
d. TV : news

8. *bread* : *flour*
a. TV : gadget
b. book : paper
c. wall : cement
d. river : rain

9. *light* : *darkness*
a. medicine : cure
b. knowledge : ignorance
c. food : energy
d. friend : enemy

10. *plant* : *leaf*
a. calender : date
b. camera : picture
c. paper : news
d. body : arm

11. *sock* : *foot*
a. glove : arm
b. sweater : cold
c. cloth : body
d. lip : mouth

12. *knife* : *fork*
a. cup : saucer
b. bread : butter
c. fire : warmth
d. kitchen : cooking

13. *fire* : *warmth*
a. rain : cloud
b. cold : numbness
c. earth : river
d. chair : comfort

14. *prune* : *hedge*
a. trim : hair
b. cut : boquet
c. reap : crop
d. shave : moustache

15. *euology* : *praise*
a. comedy : laugh
b. epic : contempt
c. tirade : awe
d. elegy : lament

16. *satire* : *ridicule*
a. hyperbole : exaggerate
b. comedy : laugh
c. camera : click
d. hoe : dig

17. *start* : *finish*
a. begin : stop
b. born : die
c. produce : destroy
d. bath : dress

18. *open* : *close*
a. smile : weep
b. sow : harvest
c. grow : mature
d. talk : quiet

19. *food* : *hunger*
a. police : criminal
b. teacher : knowledge
c. water : thirst
d. lie down : tiredness

20. *bed* : *rest*
a. book : print
b. lamp : read
c. house : enjoy
d. dress : wear

Degree relationship

21. *admire* : *idolize*
a. weak : strength
b. dislike : hate
c. mumble : talk
d. pray : worship

22. *adamant* : *dogmatic*
a. weak : firm
b. love : hate
c. happy : ecstatic
d. sour : bitter

23. *attachment* : *love*
a. frugal : parsimonious
b. ordinary : magnificent
c. trite : cliche
d. shout : thunder

24. *warm* : hot
a. jump : fly
b. purloin* : pilfer
c. firm : dogmatic
d. wind : tornado

A few more in this class

emotion : fervour
breeze : gale
appreciate : admire
fear : terror
lapse : blunder
(slight mistake) : (gross mistake)
gift : largesse
saunter : stride
dawdle : race
provision : plethora
dime : dollar
decade : century

cause and effect

25. *sun* : *heat*
a. jump : catch
b. generosity : cautious
c. glass : break
d. slap : pain

26. *drug* : *cure*
a. murder : jail
b. eat : sleep
c. generosity : gratitude
d. blabber : blunder

27. *cloud* : *rain*
a. mischief : jail term
b. chair : sit
c. water : grow
d. prevaricate* : quibble

28. *throw* : *break*
a. drownsiness : eat
b. muffle : sound
c. smatter* : superficial
d. ego : vanity

a few more in this class

vaccinate : immunity
sleep : rest
read : understanding
rub : friction
thought : action
education : refinement

part of

chapter : book
stanze : poem
tuber : plant
foundation : building
movement : sonata*
wheel : car
leg : body
table : legs
compartment : train
galley : ship

Type of

table : furniture
football : sport
sword : weapon
ode : poem

person/thing-characteristics

zealot : fervour
baby : helplessness
giant : bigness
surgeon : dexterity
athelete : agility
pigmy : tiny
purgatory : purge
poem : rhyme

general - specific

person : boy
vehicle : bus
poem : sonnet
wood : mahogany

user-tool

farmer	:	hoe
dentist	:	drill
paintbrush	:	artist
teacher	:	chalk
writer	:	pen
mechanic	:	spanner
reaper	:	scythe
woodcutter	:	axe
carpenter	:	saw

Note: Words ending in -logy and –graphy should also be learnt.

Synonyms

admonish	:	reprove
prig*	:	conceited
terse*	:	smooth
nebulous	:	turbid*
terminal	:	fatal
extant	:	exist
squeamish	:	fastidious*
nebula	:	defective vision
squirm	:	wriggle
nomenclature	:	catalogue
squelch	:	disconcert
podgy	:	fat
purloin*	:	pilfer / steal
variegated	:	dappled*
motif*	:	distinctive
tortuous	:	curves
moulder*	:	decay
staid	:	sedate
pique	:	irritate
vellum*	:	parchment

Antonyms

reckless	:	cautious
gibberish	:	sensible
strident (loud)	:	quiet
earn	:	filch*
surfeit	:	dearth
creduolus	:	dupe
extravagant	:	miser
metaphor	:	literal
melody	:	spoken
poseur*	:	sincerity
flirt	:	decency
levity	:	seriousness
acerbic*	:	sweet
staid	:	jaunty
manacle	:	freedom
ineluctable*	:	avoid
lethargic	:	stimulate
vacillate	:	steadfast
breach	:	dam
sedulous*	:	piquancy*
obscurity	:	light

Note: We can make an almost endless list of such pairs. I made this listing only to impress upon you the significance of learning odd synonyms and antonyms. It is desirable to have the concise Oxford Dictionary on your reading table because it has all odd expressions that other dictionaries may not list.

A few other relationships

Function of

brain	:	thinking
TV	:	entertain
newspaper	:	inform

sign of

grimace	:	pain
mature	:	grow
reward	:	action
medal	:	bravery
trophy	:	championship
virtue	:	failing
fortitude	:	cowardice
creator	:	creation
artist	:	picture
poet	:	poem

There are of course several others.

Exercise 31(Continuation)

29. *hypothesis*	:	*proof*
a. statement	:	expression
b. promise	:	fulfillment
c. urging	:	need
d. execution	:	intention
30. *copyright*	:	*author*
a. license	:	driver
b. passport	:	citizen
c. patent	:	inventor
d. gavel	:	chairperson
31. *code*	:	*meaning*
a. safe	:	valuables
b. confidence	:	secret
c. camouflage	:	location
d. briefcase	:	documents
32. *diary*	:	*person*
a. log	:	ship
b. journal	:	science
c. calendar	:	year
d. bankbook	:	deposit
33. *scenario*	:	*play*
a. medley*	:	song
b. sketch	:	painting
c. index	:	book
d. pirouette*	:	ballet
34. *ratiocination*	:	*thinking*
a. supposition	:	theorizing
b. emulation	:	idolizing
c. jubiliation	:	pleasing
d. articulation	:	talking
35. *adulterate*	:	*purity*
a. modify	:	essence
b. exonerate	:	crime
c. ascertain	:	validity
d. enervate	:	vigour
36. *itinerary*	:	*trip*
a. resume	:	job
b. portfolio	:	document
c. legend	:	map
d. syllabus	:	course
37. *awl**	:	*pierce*
a. lathe	:	penetrate
b. drill	:	flatten
c. pestle	:	mash
d. sickle	:	smooth
38. *surgeon*	:	*dexterity*
a. engineer	:	clarity
b. sailor	:	navigation
c. industrialist	:	capital
d. acorbat	:	agility
39. *credulous*	:	*dupe*
a. insensitive	:	boor
b. argumentative	:	lawyer
c. spontaneous	:	extrovert
d. extravagant	:	miser
40. *superimpose*	:	*above*
a. permeate	:	beside
b. focus	:	around
c. insert	:	between
d. fuse	:	behind

41. *courage* : *rashness*
   a. generosity : prodigality
   b. temperence : modesty
   c. honour : humility
   d. compassion : contempt

42. *cow* : *herd*
   a. grass : green
   b. child : family
   c. bald : hair
   d. horse : jockey

43. *bird* : *ornithology*
   a. zoology : animal
   b. stars : galaxy
   c. archeology : antiquity
   d. plant : botany

44. *tree* : *trunk*
   a. pen : ink
   b. car : chassis
   c. cabin : log
   d. arm : body

Note: It's good to learn to arrive at the right choice by elimination process because you may not know every expression in the test item and the choices.

3. Group Discussion

3.1 Body language

3.1.1 Definition

We communicate also non-verbally. This is known as non-verbal communication. What does this mean? When messages are passed on from one person to another without using words or speech, they are termed **non-verbal**. In other words, non-verbal communication is a process of sending and receiving wordless messages.

Non-verbal communication is equated with 'body language'. This is because most of it occurs through the use of the body. Body language also includes 'gestures' that we do with different parts of the body. However, there are also certain other means of communication that are non-verbal. These we shall discuss after learning about body language and what it means and implies.

3.1.2 Use

Communicating non-verbally must be older than verbal communication. Our human ancestors must have used their limbs—body parts—to communicate with each other long before they were able to use sounds to form words, to create and use words to form sentences. For thousands of years, we have been using languages and improving them everyday to communicate. Even after such long use of languages, non-verbal communication has not died; in fact, we've been using it like before.

We have improved our languages over centuries through continuous creation of new words and use of sentence structures innovatively. And yet, we use non-verbal communication alone [by itself] or along with the verbal. Why is this?

3.1.3 Role

Because, as we will learn in the next few pages, non-verbal communication can strengthen, confirm or contradict verbal communication. And by itself [that is, without words] it can give messages with force, accuracy or clarity.

Moreover, it clearly reveals the personality of the person concerned. It depicts the behaviour pattern[s] of the person. Various aspects of a person's character go to make up personality. Things like perception, attitude, motivation, involvement, consistency, persistence are part of personality. Non-verbal communication reveals such aspects.

3.1.4 Characteristics

Non-verbal communication and behaviour can be **involuntary or voluntary**. It's voluntary when we are conscious of what we're doing with our body or when our body is under the control of our will. For instance, in normal conditions, we walk when we want to, we read the newspaper because we want to, we lie down because we want to rest our body and so on. Children throw stones to chase dogs away. These and other similar actions are the result of conscious decision-making. In other words, we know what we're doing.

Non-verbal communication is also involuntary when our will has no control over body movements. For instance, when we are in deep thought, we don't know what our body is doing; we may be walking without knowing we're walking, we may pick up the newspaper and turn the pages without knowing that we're doing it. We may cross the road without being aware of it. Our eyes may be looking at someone but our mind doesn't register the person.

Non-verbal messages may **accompany** [=go with] verbal [oral] messages. We say "congrats!", we also smile and/or shake hands. We say "please come in!" and we indicate the welcome with a smile and an arm gesture. Parents show anger with words and body language like slapping, hitting or beating. To add effect to what we're saying, we lower our voice and whisper.

Non-verbal messages may **not accompany** verbal [oral] messages. Such absence of nonverbal also sends messages. We may say "I'm leaving" but we may have no intention of leaving. When someone knocks and seeks permission to enter, we say "come in!" without getting up or stopping what we're doing. Because we know our subordinate is coming in. Or because we know who is coming and we want to show our unhappiness or some other feeling towards that person.

Very often we communicate only nonverbally. We may enter a place without permission to show there is no formality or to show authority. We may leave a place without putting it in words. We may throw or pretend to throw an object at a person seriously or for fun.

3.1.5 Aspects

Here, we'll talk about **body language**. We shall also learn about **proximity, touch, posture, voice, sound symbols, orientation, physical characteristics, time, silence.**

The study of language is called linguistics. This branch of knowledge studies, investigates, analyses and describes language, its formation, its function and so on. Similarly, various aspects of nonverbal communication are being studied, investigated, analyzed and described. **Kinesics** studies body language. **Proxemics** studies personal space. **Haptics** studies touch, **Oculosics**, eye contact, **Chronemics**, time, **Vocalics**, voice.

Body language[kinesics]

This is a broad term for different forms of communication using body movement or gestures instead of or in addition to verbal expressions. Such messages are known as paralanguage.

This includes facial expressions, gestures, eye contact, nodding.

Physical characteristics

Physical appearance is the first source that gives shape to mental images of people we come into contact with. It's not possible to store a person in our memory just by name or position. Until we see the person, we automatically indulge in image-forming. That we do this is evident when we are surprised by the difference between our image and the actual person. We may even be disappointed or annoyed that the person looks very different from the mental image we formed.

Height, weight, colour, hair, beard, unkempt hair, thick or thin eyebrows, dress, dress colours, its quality convey messages to others. The viewer combines all these or some of these to add or delete value to the image of the person he/she has in mind. Fair colour is generally a plus, Fatness is generally a minus. A beard can make one handsome or ugly. Thick eyebrows are generally unfavourable. A well-dressed person is generally liked.

However, how someone views physical characteristics will depend on their perceptions or how they look at these characteristics.

Facial expressions

They convey emotions or feelings. They can be as different as concentration, anger, contempt, disgust, desire, doubt, greed, excitement, fear, joy, confusion, sadness, surprise, frown, glare, shock, smile, sneer. Expression of feeling or emotions can bring sympathy, understanding, help as support and thus reduce mental, psychological or emotional disturbances. Or it can result in negative reaction like disassociation, enmity and the like.

Winking, rolling the eyes, raising the eyebrows, twitching the nose, scratching the head, gnashing the teeth, putting the tongue out, closing the eyes, intentional coughing, tapping the forehead, massaging temples, face turned away, bent head, head shaking, raising the chin, using fingers or arms to go with what we're saying, nodding are gestures that send meaningful messages.

Winking expresses amusement or understanding between two, not known to others . Rolling the eyes indicates disbelief or mockery. Raising the eyebrows shows doubt or seeks more explanation or information. Twitching the nose indicates irritation, dislike or disgust. Scratching the head expresses difficulty in getting a solution. Gnashing the teeth occurs as a result of extreme anger. Intentional coughing draws attention. Tapping the forehead says 'the credit goes to thinking'. Massaging temples highlights anxiety. Bent head expresses shame or is a form of greeting with respect. Inclined head indicates interest in what's being said. Nodding is generally a sign of confirmation. It's also a 'hello' gesture, indicating informality. We nod as a sign of encouragement or attention when someone is speaking to us. Otherwise that person might think we have no interest in him or what he's saying. We say 'Look over there!' with the forefinger pointing in a given direction. We use the forefinger while asking a person to leave the place. We use arms as additional sign of welcome. We shake hands as a sign of greeting or happiness. We use our arms as we give a speech or lecture for such gesture lends strength and life to what we may be saying. Arms are a necessary tool when communicating to a dumb and deaf person.

We threaten with a shaking fist. We wave our hand to show affection. We pound a table for emphasis. We lean forward to show interest. Leaning back in the chair exhibits disinterest. Moving away from a group or our partner in conversation is a clear sign of disinterest, disassociation, unwillingness to continue the conversation and so on, depending on the context. Our eyes widen as we wonder at what we're seeing or hearing. A quick wink may tell stories that words cannot fully express. Finger-tapping shows impatience. We pace the floor with restlessness. We shrug our shoulders indifferently. We slam a door in anger. We clap to appreciate or to ask a performer to stop!

So how well we manage people through communicating depends on how well we respond or react to what the speaker is communicating.

Eye contact

This is a very essential body language for socialization purpose and managing people through communicaing. It is a positive sign seeking contact, acquaintance, friendship, business, relationship, understanding, appreciation, criticism. Without eye contact, we cannot succeed in an interview, for instance. We need to look at the interviewers as we speak. Again, we should not get into the habit of looking at only one person when there are several. This would mean we are ignoring the others and don't recognize their presence. They will be hurt and naturally you'll lose them in due course. "Look me in the eye" is what we say when we suspect someone lying to us. It indicates you have nothing to hide and that you are open-minded. It also sends a message of confidence to the speaker. It also helps retention and recall of information because it links one mind with another and it is a sign of attention as well.

Nodding

When we speak, we expect listeners to look at us and nod so that we know they are listening. Nodding confirms listening and encourages the speaker to continue. This is a very important responding act in managing people through communicating. Confirmation through nodding, however, may be culture-dependent. We Indians expect our partners to nod often or express confirmation through vocal responses.

Posture

When we keep our body in a particular position, when we hold our body in a particular way, posture happens. Postures communicate social or official status, dominance or submissiveness.

We indicate superior status or dominance when we are seated and the other person keeps standing. When the other person stands hands folded across the chest even when we are standing, it shows our superior status and the other person's submissiveness. We stand as straight as possible before our superiors. We bend our back forward to explain a point or to direct our superior to a particular part of a visual or a piece of writing or a balance sheet. During job interview, the interviewer sits leaning the body on the back of the chair while the interviewee is expected to sit with a straight back or rest his/her back lightly on the back of the chair. Resting the back against the back of the chair will lead to the body sliding down a bit and that is not considered appropriate posture for an interviewee to take.

Some postures are difficult to read. For instance, if we stand with our arms crossed at our back and a bent head, it may indicate shame, shyness, sadness or modesty. It could also mean that we are very self-conscious. If we stand with our feet apart and arms on the hip, it could mean authority, pride or confidence. When we sit slouched [in a drooping fashion], it could mean accepting defeat, confusion in the mind, helplessness or disappointment or even boredom. To interpret such postures, we need to take into account other aspects like the person's personality, attitude, confidence-level and the context or the situation the person is in because we want to manage people through communicating.

---

*Proximity **[proxemics]***

This refers to physical space that we have in mind and put to use when we are with others in a given place. That is, 'space' refers to the distance we would like to maintain between others and us. The nearer we are to each other, the more intimate we are to each other. The more the distance we are at, the more the distant the relationship is.

Some of us may be particular about the distance. We may not like others coming or moving closer to us. If someone did reduce the distance they have in mind, we would move away. Such moving away is probably more reflexive than intentional. So we need to be watchful and avoid embarrassing such people because we want to manage people through communicating.

We also need to be careful about personal space when we are at a gathering, at a party. We should be conscious about this aspect of non-verbal communication. Otherwise, we may not understand why someone moves away from us. A guest may be standing alone or away from the rest of the guests. Seeing this, another guest might try to engage that person and become unhappy for not getting any response. But we should respect someone's wish to be aloof because it may be their nature. Again, when we try to join a group, its members may not like it and show it by body language.

There is another possible interpretation of proximity. We are likely to develop a closer relationship with those nearer to us than with those who are far away from us. When we trust someone, we are likely to not bother about personal space. When we are not particularly interested in someone or when we dislike someone, we are likely to maintain distance from them.

---

*Time **(chronemics)***

By 'time', we refer to the amount of time we take to respond. We may take less or more time. The partner will interpret the 'time' according to the situation, his/her mental make-up at that moment and understanding of the person responding. 'Pause' is another useful tool to communicate. When we say something important and we want our partner to understand its importance, we stop speaking for a few seconds. But we should not stop too often when we are speaking because this will give the impression that we are unable to convey messages properly.

3.1.6 Why is non-verbal communication important?

We use both verbal and nonverbal messages to communicate with others. But it is believed that generally speaking, we derive meaning from nonverbal messages rather than from the verbal.

Because the former is more natural, instinctive, involuntary and automatic. Words may lie. Verbal messages may hide our thoughts or feelings. We may speak, converse and continue our relationship with a person even when we hate that person. We may call someone names but we don't mean them. We may say "I'll kill you" but more often it stays at the threat level. We may bless someone while in our mind we're actually cursing that person.

Non-verbal communication does not usually lie. Very rarely do we plan it. But it may lie when we want to intentionally deceive or when we have in mind some gain for ourselves or our close ones. We may embrace a person to show friendship or relationship, but we may actually be planning how to steal their property.

If we made it a practice to observe how we use our body to communicate and how others use theirs and learn from the observation, we would be able to handle different relationships better and enjoy harmony with others. We would also be able to monitor our own signals and achieve better control over ourselves and so function more effectively.

There is another aspect that should be remembered constantly. The interpretation of non-verbal communication is likely to differ from culture to culture. For instance, a French man may look at a woman for a longer time than an American might. The Frenchman may be appreciating beauty while the American would consider the look bad manners.

It's also necessary to remember constantly that the messages that non-verbal communication conveys need not be the same for all the members even in the same community.

3.2 Job Selection Process

3.2.1 Introduction

Today, employees need to work in groups, not in isolation.

Group Discussion is being used as part of selection process by organizations in their search for right candidates to help do their business and, of course, grow with them. In other words, G.D. is used as a *qualifying test*. It is used as a means to evaluate your ability to work with your colleagues.

Between five and ten of you are thrown together in an arch or a circle formation and given a current or controversial topic to discuss. It's possible that you are given case studies or a serious situation requiring a solution. In this case, there is no right or wrong solution. The representatives of the prospective employer observe you closely and note how each of you fare as a member of the group.

Employers expect you to show your knowledge about the influence of environment—political, social, cultural, economic, trade—over business activities. So you should have a sound general knowledge. Next they expect you to have the right mental abilities: **thinking, analyzing, arguing, convincing, persuading.** They also expect you to demonstrate your ability to use English as a listening and speaking medium. Finally, they expect you to use GD skills to:

- perform among strangers
- survive in competition
- listen well and indicate this through communication
- contribute to discussion
- use intelligible language
- speak clearly, briefly, precisely, relevantly, convincingly
- use tone and pitch properly
- use body language appropriately:
  lean forward, use hands, smile, nod, keep face alive
- reenter smoothly, refocus
- show leadership:
  - initiate discussion with appropriate lead
  - summarize ideas at stages
  - direct discussion in different angles
  - conclude.

3.2.2 Time Limitation

G.D. generally lasts only for anything between ten and twenty minutes. Since there'll be a minimum of five or six in the group, you may not get, on an average, more than a minute or two to show that you are a good G.D. player. You have to

- listen extremely carefully,
- analyse what you're listening to,
- think quickly, and
- talk briefly, precisely, relevantly.

For all these, a minute or two will not be sufficient. You have to manage more time. How can you do this ? The member you're listening to will have to pause (= stop for a second or two) between sentences. As you're listening, think and plan your ideas and **enter the discussion at the pause time**. Now you'll not be interrupting. In fact, you'll be entering the discussion smoothly. Such entries will give you more time.

3.2.3 Preparing for the G.D.

Now selection criteria in detail. How do you meet your employer's expectations?

1. **General knowledge is important;**

   Read newspapers. Watch the BBC and CNN and other English channels. Read magazines. Gather and **retain** information about important events in economics, commerce, politics, sports, and others. Think, analyse and **form opinions.** Be **objective** in your conclusions. Only then you can exude confidence.

2. **Expression is very important;**

Right from the beginning of your third Semester, if you have not done so already, **start using English** for all your communicating acts with friends, seniors and faculty. Don't mind if they look at you strangely or if they find fault with you. Continue **speaking**. Take up news items and discuss them, especially with your friends. Don't speak in a dull voice. Put life into your speech. Show your **involvement.** Remember how you talk, **how expressive your face and hands and tone become** when the subject is your favourite hero (heroine), politician, cinema or serial. Use your body language now in a similar manner. Let the body language add meaning to whatever you are saying and strengthen it. But don't shout, don't threaten.

3. **G.D. Skills are most important;**

If you can, **initiate** the discussion. State (say) what you know (not everything at once) and your opinion. If somebody speaks up, don't cut in (don't say: wait, wait, I haven't finished). Wait for sometime. Keep listening. Use your eyes and hands to show you are listening. Smile or nod in appreciation

Show you are a team player. As soon as you can, speak again without stopping a partner rudely. But don't, don't repeat either what you had said earlier or what the previous speaker was saying. You are wasting valuable time. You have only a few minutes. **So say something that continues the discussion**.

When necessary, make out a brief summary and start off in another angle. Again, don't continue speaking if someone speaks.

Keep watching for time. The group will be given 10 or 15 minutes only. When it is almost time for G.D. to end, if you can, summarise quickly and bring it to a **conclusion.**

Throughout G.D. it is speak and listen and listen and speak. Starting, continuing and concluding the G.D. are major activities. See that you **do** at least **one** of them. Make **useful** and sensible **contribution** to the G.D. **Exhibit** a high level of **confidence.**

To be successful in G.D. you need:

- some do's and don'ts
- a few expressions for G.D.

3.2.4 Some Do's and Don'ts

Do's	Dont's
Seat yourself in the centre.	Avoid sitting in corners.
Initiate discussion, if you can.	Don't cut into another's speech.
Take notes.	Don't become emotional.
Use appropriate gestures.	Don't be silent for too long.
Be polite.	Don't silence others.
Be firm.	Don't be dogmatic.
Allow others to talk.	Don't talk for long.
Keep eye contact.	Don't look only at one person.
	Don't repeat what's already said.

3.2.5 A few Expressions to use in G.D.

Activity	Expressions
• Lead the discussion	• It's not difficult to understand that a problem exists in…… • The world / India is a facing a problem…. • The problem is ……… we may begin by looking at……….
[How exactly to begin the discussion depends on the topic]	
• Draw someone into discussion	• What do you think? • What's your opinion? • Do / Don't you agree?
• Refocus the discussion	• Shall we look at the topic from another angle? • For instance,……. • I think we are off the track…….. • I think I'm afraid we are moving too far away from the topic……
• Involve others in the discussion	• How will you…..? • Do(n't) you think there is (no) other way / another way we can ……
• Help someone to participate	• Yes, you are right. • Please, go on. • Yes, you were saying…….. • Can you elaborate ?

	• Please give an example. • I think you mean...... don't you? • You have a point there, I think.
• Make suggestions	• What about.........? • How about..........? • Shall we.......? • Let's ....
• Intervene in the discussion	• Let me add a point here .... • Excuse me, aren't we overlooking a previous point....... • Before we go further can I say something?..... • But there is a problem here......
• Summarise	• It's time to summarise what we've been saying....... • Since there're other things to be discussed, let's summarise quickly......
• Conclude	• We've spoken at length on/about the topic. In conclusion shall we say that .... • It's time to conclude......
• Make predictions	• In all probability, what will happen is...... • I predict that........ • I expect......to happen.
• Seek clarification	• Can you say something more? • Just a moment. I don't understand. • If you don't mind, do you mean......? • If I understand you correctly, you are saying that....
• Express opinions	• I doubt it because....... • I agree with you there. • I'm afraid I'll have to disagree. • I don't think so. The reason is .... • What you are saying sounds appealing but.... • Yes, you are right. • Nod or shake your head, raise your eyebrows. • Well, probably.

You'll of course have to have **several practice sessions**. Your English teachers and others can help.

3.2.6 Some G.D. topics

Form groups of five or six. Using these topics practise participation in G.D.

Exercise 32

1. peer pressure
2. reservation and merit
3. ads and the public
4. pollution—live with it!
5. India and Olympics
6. classroom learning versus learning via WWW
7. learning without a teacher
8. eighteen year olds and the right to vote
9. television has harmed more than helped
10. degrees and jobs
11. foreign trade is essential to a country's growth
12. God created man or vice versa?
13. modern youth—a selfish and confused lot
14. impact of cable TV
15. old age homes are increasing!
16. evaluation—internal and external
17. hunger first, ethics later!
18. reservation for women is unnecessary
19. multi-party system
20. We pay but don't get education
21. life is a comedy of errors but a tragedy of blunders
22. life is groping in the dark?
23. ignorance is bliss?
24. life and ethics

4. Interview Skills

4.1 Introduction

This is generally the last stage of job selection. A few organizations may use this as the only means. The time limit could be anything between ten minutes and an hour. Here your performance is at an individual level. Here you will be facing a group of elderly and experienced interviewers who will ask questions and expect answers, who will be observing your expressions, evaluate your responses, and who will watch out for appropriate behaviour.

They will be **testing** you for:

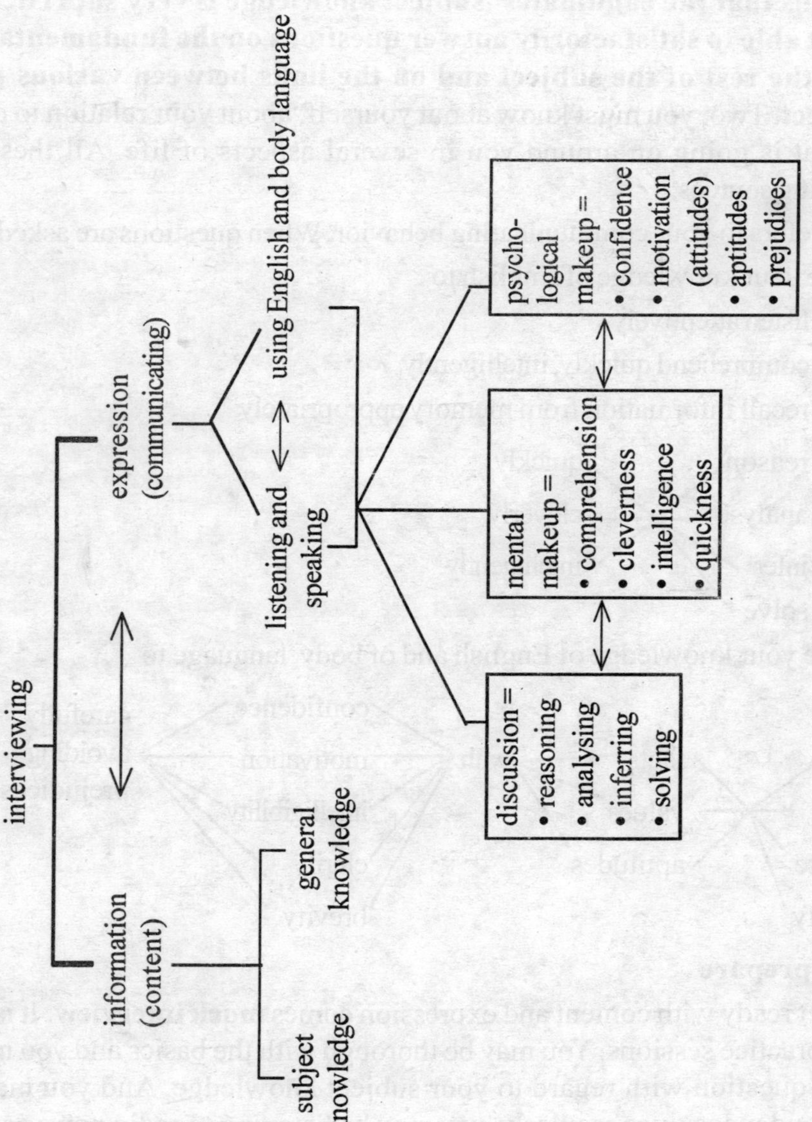

4.2 Preparing for interview: (What you require)

Attending an interview successfully depends primarily on two important things you should have and use:

Content and **communicating**. Content is the fund of knowledge you have gathered over the years. It refers to information you have at your disposal. This information is related to two areas: subject knowledge and general knowledge. Subject or general, you must have sound knowledge. One, you must be thorough with **the basics in your major subject** and others closely related to it. Because **there is a general complaint from visiting organizations that the candidates' subject knowledge is very superficial and that they are not able to satisfactorily answer questions on the fundamentals and their relation to the rest of the subject and on the links between various parts of the major subject**. Two, you must know about yourself, about your relation to others, about life and what is going on around you in several aspects of life. All these form your communicating sources.

Expression refers to your communicating behavior. When questions are asked, you need to

- use your knowledge of English to
  - listen attentively
  - comprehend quickly, intelligently
  - recall information from memory appropriately

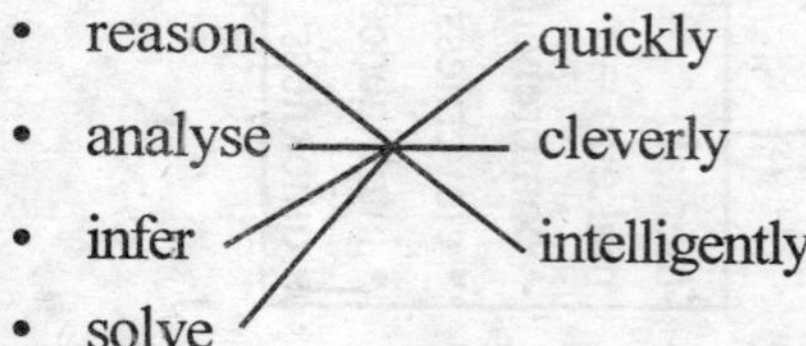

- use your knowledge of English and of body language to

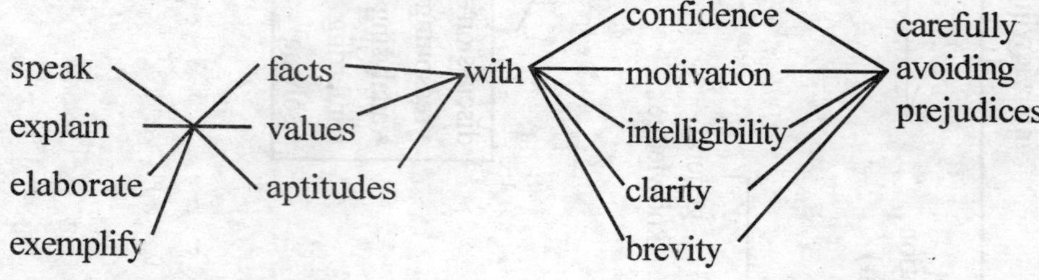

4.3 How to prepare

After you get ready with content and expression comes **mock interview**. It is necessary to have a few practice sessions. You may be thorough with the basics and you may be able to answer any question with regard to your subject knowledge. And you may be reading newspaper and magazines regularly, you may be listening to radio news or watching the

BBC or CNN and other channels and you may be ready to answer questions related to general knowledge. You may know your strengths as a person and be able to use them in the interview to your advantage.

In spite of such readiness, you may fail. Remember you are facing strangers; in a way, your future lies in their hands. **Facing** them and answering questions requires **tension-free behaviour**. You must not be nervous nor feel tensed. This can spoil the whole show.

A few practice sessions will definitely help reduce, if not remove completely, this nervousness or tension. Your faculty can help here. They can come together as a panel of interviewers and conduct at least three or four interview sessions. They can seek the help of a few senior executives from public and private sector to join them in conducting mock interviews.

With their help you can have a post-mock interview **discussion session**. Here your faculty can discuss with you first your plus points and congratulate you and next your weaknesses or problems and suggest solutions. To make this discussion more meaningful and fruitful, mock interview sessions could be **videoed** and **played back** so that you can see for yourself how you have performed. You may not believe others but you will have to believe the video tape. You can play it as many times as you wish, listen to questions and the quality of your performances, you can see what is lacking, you can identify your problems, note them down and try to avoid them in other mock interviews. You can learn if your listening was poor, if you misunderstood the questions, if you assumed the meanings of questions, if your English was good or poor, if your answers provided all the information that the questions expected, if you entered properly, if you sat properly, if your eye contact was good, if you were sitting like a statue, if you were taking too much time to answer one question, if you were beating around the bush, if you were waiting patiently for the interviewer to finish his question, if, before you left, you put the chair in its place without noise, if you thanked them before leaving, if you closed the door without noise, if you smiled at all, if you indicated that you were looking at everyone of the interviewers even though only one or two spoke to you, if you kept your arms folded or used them appropriately.

4.4 Additional preparation

There is yet another aspect of the interview that you must remember and prepare for. The interviewers can also ask any of these questions:

- Can you say why we should employ you?
- Why should you wish to build a career with us?
- What do you know about our Organization?
- Can you state your career goals?
- You may have some personal problems. Wouldn't they interfere with your job performance?

In these mock sessions, you can prepare yourself to answer these questions. To the first question, you might talk about your academic performance, your project, your interest in co-curricular and extracurricular activities, your qualities and attitudes and your readiness to contribute to the organisation's growth. But be brief and precise. To the next question you might say:

> Yours is a young organization. I can grow with the organization. There'll be plenty of opportunities for my contribution.
>
> or
>
> Yours is an organization of repute. You are among the top five in the field. I believe you treat newcomers with understanding.

The answer to the third question will be factual. Talk about their product(s), their performance in the market etc. Answer to the fourth is not difficult. In your answer to the last, you will have to be tactical. You may say something like:

> I am eager to start working, learn and gain experience. I won't allow anything to come in between me and success. It'll not be easy but I think I'll achieve it, with guidance from colleagues and superiors.

So then, perform and learn, learn and perform and they make your practice useful to you so that in a real interview you can perform easily and confidently.

4.5 Performing in the interview

Your communicating behaviour starts the moment you are called. On being called, knock gently on the door. Seek permission to enter, wait to be called, enter, move towards the interviewers with a smile and, depending on the time of the interview, greet them with good morning/afternoon. Keep standing and be seated only when asked to do so. If the chair is too close to the interviewers, don't drag or pull it backward but lift and place it at a comfortable distance. Seat yourself with a straight back – not slumped or with a stiff back like a solider – that is, lean your back lightly touching the chair's back rest and cross your legs at the ankles with the arms on the sides or holding your certificates in your lap. This posture will help to lean forward when necessary to hand the certificates if necessary and to use your arms for gestures to accompany your speaking. Don't cross your arms across the chest. This will prevent you from using them. If a drink is offered you may accept it with a 'thank you' or decline it with a 'no, thank you'. Sip through the drink without noise and spilling. Wait for the interviewer(s) to address you.

The interview may begin with a few questions about yourself to loosen you up, to reduce your tension, to put you at ease. Answer them well. When the actual interview begins, listen to the questions fully and attentively, understand them and form your answers in your mind, wait for a second or two and then reply. If an interviewer makes a long statement listen carefully, nod your head to indicate you are following what he or she is saying, break it into smaller parts and get your answers ready. There is no harm asking for the question to be repeated; there is no shame in this but don't ask them to repeat very often. Keep your answers to the point. Be brief in your content, be clear in your language. If you don't know, if you don't have answers, tell them so – there's nothing wrong in this. Never feel shy and give wrong answers. If you are asked to state your weaknesses, mention one weakness that is not a serious one, that will not harm your chances – that you are a bit reserved type, that you take time to take decisions or to make friends.

Throughout the interview, keep eye contact with everyone present. When you respond to a question, have eye contact with that person for a few seconds and begin your answer. And as you are talking, have eye contact also with other members of the panel. Move only your eyes, not your head. Use your head to nod, use a smile, eyebrows, arms and eyes to express your feelings and reactions. **Your every word, your every movement, your every response must reflect your confidence, must indicate that you are sure of what you are saying.** Be calm, be cool, don't get excited.

Towards the end, the interviewers may themselves give you information about their organization. If they don't, don't risk asking for this information because such Western Culture may not be viewed favourably.

You will know when the interview is coming to an end. They may say: "well, we'll offer you ……." or "Thank you. We'll intimate to you" or "please meet Mr ……. on your way out". Thank them, collect your papers, put the chair back in its place, if necessary, and leave closing the door gently behind.

---

5. Resume Writing

5.1 Sample CVs with cover letters (without experience)

Like any other field of activity, applying for a job is no longer based on the traditional presentation of information; it has become a professional activity. For exactly this reason, job seekers approach some agencies or individuals to prepare their job applications letters, and pay for it.

It's not difficult to prepare your own CV and a cover letter.

5.1.1 A traditional CV with a cover letter [without experience]

A biodata

Biodata

Name	:	A. R. Lakshmanan
Age and Date of birth	:	20, 16.04.1989
Education	:	BA History, first class, 2006, University of Madras
Curricular	:	presented a paper on Thanjavur temple
Cocurricular	:	organised education tours
Extracurricular	:	member, college volleyball team-2005-2006
Achievements	:	highest collection for Tsunami Relief Fund
Interests	:	tennis, science fiction
Address	:	2 Swamy Street K.K.Nagar Chennai 600021 Phone: 044-25327468

A cover letter

20 August 2008

From
A. R. Lakshmanan
2 Swamy Street
K.K.Nagar
Chennai 600021

To
The Human Resource Department
____
____

Dear Sir
I am applying for the post of Front Office Assistant as advertised in The Indian Express dated today.
I am a graduate in history. I have presented a paper. I was a member in the volleyball team.
I am enclosing my biodata.
I hope you will consider my application favourably. If selected, I will work to the fullest satisfaction of my superiors.
I thank you in anticipation
Yours faithfully
A.R.Lakshmanan

Enclosure: 1. biodata
2. certificates

This biodata gives some idea about the applicant. The cover letter is also in the traditional format. It doesn't add anything new to the biodata. It only repeats the information given in the biodata. And the last paragraph of the letter is totally out of place.

Don't prepare your biodata and the cover letter like this.

You'll see in the next few pages samples of how to prepare CVs and cover letters as an applicant without experience and with experience. You can prepare yours in a similar manner using information about a particular job.

5.1.2 A good CV and cover letter [without experience]

A. R. Lakshmanan

born: 16 April 1986

2 Swamy Street
K.K.Nagar
Chennai 600021 phone 044 - 25327468

Objective

Front Office with a career growth in customer care

Qualification

communication — my paper on Thanjavur temple was appreciated for its clarity and simplicity of expression and also for the content

working together — improved my attitude towards working with people not close to me

organising — learnt that patience is a very important part of behaviour when dealing with new people.

languages — can speak, read and write Thamizh, Malayalam fluently

Education

June 2006 B A History, I class, University of Madras

Achievements

Highest individual collection for Tsunami Relief Fund in the college

2 Swamy Street
K.K Nagar
Chennai 600 021

20 August 2006

____
____
____

Dear Sir

I would like to apply for the position of Front Office Assistant, advertised in today's Indian Express.

During the three years of my stay in college, I have learnt a lot about moving with superiors, close friends and not so close friends. Living together requires patience and compromise. I have realised the importance of this in being successful.

I am used to receiving and giving messages on behalf of my parents and make telephone calls accordingly. So I can handle this job along with taking care of customers and others who may come to do business.

I enclose my CV and photocopies of certificates. I am prepared to appear for an interview at any time.

I thank you for considering my application.

Yours faithfully

....

A.R. Lakshmanan

enc. as stated

The item 'objective' shows that you have a long term plan, not just getting a job. It tells the reader you're not an aimless person, you're preparing yourself to become 'somebody' in a profession of your choice. This is a plus for you. At least you'll be called for interview where you can probably impress the interviewer[s].

The item 'qualification' may be new to you. Here you mention the **'skills'** you have and will use to perform as a person. This presents to the reader what you can do to help the organisation grow if you are appointed. If called for interview, be ready with concrete instances to support your claims here.

Use the item 'achievements' **only if** you have something special to mention like 'awards', 'honours' or something that you can be proud of. CVs of 3, 4, and 5 do not have 'achievements' column.

The cover letter should not merely repeat the information available in the CV. It should provide a picture of yourself, supporting and adding to the CV. The middle paragraphs in the letter picture to the reader how you **think** about yourself and how well you can do the job.

5.1.3 A good CV and cover letter [without experience]

A CV

Nikhil Yadav

born: 26 July 1986

Venkatesh Apartments
193 Trimurti Colony
Nagpur 440 022 phone 22367468

Objective

Become a GM[finance]

Qualification

working together — improved my attitude towards working with people not close to me

organising — learnt that patience is a very important part of behaviour when dealing with numbers and when explaining the meaning of numbers.

Education

June 2006 B Com, Commerce, I class, University of Madras

May 2005 Diploma in Tally

June 2006 Diploma in MS-office

A cover letter

Venkatesh Apartments
193 Trimurti Colony
Nagpur 440 022

20 August 2008

____
____
____

Dear Sir

I would like to apply for the position of Accounts Assistant, advertised in yesterday's Hindustan Times.

As a result of the three years of my stay in college, I have developed a respect for numbers and the messages they convey in terms of deficit, growth and prosperity. Words may lie but numbers don't. Numbers tell you how important budgeting is.

College life has taught me how to be polite and courteous to superiors. I have also learnt that patience and compromise are essential to realising goals.

I am quite comfortable with the computer. I am quite conversant with Tally and Ms-office. In fact, our College accountant has helped me a lot. With experience and guidance, I will be able to prepare reports as well..

I enclose my CV and photocopies of certificates. I am prepared to appear for an interview at any time.

I thank you for considering my application.

Yours faithfully

………………

Nikhil Yadav

enc. as stated

Samples 2 and 3 are similar in format but different in content. From this you should understand that what you write in the CV and the cover letter depends on your education and the job you're applying for. Lakshmanan wants a career in handling people whereas Nikhil wants a career in handling numbers. And there is no'achievement' column in the CV because Nikhil has nothing to mention.

The content of cover letters of 2 and 3 helps the reader to form images of Lakshmanan and Nikhil.

5.1.4 A good CV and cover letter [without experience]

Manveer Jain
born: 26 July 1986

9-3-13/B Brahmin Street
Vijayawada—520 001
phone 26367458

Objective

Run a call centre by 2020

Qualification

working together — improved my attitude towards working with people not close to me

good listener — learnt when to listen and when to respond and if necessary how to interrupt

good communicator— learnt to use a word of praise, a word of sympathy, a word of understanding

Education

June 2006 B A Economics, I class, University of Madras

May 2005 attended a communication workshop and learnt about the key role of tone

---

9-3-13/B Brahmin Street
Vijayawada—520 001

20 August 2008

____
____
____

Dear Sir

I would like to apply for the position of Customer Service Executive, advertised in The Indian Express of 17 August.

I have had my education through English. And language comes naturally to me. I am good at Telugu, Hindi, besides English. I like American movies, and I have watched several of them, so I can easily follow a conversation. I cannot, as yet, speak like them but with training, I will.

College hostel life has taught me how to be awake during nights and not feel tired next morning. I have also learnt that patience is a virtue while speaking to strangers.

I enclose my CV and photocopies of certificates. I am prepared to appear for an interview at any time.

I thank you for considering my application.

Yours faithfully

……………..

Manveer Jain

Sample 4 has the same format as those of 2 and 3 but very different in content. From this you should understand that what you write in the CV and the cover letter depends on your education and the job you're applying for.

Manveer clearly knows the demands of the job he's applying for. He says he is a good listener and knows what to say when. He says in his cover letter he has some idea of how native users of English speak and he expresses confidence in himself. These are the 'skills' that the employer would expect a candidate to have.

5.15 A good CV and cover letter [without experience]

A CV

Tejaswini Sawant
born:16 June 1986

16/67 B Kranti Lane
Near Income Tax Office
Kanpur –208 001 phone 26367458

Objective

Executive Engineer with career growth in R&D

Qualification

communication — gave seminars on major discipline and allied areas.
presented a paper on …………..
……………………at

working together — improved my attitude towards working with people not close to me.
captained college volleyball team and won a Trophy.
got allowances for my team mates

organising — as part of tour programme arranged for passports and visas

Education

June 2006 B E Information Technology, I class, JNTU, Hyderabad

A cover letter

16/67 B Kranti Lane
Near Income Tax Office
Kanpur –208 001

20 August 2008

____
____
____

Dear Sir
I would like to apply for the position of Executive Engineer, advertised in The Hindustan Times of 15 August. I believe I have the right qualifications.

My seminar experience helped me get rid of my stage fear and enabled me to come out of my shell. I realised that I could also use English as well as others, if not better. This has also enabled me to go beyond the syllabus and learn to use the library to strengthen my knowledge base.

My teachers and batchmates were very understanding and helped me grow as a person and as a student. I am sure a similar atmosphere prevails in your organisation.

I enclose my CV and photocopies of certificates. I am prepared to appear for an interview at any time.

I thank you for considering my application.

Yours faithfully
………………
Tejaswini Sawant
enc. as stated

The blanks in 'communication' should be filled in with the title of the paper and the place where it was presented.

Sample 5 has the same format as those of 2, 3 and 4 but very different in content. From this you should understand that what you write in the CV and the cover letter depends on your education and the job you're applying for.

Tejaswini mentions 'skills' under 'qualification' that she can support during the interview. She also talks, in the cover letter, about how she became a better person through experiences in the college and help from others. She goes one step further and says she expects a similar atmosphere in the employer's organisation. This will please any employer.

5.1.6 Cover letters or application letters without experience

'Cover letter' is also known as 'application letter' or 'letter of invite'. It should be a **one-page** letter.

You've already seen the cover letters for 2, 3, 4 and 5. Now you must have some idea of how to write cover letters when you have no experience at all.

In addition to these, you see below some possible **variations** you can use to write cover letters when you are a fresher.

A cover letter usually has three paragraphs:

First paragraph

> I wish* to apply for the position of ——1——advertised in ——2—. I believe I have the right qualifications.
>
> * you can write 'I would like' instead of 'I wish'.

notes:

1. fill in the job title[and any reference number that may have been given in the ad.
2. today's/yesterday's——[source name]
   [or]
   the————of——
   [the source, the date without year]

> I am responding to the position advertised in ——2*—— for a ——1————. I am enclosing my resume for your consideration.

Fill in 2 and 1 as in the previous sample.

Dear Sir

_______________ [mention here name of the position]

I wish to apply for the above post, advertised in ——1—— .

1. write here 2 as in the first sample

All the three samples above respond to an advertisement placed in a newspaper.

But it's possible that you hear from someone about a vacancy for a position in an organisation. For this, paragraph 1 should be something like:

I recently learnt from ———1———, ———2———at———3———that you are looking for————4————. I know that your firm is number one in the region* and I feel that your organisation is the right place for me to develop my talents and skills.

One of your marketing executives, ———1———, a batchmate of mine at college informed me of a possible opening for a —2—— in your marketing division. I think I have the right competencies to apply for it.

* you can also say 'I know that your organisation is among the top ten in the country.'

1. mention the name of the person 2. the position of that person 3. the name of the organisation where that person works 4. the position vacant

1. mention the name of the person 2. mention the position vacant

Middle paragraph[s]

This is where you show why you are the right person for the advertised position. This is where you sell yourself with specific aspects of your work history having a direct bearing on the job you're applying for, like the responsibilities you carried out, the skills that enabled you to promote the interests of your workplaces and that qualify you for the position you're seeking. This is where you thus convince the reader about your usefulness.

But you are a fresher. Naturally you have no work experience. What do you write here?

Since you have no working experience, you cannot talk about professional or job skills. But you can definitely talk about skills you developed or improved as a person or an individual during your stay in an educational institution. Any potential or prospective employer will surely be interested in how you grew or how you matured as an adult.

You already have some idea about what to write from letters 65, 66, 67, and 68. Let's see what else you can write:

1. Did you work or participate as a member of a group in any
   - college activity like Sports Day, College Day, Hostel Day, Independence Day Celebrations, cultural activities [or]
   - College Association like Student's Association or Association of your major Department, RSS [or]
   - sports team or NCC ?

   If you did, you can say some things like these:

You can also use other college situations or experiences and say things like these:

As a team player in my Department Association, I have learnt to appreciate the need to complete a job within a time frame, to interact with outside world courteously and patiently and not to allow my ego to come between my task and me. **1**

As a member of the football team, I have learnt to accept that other members and their ideas are as important as my ideas and me. **2**

As a member of the Table Tennis team, I saw our Physical Director doing injustice to me; I felt hurt when he did not make me captain. I took this positively and decided that when I got an opportunity, I should not behave like him. **3**

When I joined college, I was shy and would not easily mix with others. Jerome, a close friend of mine now, was the one who showed me that I could be like anybody else and achieve things. So when I get an opportunity, I will do for someone what Jerome did for me. **4**

As Captain of the college volleyball team, I realised that for any leader to be successful, he would need the full cooperation of his team. **5**

I was the Student President for 2005-2006. This was when I learnt how difficult it was to be a good leader. I made a few mistakes initially but learnt from them. **6**

From my history teacher, I learnt to give equal importance to others and their ideas, and became a good listener. **7**

I have learnt that having an opinion different from others is not wrong but not respecting the individuality is. **8**

As an organiser of an event or two, I realised the need for tact in dealing with superiors and students whom I did not like.

As an organiser, I realised that convincing is better than commanding. **10**

As an implementer, I realised that when I focused on the objective to be achieved, I was able to do a better job. **11**

As an implementer, I realised that achieving a goal was easy when I went to the right people or the right sources. **12**

I think I am a good listener. I do not interrupt when somebody speaks. I let them complete what they want to say. I think I have a lot of friends because of this. **13**

I learnt this in college: Success depends to a certain extent on how you behave with others. Be formal with formal people and be informal with informal people. Never mix them up. **14**

My college life taught me that being aloof or shy drives others away from you; makes you feel more lonely and you become a problem to yourself. **15**

I saw some of my friends enjoying each other's company and some others fighting all the time. "Forgive and forget" is difficult to practise but yields happiness. **16**

I interact well with people. I enjoy working with others. I learn a lot from how others do their jobs. **17**

I possess good communication skills. Whenever guests came to college, I was the one to introduce them to the students. **18**

I am strong in ——1——. I am also interested in ——2——. Whatever job I may get, I think I will find time to read further and enjoy my reading. **19**

1. an area in your subject where you got good grades grades. 2. an area in your subject about which you think more and want to know more.

The third sentence clearly indicates your interest in reading and knowledge for the sake of knowledge.

I was lucky to have good teachers. They were good subject-wise and guided us in the right direction with a friendly attitude, without using their authority. Because of them, I have developed a positive attitude towards others, seeing the good side of others rather than their weak side. **20**

These twenty items tell you that you have a lot to write about yourself even if you ***have no work experience***. So think about the three or four years of stay in college, remember your interactions with others and what you have learnt about yourself and others, the strengths and weaknesses and how these have shaped you to become a better person. You can use college experiences to say things like these in paragraphs 2 and 3 of your cover letter. Of course, if you get a chance to be interviewed, you should be able to cite instances from your college life to support your claims about your growth. The prospective employer will want to know about the human side of your life because like college, the workplace is a place where you have to move with people, mix with them, get along with them and perform your job.

Last paragraph

This is where you talk about interview dates and close it with an appropriate statement.
Here are some sample last paragraphs:

I would welcome the opportunity to discuss this letter and my enclosed curriculum vitae. The telephone number I have given is our landline and all calls are answered.
I look forward to hearing from you. **1**

I look forward to an interview at your convenience. I will call your office next Monday to arrange an interview. **2**

I would appreciate the chance to interview with you at your earliest convenience. If you have questions or would like additional information., contact me at ———— any Tuesday or Thursday after 10 a.m. or e-mail me at ————. Thank you for your time. **3**

I would appreciate the opportunity to meet with you to discuss your ———— [job]. If you have questions or would like to speak with me personally, please contact me at ———— [phone] any weekday after 3 p.m. Thank you for your time and consideration. **4**

I would enjoy meeting with you at your convenience to discuss this career opportunity further. Also, I have many references that I encourage you to contact. Feel free to call me any weekday morning or e-mail me at ———— if you have any questions, need further information or would like to set up an interview. Thank you for your consideration. **5**

I would like to discuss my qualifications in an interview at your convenience. Please write to me, telephone me at ———— any weekday or e-mail me at————. **6**

Sample 1 is British style. The other five are American. You may use these if you're sure you're applying to a British firm or an American firm **overseas**. In this case, personal interview may not be possible. Telephonic interviews are, however, occurring for selecting right candidates. So you may add 'telephonic' before 'interview'.

But in **our** environment, it's safer to write something like this in the final paragraph:

I enclose my CV and photocopies of certificates. I am prepared to appear for an interview at any time.

I thank you for considering my application. **7**

Don't write something like 8 or 9:

If I am appointed, I will be honest and sincere. I will work to the fullest satisfaction of my superiors. I will be grateful if you consider my application favourably. I am waiting for a favourable reply. **8**

I promise to work honestly and sincerely and to the fullest satisfaction of my superiors. I hope that you will reply by return of post. **9**

8 or 9 is meaningless because the prospective employer assumes that you will be loyal, sincere, honest. And a response cannot be demanded.

5.2 Cover letter or application letter with experience

There is no difference in the first and the last paragraphs of cover letter without experience or with experience.

The difference is, however, in the middle paragraphs. This is where you show why you are the right person for the advertised position. This is where you sell yourself with specific aspects of your work history having direct bearing on the job you're applying for, like the responsibilities you carried out, the skills that enabled you to promote the interests of your workplaces and that qualify you for the position you're seeking. This is where you thus convince the reader about your usefulness.

There can be no possible model for the middle paragraphs. Because what you will decide to write and how you'll present it will depend on

- the job and the responsibilities that go with it
- the jobs you have held and the responsibilities that go with them
- the kind of **matching** you'll have to do between these two
- the role of your contribution to the success of the workplaces.

However, cite instances to show your role in the growth of the firm where you worked and/or are working. Mention quick promotions you received or substantial increase in your salary or any specific training you underwent.

You can also mention, if any, academic or sports honours or any other meritorious recognitions, responsibilities you discharged as a member or a leader in any of the college associations.

A cover letter should not go beyond a page. So, remember not to write too much. The reader may not have the time or the patience to go through a long cover letter. Be selective in the choice of your experiences, instances that will project you as an achiever in relation to the position you're seeking.

There should be enough specific details focusing on what you are and how you can fit into the new organisation. If you have a lot to say, write them all down, read it as many times as you can, edit it—make it brief and crisp.

Have a good mix of simple, complex and compound sentences, appropriate to the thoughts to be expressed. Don't go for obscure or high-sounding words. Use positive expressions.

Also you need to proofread or edit and correct any spelling, grammatical or punctuation errors. Error-free letter will indicate you are a thoughtful, careful writer and so a useful employee.

5.3 CV with experience

Below you have two kinds of CV with experience.

5.3.1 A chronological CV

T V Ramkumaar
G-2 Fortune Enclave
22 Rukmani Street
Krishnapuram
Ambattur
Chennai 600 0053
Tel: 26584233
e-mail: antelope_26@yahoo.co.in

Experience

2000—present
Regional Sales Executive in charge of Tamilnadu, Kerala and Goa, India Pistons Ltd. Responsible for achieving set targets, improving sales, satisfying customers, launching new products, product moving trend analysis, planning and implementing appropriate schemes for mechanics and reborers.

1997—2000
Executive-logistics, India Pistons Ltd. In charge of warehousing and outsourcing it.

1995—1997
Executive-marketing, India Pistons Ltd. Coordinated with production dept., executed inter-depot stock transfers, carried out depot inventories

1994—1995
Executive-accounts, India Pistons Ltd. Maintained sales and F.O.C. invoices, sales day-book

1993—1994
Management Trainee, India Pistons Ltd. Trained in all operational departments.

Qualifications and training

PG Certificate in Sales and Marketing, IIM, Kozhikode	2005
Diploma in MS Office, Lotus notes	1998
Bachelor of Arts in Economics, University of Madras	1992

Interests
Cricket
Travel
Meeting people

Referees

________________ ________________
________________ ________________

5.3.2 A functional CV

T V Ramkumaar
G-2 Fortune Enclave
22 Rukmani Street
Krishnapuram
Ambattur Tel: 26584233
Chennai 600 0053 e-mail: antelope_26@yahoo.co.in

Profile

Enthusiastic, innovative, committed, practical, outgoing, self-driven person wishing to reach the pinnacle in sales and marketing. Able to work as a team member and a team leader to set targets, to initiate action and to realise goals in a given time frame.

Training

Has recently completed a PG Diploma in sales and marketing at IIM, Kozhikode.

Skills gained

- achieving sales targets ahead of time-schedule
- planning and organising training programmes
- managing distributors and dealers effectively
- setting and achieving performance standards for self and team
- ensuring smooth labour-related environment
- applying cost control in purchases, transportation
- employing successfully third-party logistics
- willing listener
- including suggestions from team in action plans
- employing inventive strategies to draw end-customers
- improving customer database

Experience

- Seventeen years' work experience with Indian Pistons Ltd., known for its quality products
- Responsible for achieving set targets, improving sales, satisfying customers, launching new products, product moving trend analysis, planning and implementing appropriate scheme for mechanics and reborers.
- In charge of warehousing and outsourcing it
- Maintained sales and F.O.C. invoices, sales daybook

Education

Bachelor of Arts in economics, University of Madras 1992

Interests

Cricket, Travel, Meeting people

Referees

________________ ________________
____
________________ ________________

5.4 Electronic/Online Version of a CV

The CVs we've seen so far are known as traditional paper resumes. 'Paper' because they are printed on paper. 'Traditional' because the CVs in 3.1 and 3.2 are contrasted against the latest medium which is 'electronic'. We usually mail them by post or send them via e-mail.

Do not send it by e-mail as an attachment unless a company requests it. Because of the danger of viruses on attachments, several companies, as a policy, delete attachments before opening e-mails. So paste your CV to the e-mail, and then reformat it to suit the e-mail message window. Or get ready an electronic version of your paper CV and put it on the e-mail.

To widen your job search, you may respond to ads in the print media, in the electronic media, to post your CV on job boards on the Internet or to post it on your Web page if you have one.

The traditional paper CVs will do for land or air mail. You'll need an electronic version prepared in a specified format to send it via e-mail or the Internet.

An electronic version should be an ASCII [American Standard Code for Information Interchange] document. While preparing such a document, you

- must not use things like graphic lines or boxes, bullets, underlining, italics or boldface,
- should use only simple font styles and sizes between 10 and 14 points,
- should replace bullets with hyphens or asterisks and use white spaces between sections rather than indenting,
- should set the margins so as not to go beyond 65 characters per line, including spaces between words,
- should save your document as an ASCII or MS-Dos text document using the .txt extension.

But if you have to submit a CV with special design features, you may scan it as a PDF file.

Your electronic version may be scanned or downloaded into a company's database. Such companies prefer to see 'nouns' rather than 'verbs' to describe experience and skills

[*supervisor* and *refinement* rather than *supervised* and *refined*]. So you may include a separate section titled 'keywords' [also known as '*descriptors*'] in your resume to refer to your experience and skills. Use a maximum of 50 terms for this purpose. Place this section below the 'heading' or above 'references'. See a sample in the next page.

[5.3.1, 5.3.2 and 5.4.1 are based on information in "Handbook of Technical Writing" by Gerald J. Alred et al, St. Martin's Press, seventh edition, 2003]

5.4.1 A sample electronic version of a resume

K R Lakshminarayanan
2 Thirumal Nagar Extn. 1
Poonamallee, Chennai 600 056
India
(91-44-2649 1052)
klnsurt29@yahoo.com

Job Objective
Language Expert—English, Asian Region

Keywords
Curriculum and course writer, course/programme coordinator, language skills trainer, student counsellor, test items writer, answer scripts evaluator, English teacher—class 6 to UG, coursebook writer, 'communication' books writer for the public, researcher.

Education
**1994 Certificate as 'induction' trainer ISTE, Delhi
**1990 PGDTE *(English)* CIEFL, Hyderabad
** 1988 PGCTE *(English)* CIEFL, Hyderabad
**1987 Basic Cert. AIU, Delhi
[Methodology and]
[Examinations]
**1986 *B.Ed [English]* Annamalai University
**1986 PG Diploma ISSR, Salem
[Edu. Admn.]
**1966 M*A [English]* Madras University
**1962 *BA [English]* Madras University

Employment Experience
** English professor—1985-2005
Sri Venkateswara College of Engineering, Tamilnadu, India
** English teacher—1968-1984
Ministries of Education, Kwara and Bauchi States, Nigeria
Ministry of Education, Ethiopia
** English tutor and lecturer—1962-1968
AM.Jain College, Chennai, Sri Palniandavar College of Indian Culture, Palni, Tamilnadu

Publications and conferences
** articles on ELT and topics of general interest in the States, Ethiopia and India
** English coursebooks for UG engineering students, recommended for study
** The Communicating Art—2004
** Speak in English you can!—2006
** in press
English for Competitive Examinations [co-author]
Puzzles and Games for Children—5-12
Edit your writing
Pen your letters

Further information
**References, writing samples available on request

6. Reading Comprehension

6.1 Why do you read ?

You read because

- reading is part of being literate
- you receive messages, information, knowledge, entertainment in print/manuscript
- you wish or need to respond to these messages
- you want to enjoy these messages.

6.2 How do you read?

To comprehend or understand a reading passage, you need to use three reading skills: **skimming, scanning** and **studying.** Skimming occurs when you read a written piece quickly in order to find a particular point or the main points. Summarising is a kind of skimming. Scanning occurs when you read a written piece in order to look for specific pieces of information, for important details that make up the more important details. Studying occurs when we do serious reading in school or college or for research purposes.

Using these skills to good effect is only the third step. The first step is to recognize and pronounce loudly or in our mind [silently] the sounds that the letter symbols represent and make meaning from bunches/groups of these sounds. The second step is *how well* you read. That is, do you read word by word or words in groups?

Read this passage:

> Read through this passage very quickly and from the ideas expressed, gather the topic. This process is known as skimming. When you scan, you're looking for specific pieces of information, for important details that make up the more important ideas. The process of identifying these ideas is known as scanning.

Did you stop at every word? Or every two or three words?

Did you go back to your left while reading?

Did your lips move as you read?

Did you use your finger at the words?

If any of these happens to you while reading, you have reading problems.

6.3 What do you do about this?

To improve your reading and comprehension, you should become a good reader.

Good readers do not read every word separately; they read in **chunks**, large and small, as their eyes take short and long jumps. That is, they do not pause [=stop briefly] at every word. They read words *in* groups which we call *sense groups*.

The passage you read a while ago is now divided into chunks [sense groups]. Before you attempt to read the passage with the slashes, **listen to it on the CD on track 4** you've been provided with this Book. Stop at every slash as you read, you'll find that your reading speed is getting better.

1. Read through/ this passage/ very quickly/ and/ from the ideas/ expressed,/ gather/ the topic./ This process/ is known/ as skimming./ When you scan,/ you're looking for/ specific/ pieces of information,/ for important details/ that make up/ the more important ideas./ The process/ of identifying/ these ideas/ is known/ as scanning./ [23 stops]

The above passage is now divided differently with more words in each chunk. Again listen to this on the CD. Now Read and stop at the slashes.

2. Read through/this passage/very quickly/and from the ideas expressed,/ gather the topic./This process is known/ as skimming./ When you scan,/ you're looking for/ specific pieces of information,/ for important details/ that make up/ the more important ideas./ The process of identifying/ these ideas/ is known as scanning./ [16 stops]

In this attempt you'll find the slashes [stops] further reduced. Listen to the CD. Read.

3. Read through this passage very quickly/and from the ideas expressed,/ gather the topic./This process is known as skimming./ When you scan,/ you're looking for/specific pieces of information,/ for important details/ that make up/ the more important ideas./ The process of identifying these ideas/ is known as scanning./ [12 stops]

Now you'll find stops still less. Listen to the CD. Read.

4. Read through this passage very quickly and from the ideas expressed,/ gather the topic./This process is known as skimming./ When you scan, you're looking for specific pieces of information,/ for important details that make up the more important ideas./ The process of identifying these ideas is known as scanning./ [6 stops]

Your present reading ability may be at any of these stages—from 1 to 4. If you are at 4, you have no problem at all. If you are not, practise reading 2 to 4 until you reach stage 4.

A word of caution. Picking up reading speed, being able to read in proper chunks, reading words in sense groups is the normal goal because that's how we normally read. But this 'normal' refers to *general reading* like novels, non-fiction, newspapers, magazines. Here you have the liberty to skip words, sentences, why even pages occasionally. But you cannot read certain material fast because you should not. You should not read them fast because they are meant to be read slowly, because they are meant to be understood fully. Can you read your coursebooks or textbooks, articles in technical or scientific journals like you read fiction? You cannot, you should not because you don't read them, you **study** them. You study them because you don't want to miss any information or fact or argument. Why sometimes, you do reread certain portions of 'light reading' for better enjoyment or appreciation.

6.4 Role of Reading

To learn a language, you need a live environment where it is spoken, listened to, read and written. Being conversant in Thelugu in Andhra Pradesh is easy because there is a live environment around you—you hear and speak it all the time, you read and write it all the time. But to be conversant in Thelugu in Punjab, for instance, is very difficult because there is no live communicating environment in Punjab, except your family. How then do you become conversant in Thelugu in Punjab? You need to provide yourself with a substitute 'environment'. Read as many books in Thelugu as you can.

So is your case with being conversant with English in Andhra Pradesh. If you've lived in an environment where English is not spoken and so not heard and if you wish to acquire some command of English, you should not stop with reading English textbooks but do a lot of extra reading. Read story books, novels, non-fiction, newspapers, magazines. ***This reading keeps you in touch with the English language as it is used for communication.***

6.5 Passages for practising reading comprehension

Reading these passages and answering the comprehension questions will help you develop the skills that you can apply successfully in answering questions on reading comprehension in **TOEFL**.

1. Liberalization and Globalization

Immediately after getting political independence, India had to choose one of the two paths to development: market-led or state-led. The difference between the two lies in the extent of state intervention. India chose the 'mixed economy' model, which sought to combine the virtues of both models. The public sector was to play a dominant role in the industrialization process and would be complemented by the private sector. Private sector would be heavily regulated by the state through a variety of procedures; the most [un]popular of them was the industrial licensing procedure. In fact, the licensing system was later dubbed as 'license-raj'. The licensing system decided on what and how much the private sector would produce. It was felt that since industrial development had begun only after independence, chances of selling our goods in the international market were not bright.

Besides, our foreign exchange reserves, required to finance imports, were scarce. India would depend on its own resources, goods and services and conserve the scarce foreign exchange. Based on the principle of self reliance, the government adopted an import-substitution industrialization strategy. This model offered protection to domestic industries from tough international competition. It was seen to suit the needs and constraints of an under developing economy like ours.

This model worked well initially. However, the poor performance of the industrial sector and the inefficient running of the public sector were seen to be the inevitable outcomes of the over-regulating industrial policy and protectionism. The licensing system not only severely restrained the freedom of the private sector but also bred corruption. Three policy implications flowed from this realisation.

Firstly, constrictions imposed on the private sector had to be minimized and the private sector had to be given a greater and more meaningful role in making India a viable and vibrant economy. This in fact is what is called 'liberalization', that is, freeing private sector from the control (if you wish, stranglehold) of the government. Industrialists had long been pleading for free economic environment. They wanted freedom to decide what to produce, where to produce, how much to produce and so on.

Secondly, the public sector should be reformed and reorganised to improve its efficiency. It was also argued that the government should reduce the size of public sector participation in production of goods and services. (This is known as privatization argument).). Privatization in simple terms means transfer of ownership from government to private hands. In India the term 'disinvestment' is popularly used to indicate divestment of some portion (minor or major) of the shares to private agencies. Pro-reform economists and private sector firms advocate privatisation on grounds of efficiency. A number of public enterprises are incurring losses and they impose a heavy burden on the public finance of the government. They should not be producing goods that could be produced more efficiently by the private sector. Private sector firms are likely to be more efficient than public enterprises for a number of reasons. They are subject to market scrutiny and the loss-making firms face the threat of bankruptcy or take-over. Contrastingly, loss-prone public sector firms enjoy government financial support (through budgetary support).

Thirdly, India should concentrate on promoting exports. It was argued that the closed economy model, that is, restricting imports and limiting exports was a failure and that India should be promoting exports more vigorously than before. The East Asian economies such as South Korea, Taiwan achieved faster economic progress by encouraging exports.

It is important to remember that India had, in fact, started introducing some of these reforms in the mid-1980s. But what tilted the balance towards reforms was the balance of payments crisis faced by the Indian economy in 1990-91. India fended off the crisis by taking a loan from the International Monetary Fund (IMF) in June 1991 under the Structural Adjustment Programme (SAP). The SAP loan stipulated some conditions for sanctioning the loan and the Indian government was obligated to implement them. The New Economic Policy introduced by the Narasimha Rao government initiated the reform process by considerably liberalizing the procedures in the industrial sector. The privatization drive soon gained momentum. The formation of World Trade Organization (WTO) in place of General Agreement on Trade and Tariff (GATT) in 1995 provided rules for a free trade and capital regime. A free trade regime means international trade taking place with least restrictions. Particularly, it meant removal of restrictions on the 'quantity' to be imported (called as 'quotas'). Equally importantly, it also meant free movement of capital. These developments opened up markets for goods, services, capital and, in some sense, opportunities for workers. In one word, this is 'globalization'.

Globalization is expected to benefit the economic agents in various ways. The consumers stand to gain most as they will enjoy a range of quality goods and services at cheaper prices. Firms can compete in wider markets, use better technology, have more choices for operation and so on. Economies can exploit the foreign capital inflow, the smooth technology transfer, and the available skilled workers. Trade is thus thought of as an 'engine of growth.

But the actual scene does not appear to be as rosy as this. Globalization has its critics. Critics argue that globalization has not kept its promises. Big multinational enterprises[MNEs, also called as transnational corporations, TNC] are seen to be dominating the global business. They seem to be flexing their muscles and coercing weak governments (especially, developing countries) into giving concessions that often work against the interests of people, especially workers, in these countries. Much of foreign capital movement seems to be within and among developed countries. Transfer of technology is limited and MNEs keep core business such as research and development in the 'origin' countries. Most global trade is within the MNEs (called 'intra-firm') and within the 'triad' consisting of the United States, Japan and Europe. More importantly, globalization has worsened the economic inequalities. Genuine globalization is really not happening. For instance, there is a big hue and cry against 'outsourcing' by US firms to firms in India. Globalization is seen to hurt the interests of workers in developed countries as firms therein seek to relocate their business activities to cheaper regions in the South. The protectionist tendencies still seem to be present even in the countries that preach free trade regime.

Back home, in our country, the debate over the impact of liberalization is on. Under liberalization, the performance of the industrial economy has not been as impressive as it should have been. However, our industrial growth has climbed to around 8 percent, comparing favourably with the performance of industrial sector in China. Notwithstanding the controversial database, there is some truth in the official picture as there has been a reduction in the number of people below the poverty line (defined in terms of consumption limits). Though economic growth has been impressive, it has not been accompanied by job creation, nevertheless. This peculiar phenomenon, known as 'jobless growth', is a disturbing one. Thus there are enough grounds for both the supporting and opposing camps of reforms.

Exercise 33

Comprehension

1. Read the passage and get the meanings of these words from the context:

   intervention [interference] dominant scarce foreign exchange inevitable

   constraint constriction restriction restrain viable vibrant stranglehold

   plead incur impose scrutiny stipulate bankruptcy tilt balance (2)

   reform be obligated implement initiate momentum consumer exploit

   capital inflow flex muscle coerce concession core business preach

2. What path did India choose to run its economy?

   ____

3. What was used to control the private sector?

   ____

4. Why was India not interested in imports?

   1. ______________________________

   2. ______________________________

5. What did the licensing system finally lead to? [in one word]

   ____

6. Define 'liberalization'.

   ____

   ____

7. Why don't public sector firms care about loss?

   ____

8. Why is private sector more efficient than the public sector?

   ____

9. What benefit did South Korea receive for encouraging exports?

   ____

10. Who provided for 'globalization'?

    ____

    ____

11. Put slashes for the first two paragraphs and read to your lecturer / professor.

    [Also check your response by listening to Track 5 on your CD]

2. What's in a number?

It all started as a fun way to beat the blues. Pune-based BPO employee Jean signed up for a cell phone dating service to enjoy the thrills of chatting with a stranger.

But the stranger, a 42-year-old in Bangalore, managed to trace her personal information, including her extension number in office, and landed in Pune. When she refused to meet him, he threatened to expose their chat records to her spouse.

the number game

An airline employee took an anonymous relationship to the next level and met up with the person. He drugged her, clicked her in a compromising position and blackmailed her.

The case of Jackie, a Chennai-based businessman, is different. He was trapped by an ex-cabaret danacer, who posed as a Karnataka State Government employee, got the numbers of high net individuals, invited them for chats and made money by threatening to make their relationships public.

In all the three cases, it was the mobile numbers that landed them in trouble.

easy targets

What is there in a mobile number? "Your life," says J.Prasanna, director and joint secretary, Cyber Society of India. "Using this number, a person can gain access to the home and office address and family details. The victims are adults leading unhappy lives. They easily fall prey to the new-found happiness these anonymous chats offer,"

casual talk

The problem begins when the casual talk on such PC-based cell phone dating services turns into a relationship. "From chatting with nick names, they move on to the next level of trust, and exchange numbers. Exchanging photographs and late night chatting follows," says Prasanna.

Psychiatrist V, Ponnai Muralidharan blames it on the easy-going nature of society. "Now, everything is considered cool. Only a few guilty ones approach psychiatrists for help. In most cases, it is people with low self-esteem who look to such channels for reassurance. When they are bored with their current relationships, acknowledgement from a stranger that they are intelligent and fun to be with brings cheer. Another advantage is the anonymity factor," she says.

Though mobile culture and chatting on the web is rampant among youngsters, psychopaths out there want to target adults.

"Because family people have so much to lose—house, car, children—a spouse can even apply for a divorce citing adultery," explains Prasanna. So never give your mobile numbers to strangers.

"Even if it's going to be plain fun, make sure to check the credentials of the other person. Maintain anonymity and switch over to another Instant Messenger chats if the person asks for numbers," he adds.

cyber affairs

Be it landline or mobile chats, both create problems in steady relationships, says psychiatrist D. Srinivasan. "Don't fall for it. Though anonymity gives security in 'cyber affairs', you gain nothing in the end. It is like falling in love; you tend to overlook the negative aspects. Another problem is that one of them can easily manipulate the other into an intense relationship to achieve their hidden motives. So, you end up losing your peace of mind, he says.

pamper yourself

Unconditional acceptance of the self and spending more time with family are possible ways to steer clear of such situations.

"This is an impulsive behaviour of the super ego, which deals with the pleasure-oriented instincts. Such relationship problems arise when the super ego gets stronger," says Srinivasan. In any relationship, the pillars of strength are love, respect and trust. Respect for the individuality of the other person, intensity of trust and intimacy are the other factors. When there is a fine balance of all these, there is no room for boredom.

"Things are smooth as long as love is unconditional. When it becomes conditional, the partners tend to undervalue what they get and look for alternative channels of reassurance. Even when one pillar becomes weak, the relationship turns shaky," the psychiatrist warns.

Says Prasanna: "Never take technology for granted. Like it happens in our daily lives, relationships of every kind can evolve over the technology platform too. Be wary of them."

If caught in such a situation, people can e-mail <u>cybersocietyblr@yahoo.co.in</u> for help.

[K. Jeshi's article published in the Metroplus of The Hindu of 12 March 2007]

Exercise 34

1. Guess the meanings of these words in the context of the passage:

   chat thrill extension number threaten expose spouse anonymous compromising blackmail ex- cyber victim fall prey cool psychiatrist cheer psychopath target adult divorce security overlook hidden instinct

2. What does "the blues" mean?

   ____

3. What threat did the stranger make to Jean?

   ____

4. "What is there in a mobile number?" "Your life," says J. Prasanna. What does he mean? [discuss orally]

5. Casual talk on PC-based cell phone turns into relationship. Write down the three things that indicate the relationship.

   ____

6. "Psychiatrist V. Ponni Muralidharan blames it on the easy-going nature of society." What does 'it' refer to?

   ____

7. What is common between 'falling in love' and 'cyber affairs'?

   ____

8. Mobile chatting results in ____________________
9. The three pillars of any relationship are ____________________
10. Complete the sequence:

    ____________________ → ____________________ →

    look for alternative channels → casual talk → relationship → problems
11. Use slashes to read the first two paragraphs.

    [Also check your response on listening to Track 5 on your CD]

    ____

3. The Nobel Prize

The title leads us automatically to think of a person known as 'Dynamite King' and 'Merchant of Death'. This very person did great disservice to humanity a century ago with the invention and manufacture of explosives and did great service by placing a quarter century ago nearly two million pounds in the hands of Swedish and Norwegian Trustees for the award of five prizes, later known as Nobel prizes.

Who was this person? Alfred Bernhard Nobel. How did such turnaround occur? Probably through Countess Bertha von Kinsky. Nobel was greatly impressed by her novel titled 'Lay Down Arms!' and the World Peace movement of which she was the first President. He decided to do something great for the movement.

prizes

Nobel stated in his will that the annual interest should be divided into five equal parts and each to be awarded to a person or an institution for exceptional contribution in the field of physics, chemistry, physiology or medicine, literature and international peace, and that the nationality of the candidates being considered should not be a restraining factor for awarding the prize. Nobel Foundation, established in 1900, started to award the Prizes from 1901. The Central Bank of Sweden instituted the Nobel Memorial Prize in economics with a cash award equal to the other Nobel prizes. The Noble prize includes a cash award, a medal and a diploma with the winner's name and field of achievement. Prize winners are known as Nobel Laureates.

Nobel Laureates of India

Eight Indian citizens or people of Indian origin have been honoured to date. They are:

1.	Rudyard Kipling	[Indian origin]	literature	1907
2.	Rabindranath Tagore		literature	1913
3.	Sir C.V.Raman		physics	1930

4.	Hargobind Khorana [for his work on genes]	[Indian origin]	physiology/medicine	1968
5.	Mother Therasa		peace	1979
6.	S. Chandrasekar	[Indian origin]	physics	1983
7.	Amartya Sen		economics	1999
8.	V.S. Naipaul	[Indian origin]	literature	2001

Nobel peace prize

The Prize for 2006 went to Muhammad Yunus and the Grameen Bank of Bangladesh.

Here is an interesting report by Amit Baruah in The Hindu of 17 October 2006:

> It's not often that you get candid admissions. Or that big institutions have got it wrong. A group of Indian journalists heard both at the headquarters of the Norwegian Nobel Committee, which awards the annual Nobel Peace Prize.
>
> "Our record is far from perfect and not giving Mahatma Gandhi the Nobel Peace Prize was the biggest omission," Geir Lundestad, permanent secretary of the Nowegian Nobel Committee, said on Monday.
>
> Speaking in the Nobel Committee room, where the Peace Prize for 2006 for Muhammad Yunus and the Grameen Bank of Bangladesh was decided by the six-member panel in September, Mr. Lundestad referred to Mahatma Gandhi not receiving the Nobel time and again.
>
> And the omission takes on real meaning when you look around and see the black and white photographs of all Peace Prize winners since 1904 adorning the walls. But there's no picture of the 'half-naked fakir' as Winston Churchill described the man who led India to freedom.
>
> Mahatma Gandhi was to receive the Prize in 1948, but his assassination prevented the award from coming to him, Mr. Lundestad maintained. "But that's no excuse for not giving Gandhi the prize," he explained.
>
> According to him, Mahatma Gandhi was considered not just in 1948, but in 1947, in 1946 and twice previously. "Serious consideration was given to him on all those occasions," he maintained.

When pressed further, Mr. Lundestad said that war breaking out between the newly created states of India and Pakistan could have been a complicating factor for Mahatma Gandhi not being presented with the Prize in 1948.

He also conceded that the Nobel Committee was "Western-oriented" till 1960. According to Mr Lundestad, the Committee felt so terrible it had not conferred the prize on Mahatma Gandhi that it kept looking at "other Indians" over the years.
Asked who the other Indians were, Mr Lundestad revealed that Jawaharlal Nehru and Acharya Vinba Bhave were those considered.
According to him, the Committee was governed by "common sense" and "good political judgement" when deciding on a possible Peace Prize winner. "There are many roads to peace and that's why there are different types of laureates," he stated, referring to the 2006 prize going to Mr Yunus and the Grameen Bank.
However, the Committee had not "widened" the definition of peace just because the prize had gone to the Kenyan environmentalist Wangari Maathai in 2004, Norman Borlaug for new agricultural practices in 1970 and Medicins Sans Frontieres in 1999. Mr Lundestad said the Peace Prize had also been conferred on those who helped a peace process to take shape as was the case in respect of Yassar Arafat, Shimon Peres and Yitzhak Rabin in 1994.

Asked about the Prize being given to Shirin Edbadi of Iran in 2003, he said her award showed that there were those in the "Muslim World" who worked for human rights and democracy.

In Ms. Ebadi's case, the Prize was intended to strengthen those in the "Muslim world" who spoke for human rights.

Comprehension—lexis

Exercise 35

1. Guess the meanings of these words from the context of the passage:
   award, turnaround, physiology, restrain, assassination/murder, maintain, confer,
2. You have below a set of words. Fill in the blanks with words from the passage that are antonyms to them:

A		B [words from the passage]	
service	____________	previously	____________
ordinary	____________	exclude/omit	____________
inclusion	____________	weaken	____________
autocracy	____________	war	____________
allow/permit	____________	temporary	____________

3. You have below a set of words. Fill in the blanks with words from the passage that are synonyms to them:

A		B [words from the passage]	
unique	____________	loser	____________
frank	____________	decorating	____________
broaden	____________	admit	____________
independence	____________	happen	____________

4. Copy down from the passage nouns derived from verbs:

____

____

5. Coy down from the passage words that are used as both a verb and a noun:

____

6. Copy down from the passage irregular verbs:

____

Comprehension—structure

Exercise 36

7. The last two sentences in paragraph 3 have verbs in the present tense while the rest are in the past tense. Can you explain this? [oral]

8. Read these two sentences taken from the passage:

   And the omission takes on real meaning <u>when you look around and see the black and white photographs of all Peace prize winners since 1904 adorning the walls.</u>

   <u>When pressed further</u>, Mr Lundestad said that war breaking between the newly created states of India and Pakistan could have been a complicating factor for Mahatma Gandhi not being presented with the Prize in 1948.

   Explain the difference in the structure of these sentences in relation to the use of 'when'.

9. Copy down from the passage two simple sentences:

____

____

10. Copy down from the passage passive sentences with 'by+agent':

____

____

____

11. Copy down from the passage impersonal passive voice sentences:

____

____

____

____

12. Use of abbreviated forms of passive voice is a common feature in writing. See abbreviated [shortened] passive voice structures:

You may have heard of an employee being demoted [who was demoted]

……….says R. Prasad in his article (which is) titled……" (which was) published in Science & Technology section of The Hindu of August 31, 2006.

Copy down from the passage abbreviated passive voice sentences:

____

____

____

13. The news report has very short paragraphs. This is a common feature in report writing. Discuss this.

Comprehension—discourse [direct and inferential]

Exercise 37

14. What did Nobel invent? ________________
15. How many Nobel prizes are being given? ____________
16. Nobel may have written a different will but for ________________
17. What are the two reasons cited for Gandhi not getting the Prize? (use phrases)

____

18. "Our record is far from perfect….." is connected to another sentence in later paragraphs. Write this down:

____

19. Which sentence in the passage expresses the guilt felt by the Nobel Committee?

____

20. What are the criteria the Committee uses to decide a winner?

____

21. Copy down the phrase that equals "there are many roads to peace".

____

22. The Nobel peace prize has gone, over the years, to activists from different fields. Name two of them:

____

23. Mr. Lundestad said that the Nobel Peace Prize Committee was "western-oriented" till 1960. Such attitude was against one of the conditions laid down in Nobel's will. What was the condition?

____

____

24. Which of these is false?
    a. The Nobel peace prize committee has been doing an excellent job.
    b. Gandhi almost get the Nobel prize in 1948.
    c. The Committee awarded prizes to different activists.
    d. Shirin Ebadi is a lady.

25. Use slashes to read the 'Report' by the Hindu.
    [Check your response by listening to Track 5 on your CD]

---

4. The RTI Act

It was the third week of August 2006. Of the several things that happened last calendar year, a momentous happening was that of the Indian Government's decision to defer a few amendments to the Right to Information Act because of tremendous public pressure. What are these amendments? And how tremendous was the public pressure?

The Act

The Right to Information Act [RTI] had been passed by both the Houses of Parliament and given assent to by the President on June 15, 2005. It had come into force on 13 October 2005. And India had joined the group of 55 countries to have such legislation.

The RTI Act entitles citizens to seek information controlled by public authorities. Thus it obligates every public authority to provide information. The objective is to provide a high degree of transparency and accountability in the working of public authorities and by implication to curb, if not eliminate, corruption and inefficiency in these organisations. And the Act has helped citizens to obtain official documents and to have access to government records without paying bribe or using undue influence.

History

How did all these come about?

The seeds were sown in as early as 1975 in a case "state of UP V Raj Narain". The Supreme Court had said that the people had a right to know every public act. In 1992 [Judges case] and 1995 [Airways case], The Court reiterated the right to know as implicit in the right to speech and expression guaranteed under Article 19(1)(a).

The movement—RTI—grew from the grassroots in Rajasthan. The National Campaign for People's Right to Information [NCPRI] and the Press Council of India sent in 1966 a draft of RTI law to the Government of India. In the meantime, The campaign for RTI by NCPRI continued and spread through the country. Nine States passed RTI laws: Tamilnadu(1997), Goa(1997), Rajasthan, Karnataka, Delhi, Maharashtra(2002), Madhya Pradesh, Assam and Jammu and Kashmir(2004). Though the Government of India introduced the Freedom of Information [FOI] Bill in Parliament in 2002 and got the Presidential assent in 2003, no commencement was ever notified and was thus a non-starter. So the campaign continued to press for an effective RTI.

These efforts found support in the Common Minimum Programme[CMP] of the United Progressive Alliance[UPA] which promised to make the FOI more "progressive, participatory and meaningful". The National Advisory Council [NAC], set up by the Congress Party and of which Aruna Roy and Jean Dreze were members, discussed the issue and submitted to the Prime Minister's Office a set of recommendations for amending the FOI Act after considering the suggestions from CHRI, the NCPRI and other civil society groups. An RTI Bill was introduced by the Government of India in Parliament on 22 December 2004. It became the RTI Act, 2005.

Content

The RTI Act contains 6 chapters and 31 sections. The most significant aspects of the Act are as follows:

2(f) "information" means any material in any form, including records, documents, memos, e-mails, opinions, advices, press releases, circulars, orders, logbooks, contracts, reports, papers, samples, models, data material held in an electronic form and information relating to any private body which can be accessed by a public authority under any other law for the time being in force.

2(i) "record" includes—
(a) any document, manuscript and file;
(b) any microfilm, microfiche and facsimile copy of a document;
(c) any reproduction of image or images embodied in such microfilm (whether enlarged or nor); and
(d) any other material produced by a computer or any other device;

2(j) "right to information" means the right to information accessible under this Act which is held by or under the control of any public authority and includes the right to—
(i) inspection of work, documents, records;
(ii) taking notes, extracts or certified copies of documents or records;
(iii) taking certified sample of material'
(iv) obtaining information in the form of diskettes, floppies, tapes, video cassettes or in any other electronic mode or through printouts where such information is stored in a computer or in any other device;

19 (8) In its decision, the Central Information Commission or State Information Commission, as the case may be, has the power to—
(a) require the public authority to take any such steps as may be necessary to secure compliance with the provisions of this Act including—
(i) by providing access to information, if so required, in a particular form;
(ii) by appointing a Central Public Information Officer or State Public Information Officer, as the case may be;
(iii) by publishing certain information or categories of information;
(iv) by making necessary changes to its practices in relation to the maintenance management and destruction of records;
(v) by enhancing the provision of training on the right to information for its officials;
(vi) by providing it with an annual report in compliance with clause (b) of sub-section (1) of section 4;
(b) require the public authority to compensate the complainant for any loss or other detriment suffered;
(c) impose any of the penalties provided under this Act;
(d) reject the application.

The debate

Probably all would have been well but for a serious hitch. The problem lay in **how** 'information' was interpreted. There were instances where 'file notings' were denied to citizens by public authorities. This is because the Department of Personnel[DoPT] had, through its Frequently Asked Questions [FAQs], posted on its website (www.righttoinformation.gov.in) that 'information' did not include file notings. File notings refer to comments and notes made in the files and to the reasons behind decisions taken. Officials, responsible for providing information, used this FAQ to deny file notings.

The Central Information Commission is, by law, the final arbiter on matters of information. In two cases—Satyapal Vs TCIL of January 2006 and Pyare Lal Vs. the Ministry of Railways of July 13, 2006—the Commission ruled that a combined reading of sections 2(f) and (i) and 2(j) indicated that a citizen has the right of access to a file of which the file notings are an integral part. But this fell on deaf ears. In its July 13 order, the Commission directed the Secretary, Ministry of Personnel & Public Grievances, to remove from the website the instruction relating to non-disclosure of file notings. It warned that failure to comply with this directive would force the Commission to proceed against the Ministry of Personnel.

Soon after, the Union Cabinet approved a set of amendments to the RTI Act. A critical amendment related to barring the disclosure of file notings. There were certain arguments in favour of the amendment:

(1) The President was concerned over whether the government was aware of the distinction between "sharing information or decisions taken" and "sharing of information on how the decision is actually arrived at".

(2) The three Service Chiefs believed the new information regime would not simply work in the defence services.

(3) The new "information" tool has been used by a section of the bureaucracy to settle internal feuds.

However, there have been weighty arguments against barring the disclosure:

(1) Central Chief Commissioner, O.P. Khajriwal, had said that information without file notings amounted to taking the life out of the RTI Act.

(2) A former Chief Election Commissioner, T.S. Krishnamurthy, and a former Secretary to Government, A. K. Venkatasubramanian, spoke against the proposed amendments.

(3) L.C. Jain was also against the amendments and wanted Indians to protect the right to information with their lives.

(4) Ms. Aruna Roy said the question of blackmail would arise only if there was something to hide.

(5) Civil Liberties lawyer, Prashant Bhushan, pointed out that so far not a single case of misuse of notings had come to the Government attention.

(6) Social activist, Anna Hazare, went on a hunger strike.

Mrs Sonia Gandhi and Dr Manmohan Singh received many representations opposing the amendments. So the Union Government yielded to the pressure from the public, social activists, notable personalities, and deferred its move to amend the RTI Act. It has been decided that the issue should be discussed with all stakeholders.

There's been only a semi-colon. When will the full stop come, if at all?

> Note: If you're interested in reading the RTI Act go to: righttoinformation.info/rti_act_final_checked doc.
>
> And if you're interested in knowing the procedure, go to Indiahowto.com/right-to-information-rti-faq. html

Comprehension—lexis

Exercise 38

1. Guess meanings of these words from the context of the passage:

   defer amendments assent/consent obligate transparency accountability curb eliminate highlight hitch arbiter constrain blackmail stakeholder bureaucracy

2. Match words in A with those in B:

A	B	A	B
1. momentous	a. promise	2. defer	b. device
3. reiterate	c. very important	4. accountable	d. responsible for decisions made
5. instrument	e. postpone	6. guarantee	f. restate

3. Fill in the blanks with the antonyms:

1. assent	____________	2. progressive	____________
3. curb	____________	4. public	____________
5. transparent	____________	6. democracy	____________
7. ease	____________	8. support	____________
9. internal	____________		

4. You find 'corruption' in paragraph 3. In the same paragraph you'll find two phrases related to it. Write them down here:

   ____

5. Write two gerunds from the passage: ____________ ____________
6. Both 'tremendous' and 'momentous' have 'ous' as suffix.

   a. true b. false

Comprehension—structure

Exercise 39

7. Copy down from the passage abbreviated passive voice statements:

____

____

____

____

____

8. Discuss the reason for the use of past perfect tense in paragraph 2.

9 "Probably all would have been well but for a serious hitch."
Rewrite this sentence into an 'if' sentence.

____

10. ".... the Commission ruled that a combined reading of sections 2(f) and (i) and 2(j) indicated that a citizen has the right of access to a file of which the file notings are an integral part." Here the reporting verb is in past tense and the reported speech is in present tense, which should normally be in the past tense.

11. For each of the following sentences fill in the blank with i. simple sentence ii. complex sentence iii. compound sentence:

[a] Social activist, Anna Hazare, went on a hunger strike. ____________

[b] The three Service Chiefs believed the new information regime would not simply work in the defence services. ____________

[c] Probably all would have been well but for a serious hitch. ____________

[d] The Right to Information Act [RTI] had been passed by both the Houses of Parliament and given assent to by the President on June 15, 2005. ____________

[e] Though the Government of India introduced the Freedom of Information [FOI] Bill in Parliament in 2002 and got the Presidential assent in 2003, no commencement was ever notified and was thus a non-starter. So the campaign continued to press for an effective RTI. ____________

[f] The National Advisory Council [NAC], set up by the Congress Party and of which Aruna Roy and Jean Dreze were members, discussed the issue and submitted to the Prime Minister's Office a set of recommendations for amending the FOI Act after considering the suggestions from CHRI, the NCPRI and other civil society groups.

____

Comprehension—discourse [direct and inferential]

Exercise 40

12. This passage is essentially about _____

    [a] the RTI Act [b] the debate on file notings

    [c] pressure on the Government [d] public involvement in making laws

13. The best inference from the passage is _____

    [a] very few countries in the world have RTI laws.

    [b] citizens can now ask for 'information' they want.

    [c] the government will function far better.

    [d] power ultimately rests with the people.

14. Who set the ball rolling for the RTI Act?

    _____

15. _____ was just a paper tiger.

    [a] FOI bill [b] The Supreme Court [c] The UPA government

16. The RTI Act was possible because of

    [a] UPA Government, CMP, NCPRI, the Supreme Court, NAC, Sonia Gandhi

    [b] CMP, NAC, UPA, the Supreme Court, NCPRI, activists,

    [c] The Supreme Court, NCPRI, activists, NAC, UPA Government

    [d] Aruna Roy, Anna Hazare, Sonia Gandhi, Dr Manmohan Singh

17. Paragraph 2 under 'the debate' has this statement:

    But this fell on deaf ears.

    [i] 'this' refers to _____

    [ii] 'deaf ears' refers to _____

18. What made the Union Cabinet decide to amend the RTI Act?

    _____

19. What is the latest position with regard to the RTI Act?

    _____

20. When did the UPA Government decide to postpone the amendments?

    _____

21. What do you infer from the metaphor used in the last two sentences? Discuss.

    _____

5. Stress Management

Why have I taken up this topic?

Because I'm as concerned about you as Mr Gopalakrishnan, Mr Mohsin Aziz and Ms Sujatha are [Read "IT boom—boon or bane" in the Hindu of 3 September 2006, "IT—some issues in stress management" in the Hindu of 17 September 2006, "IT/ITES staff face insomnia problems" in the Hindu of January 17, 2007 and "Computer jobs can cause back, neck pain" in the Hindu of 22 January 2007]. Because education should help you to face and overcome challenges in life.

Why should this topic interest you?

Because prevention is better than cure. Because I agree with Mr Mohsin's suggestion:

"The most important aspect of any stress management intervention is to give employees knowledge about stress." Now read on.

You're in your first or second semester. Before you realise what has happened, you'll have entered your seventh semester. That's when several IT firms and a few core companies land in your campus. And you'll be busy going through the process of selection. If you're good (I'm sure you'll be by then), you'll be offered a position with an attractive compensation by an IT or a BPO organisation.

If you accept the offer, you'll become part of an environment that is stressful. Let's understand what stress is and how you can manage it.

What is 'stress'?

Stress is the pressure we feel or worry we have about problems in life. It's a state [or condition] of mental, emotional or other strain. According to Stress Management, stress is a physiological response to an internal or external stimulus that triggers the "fight-or-flight" reaction. According to medical science, stress is a perturbation of the body's homeostasis. In psychology, stress is an internal state which can be caused by physical demands on the body or by environmental and social situations which are evaluated as potentially harmful, uncontrollable or exceeding our resources for coping. Pressure is what is happening to us, stress is how we react to a particular pressure.

What happens when there is stress?

Stress can be real or perceived [=imagined or understood as real]. When I have a heart attack, it is real. I can also construe severe pain in the chest as heart attack. There is stress in both situations. So my brain responds and releases stress hormones—cortisone and adrenaline. My body uses the hormones, acts and fights the stress. I or my relatives take steps to deal with the problem; the stress hormones in my blood stream or in the blood stream of my relatives are used up and I or my relatives return to normal. In the latter, my imagination runs riot in chain of stress situations that lets stress hormones accumulate in my blood stream. And my physical and mental conditions move from bad to worse. In fact, I may even be inviting a heart attack!

How do we know we are stressed?

The following conditions are the indicators:

i. loss of appetite — we have no desire to eat

ii. insomnia — we spend sleepless nights

iii. lose concentration — we are disturbed and unable to continue what we're doing

iv. memory loss — we have difficulty in remembering things

v. sudden increase in errors — we commit errors more frequently now than in the past

vi. anger — we get angry at the slightest provocation

What causes stress?

The physical, environmental and social causes[sources] of stress are known as **stressors**. They can be internal or external.

<u>internal stressors</u>

• body-related

•excessive heat or cold •poor diet •ailments •constant rushing •drugs/alcohol •sugar •too much caffeine •lack of exercise •overweight

• mind-related

•high expectations from self •low self image •loneliness/isolation •keeping to yourself[not mixing] •less time with family •financial concerns •unresolved conflicts •excessive time away from home [guilt feeling] •your unfulfilled expectations from others

•spiritual

•holding things inside that we are afraid to say openly •staying in a job we dislike •pushing ourselves to do things that we don't want to do

<u>external stressors</u>

•demands [expectations]by family and friends •pleasing others

•traffic snarls/jams •death of near and dear •divorce or separation

•ill treatment by or lack of support from family/friends/authority[school/college/office]

•workplace

•work overload •long hours •work monotony •meeting deadlines •keeping pace with technology •ambiguity in duties or rights •unnatural working hours •lack of opportunity for creativity •inability to cope with competitive work environment •pressure from superiors •unreasonable performance demands •lack of feedback on performance •partiality from superiors •little support from superiors •bullying/harassment/mockery from colleagues •not seeing eye-to-eye with co-workers •conflict among staff •office politics •burnout

Internal and external stressors are not independent of each other. They act upon each other. For instance, traffic jam may make you feel bodily and mentally tired by the time you reach your office. Your wife may have wanted your help, say, in housekeeping.

Failing to meet her expectation leads to frustration and you enter your office with it. You may thus begin your office work with stress. And workplace stresses get added to this. You feel defeated, emotionally and physically drained to put up any fight and thus accumulate stress over stress.

What are the effects of stress?

Both the body and mind suffer from:

physical : tense muscles, dizziness, rapid heartbeats, headache, allergies, hypertension, heart ailments, impairment of immune system, irritable bowel syndrome[IBS], chronic fatigue, weight loss/gain, insomnia

mental : reduction in memory/concentration/learning, cynicism, irritability, mental fatigue, feeling of helplessness, reduction in productivity, life is not worth living

How do we manage stress?

By managing stress, we'll be able to remove the imbalance created by stress and bring back our mind and body to normalcy.

<u>short-term methods</u>

1. During moments of stress, *don't think, don't exercise your mind.* But
   - breathe deeply and slowly
   - tense your muscles and relax them
   - visualise a peaceful scene
   - take if possible a quick short walk for a breath of fresh air.
2. Have a balanced diet:
   - avoid processed and/or fast foods [chemical or ill-prepared foods are injurious to health.]
   - avoid coffee; caffeine is bad for health
   - take fresh fruits and vegetables; drink fresh milk.
3. Drink a lot of water [tap water will do].

Water helps all organs including brain function properly. It helps stop dehydration due to air-conditioning or humidity.

4. Do physical exercises.

> Walking is the simplest and the best exercise. A ten-minute walk a day will do a world of good. Other exercises can also be thought of.
> Exercises increases blood flow to the brain. They produce beta-endorphin that has positive effect on how we feel. They warm and relax muscles and tissues. They distract you from feeling stressed.

5. Sleep well.

> As you go to bed, <u>close your mind to everything else</u> and say to yourself, "I'll have deep sleep." Believe you'll sleep well. This may take a day or two or even a week. But persist you must and have faith in your ability to sleep. In due course, this auto-suggestion will work. If your sleep well, duration does not matter at all.

6. Practise meditation and perform yoga.

> The former brings peace to mind and the latter brings peace to the body.

<u>long-term methods</u>

1. Learn to laugh.

> Laughter reduces hypertension and stress hormones. It removes stale air from the lungs and body tissues. It increases blood circulation and strengthens immune function [by raising levels of infection-fighting T-cells, disease-fighting proteins called gamma-interferon, and disease-fighting antibodies called B-cells].

2. Fill your mind with positive thoughts rather than negative ones. Look at life, people and situations positively. This is difficult but possible with effort and time.
3. Listen to music that touches your soul, that brings peace to you, that makes you happy.
4. Become, if already you're not, an extrovert. Spend time with friends and family.
5. Get help to know the kind of person you are.

> Most of us believe we know ourselves. Unfortunately, this is not the truth. We either underestimate or overestimate ourselves and our capacities. There are several psychological tests available. Use them to learn your limits and strengths. Work within your limits. Develop your strengths. Take steps to convert your weakness into strengths. For instance, oral communication may be your problem. But you may be good at written communication. Share your thoughts in writing initially but gradually develop your oral skills. Nothing is impossible if you keep trying, if you never give up.

6. Avoid being stressed at all.

See stress as an opportunity to judge yourself, **not** as an opportunity to judge others. When you are stressed, react to it. But don't allow it to occupy your mind completely. Don't allow your mind to mull over it. Give an antidote. Analyse your thinking, your actions, your behaviour. Don't expect others to change their behaviour. Don't say: I didn't start it. Why should **I** change? Don't think: Let him change first, then I will. This will only aggravate or worsen relationship.

We may not be able to change others. But certainly we can change ourselves. If necessary, change your perception, that is, change how you **see or understand** others, situations and yourself. Then your attitude, that is, your **opinion** will change. Then you can maintain your motivation, if not improve it.

Once you have such mental balance, nothing or no one can cause stress as you know how to handle it. Now peace and happiness will be yours.

Remember emotional health is basic to mental and body health. Don't simply keep thinking about stress. Act.

Comprehension—lexis

Exercise 41

1. Learn these words:

insomnia boon bane stimulate trigger potential snarl dizziness
visualise depression construe tackle extrovert mull antidote

2. Copy down from the passage words formed by negative prefixes:

__________ __________ __________
__________ __________ __________
__________ __________ __________
__________ __________ __________
__________ __________ __________

3. The passage uses several pairs of words that are antonymous. They are:

__________ __________
__________ __________ __________

4. Copy down from the passage nouns formed from adjectives:

__________ __________ __________ __________
__________ __________ __________ __________

5. Copy down from the passage words formed by combining two words:

______ ______ ______ ______ ______ ______ ______

6. Underline nominal compounds in the passage.
7. You'll find in the passage nouns formed from verbs. Write down these verbs here:
8. Underline in the passage adjectives not formed by prefixes or suffixes.
9. Underline in the passage past participles used as adjectives.

Comprehension—structure

Exercise 42

10. What is the role of subtitles?

______

______

11. How does listing the messages help?

______

______

______

______

12. Copy down sentence connectors from the passage:

13. Copy down from the passage sentences with degrees of comparison:

14. Copy down from the passage both kinds of passive sentences:

Comprehension—discourse [direct and inferential]

Exercise 43

15. What's the third reason for the author to take up this topic?

16. What's the role of education in a student's life?

17. What's the challenge students will soon face?

18. When does one invite a heart attack?

For 19-21, the answers are jumbled words given at the end. Reorder them to fill the blanks.

19. Causes of stress can also be called __________________ [esrcuso]
20. When we experience stress we're not ________________ [lmaonr]
21. By knowing the kind of person you are you can ____________________ your weaknesses. [dyneiift]
22. Name the three kinds of health: ______________ ______________ ______________
23. Prevention is better than cure. In relation to stress, this sentence means
    [a] not having stress at all is good.
    [b] you'll have no stress at all.
    [c] you should be prepared to deal with stress.
    [d] you need not be afraid of being stressed.
24. What does "intervention" in stress management intervention refer to?

7. Listening

7.1 Introduction

Whether active or inactive, without a listener being present, there can be no oral communication. You can't talk to empty space, can you? If you did and someone saw you, they might wonder if something was not wrong with you.

Nonetheless, in our value system, listening is hardly given importance. You wouldn't be surprised if someone said training was necessary to speak. But you'd be if someone even suggested training was necessary to listen.

7.2 Definition

Listening is stage one of responding act of a communicating event. Listening is a sustained effort to receive sound and make meaning. It opens up possibilities for continuing interaction.

7.3 Need for listening

1. Respect the speaker so that he will respect you when you speak.
2. Receive information, new or old.
3. Understand the message.
4. Respond to the message [become the speaker].
5. Give information, new or old.
6. Show emotions.[indicating involvement]
7. Receive well messages as instructions/knowledge/wisdom.
8. Benefit from the experience of others.
9. Indicate respect/affection/love/admiration for the speaker.
10. Show politeness and courtesy to the speaker.

7.4 Barriers to listening

In ideal conversations, someone speaks, the other listens, the other speaks, the someone listens. But does listening go on *all* the time? The answer is a 'no. Then we might ask: what makes us not listen? The answer is that there are certain barriers that prevent us from listening all the time.

What are these barriers?

Sometimes we are unable to listen. Some other times, we avoid listening. Still, some other times, we refuse to listen.

1. <u>We are unable to listen</u>

If we are unable to listen, it's not because we are deaf. Physically we may not be deaf. Sounds may reach our ears but they don't reach our brain for it to understand. Because we're preoccupied. In other words, our mind is already busy with something[s] or some other person[s]—problems, questions, expectations, emotions, sentiments and so on. We're so busy thinking about these things, we're so busy analyzing them, trying to understand, trying to anticipate, trying to solve.

Sekar : I don't know why these things always happen to me. People misunderstand me. The other day I met Jabbar. He was angry….. Raj, are you listening?

Raj : Sorry, Sekar. I was thinking of tomorrow's interview. You were saying?

2. We avoid listening

If we avoid listening, it's because someone is *not worth* listening to. Because we think we know better than the other person. What's the meaning of 'not worth'? What we are hearing may not be, in our opinion, important enough to pay attention to or may not affect us immediately or seriously to worry about. Or because the person may have a low status or position. The person may be younger to us in age or may be a subordinate, may be uneducated or poor or a stranger.

3. We refuse to listen

If we refuse to listen, it's because we're under the influence of prejudices or complexes.

complexes

We may feel inferior or superior to others; these complexes are the result of how we see ourselves in comparison with others around us.

prejudice

Prejudice can be in favour of someone or against someone. We're generally prejudiced in our favour. In other words, we see ourselves as positive, helpful, favourable or good. We're generally prejudiced in favour of some relatives, friends because we see them as positive or good towards us, helpful or favourable to us and to what we do. We're generally prejudiced against some relatives and friends because we see them as negative, unhelpful, bad or even evil. In other words, we like some and we dislike some. Therefore, we refuse to listen to those whom we dislike for some reason or other.

The reasons for the dislike can be hearsay or personal. We dislike some because we readily believe or accept what our relatives or friends whom we like may say about them. This is known as hearsay; we accept this report as true, and refuse to listen to them. We dislike some because we have had bad or bitter experiences with them.

So, we don't pay attention to what some people say to us or when they talk to us because

1. we're preoccupied with our own thoughts
2. we assume we have nothing to gain
3. we're prejudiced against them.

7.5 Need for training

Listening is a neglected skill and taken for granted. We may all feel that as long as we are able to hear, we can also listen, and do not therefore need to be taught.

There's a lot of stress on learning to speak, on conducting courses to train how to speak with different purposes but there's hardly any awareness about the need to listen efficiently and effectively.

There is another matter that we should seriously think about. We as listeners expect speakers to behave responsibly, to speak in such a way that it becomes an invitation for us to listen to them. But do we behave responsibly? We think it's our right to listen or not listen. We feel that speakers cannot blame us if we don't listen because listening is not obligatory. They may take the initiative on their own to speak to us or they might have been invited by our higher-ups. We didn't ask them to speak to us, did we now? Listeners have the freedom to do anything but listen.

I'm sure you've now understood the significant role listening as a skill plays in day-to-day activities. Eight exercises follow to enable you to practise, develop and use listening as a skill for general purposes, in job environment and to score well in tests on listening, say, TOEFL.

Exercise 44

Listen to Track 6. Your task is to identify the general content of the passages you'll be listening to.

Passage 1

Listen to the passage carefully, tick among the choices given below the one that conveys its general content.

a. cheerleaders

b. game of gentlemen

c. e-cricket

Passage 2

Listen to the passage carefully, tick among the choices given below the one that conveys its general content.

a. commercial world

b. entertainment standards

c. insult

Passage 3

Listen to the passage carefully, tick among the choices given below the one that conveys its general content.

a. T20

b. large crowd

c. cheerleaders

Passage 4

Listen to the passage carefully, tick among the choices given below the one that conveys its general content.

a. cricket
b. cheerleaders
c. cricket and cheerleaders

Passage 5

Listen to the passage carefully, tick among the choices given below the one that conveys its general content.

a. web designing and making money
b. Vijayanand
c. a new way of learning web designing

Passage 6

Listen to the passage carefully, tick among the choices given below the one that conveys its general content.

a. selling equipment
b. purchasing equipment
c. seeking employees

Passage 7

Listen to the passage carefully, tick among the choices given below the one that conveys its general content.

a. an essay on qualification for jobs
b. an ad attracting people to apply
c. an ad with strict regulations for job

Passage 8

Listen to the passage carefully, tick among the choices given below the one that conveys its general content.

a. Tea and China
b. Growth of tea as a drink
c. Tea Scripture

Passage 9

Listen to the passage carefully, tick among the choices given below the one that conveys its general content.

a. self introduction
b. comments of performance
c. acceptance of a request

Passage 10

Listen to the passage carefully, tick among the choices given below the one that conveys its general content.

a. about teacher's problems
b. about learner's problems
c. problems in curriculum

Exercise 45

Listen to Track 7. Your task is to identify specific pieces of information from the passages you'll be listening to.

Passage 11

Listen to the passage carefully, fill in the blanks given below with the words that contain relevant specific piece of information.

1. We need ________________ to cover our bodies.
2. We also need ____________________ .
3. We need water to ______________ our thirst.
4. We need food to ________________ .
5. With the help of _______________________ we've moved from seasonal harvesting.
6. We need to cover bodies in order to ____________________________________ .
7. Besides oxygen, we need ___________________________ .
8. We need water _______________________________________ .
9. We need shelter to ____ .
10. Science has made it possible to ____ .

Passage 12

Listen to the passage carefully, fill in the blanks given below with the words that contain relevant specific piece of information.

1. Solar energy is the world's most abundant ________________ source of energy.
2. Solar energy induces ____________________________ .
3. Hydrogen is converted to ________________ .
4. The ozone layer absorbs radiation in the ______________________ region.
5. Solar energy can be used to produce ___________________ .

Exercise 46

Listen to Track 8. The exercise below **guides** you to learn to **take notes.**

Passage 13

Listen to the passage carefully. As you listen, fill in the blank spaces. At the end of this exercise, you'll have got an idea of how to take notes and be able to do it on your own.

food shelter clothing

cover body

____

family, live/stay

____

____

water

____

cook food

role of science

harvesting: seasonal to ____________________

____________________________ : traditional to scientific

firewood and charcoal to _______________________, natural gas to ________________.

Passage 14

Food spoils : warm climate

______________, yeasts and ____________________

saving : past – salt, sun's heat, __________

now—readymade

process : canning, dehydration, ________________________

Passage 15

To make notes:

- select, as you listen, key (important) words and expressions
- don't copy/quote/repeat sentences you hear
- don't take notes in sentences

Listen to the passage on Information Technology. Write down the notes here. Remember to use key words and phrases in such a manner that later if you wish to capture it in your own words, your writing should contain all the important thoughts and arguments. In fact, it should be a good précis or an expanded summary of the passage you listened to.

Notes:

Exercise 47

Listen to the short paragraph on Track 9 on your CD and put the key information in the table below. Give a title to them.

Production in million tons	1986-1987	1987-1988	1988-1989	1989-1990
Rice	30.44			
Wheat	11.98			
Sugarcane	10.10			

Exercise 48

You'll now listen to short dialogues and understand what they mean to you.

You'll hear the speaker on Track 10 on your CD posing a question related to each short conversation. Listen to the question carefully. Listen to the speakers, understand what they say bearing the question in mind. Look at the choices here and select the correct choice.

Here is a sample:

Voice: where are the speakers?

Raja : You aren't playing well today. Anything wrong?

Sankar : I don't know. I'm just not able to move.

a. at Sankar's home b. at Raja's home c. in a gym. d. beside a football court

The answer is [d].

1. a. rail
   b. road
   c. air
   d. sea
2. a. She can wait till tomorrow evening.
   b. She's not sure about meeting tomorrow evening.
   c. She wants the tickets sent to her.
   d. She's not traveling because she's meeting him.
3. a. several
   b. two
   c. some
   d. one
4. a. She wants to know if her husband read the ad.
   b. She probably wants to buy a TV.
   c. She wants to know if her husband is interested in a TV.
   d. She wants a cheque written.

5. a. They are expensive.
   b. They are very cheap.
   c. They are neither expensive nor cheap.
   d. They are advertised in today's newspaper.
6. a. She's not interested in the news.
   b. She doesn't approve of the strike.
   c. She merely wants to know what their demand is.
   d. Generally, she's sick of strikes.
7. a. She didn't attend college.
   b. She voted for someone else.
   c. She likes elections.
   d. She didn't vote.
8. a. The boy is playing in a football match.
   b. The College football team will be decided.
   c. The boy is not worried about his selection.
   d. The girl is confident.
9. a. She will help the man.
   b. She helped him.
   c. She spoke rudely to him.
   d. She cannot help the man.
10. a. She is as ignorant about the way to the hotel as the man is.
    b. She knows the way but will not help him.
    c. She is a stranger to the man.
    d. She wonders why the man is asking **her**.

Exercise 49

Now you'll listen to short passages on Track 10 on your CD. Listen carefully to the questions based on the passages and then to the passages. As you listen, link the questions with the passages.

If necessary, listen twice. Choose the answers to the questions.

Passage one: What's the topic of the paragraph?

a. There is no one in the world who does not drink tea.

b. Tea is a popular drink.

c. We Indians drink tea with milk and sugar.

d. Preparation of tea with lemon or jasmine.

Passage two: Why did the Chinese like tea?

a. Because tea originated in China.

b. Because poems were written about tea.

c. Because it had medicinal value

d. Because the Chinese have been drinking it for centuries.

Passage three: What's the most important qualification for the job?

a. having a phone at home.

b. self confidence

c. degree in Electrical/Electronic engineering.

d. interest in selling

Passage four: What's the most important qualification for the job?

a. fancy degree

b. recommendation letters

c. gift to work hard for achieving your aspirations

d. experience

You'll now listen to two lectures on Track 10 on your CD. Read the questions to each lecture carefully, then listen to the lectures delivered by the speaker, locate the answers and select your choice.

Exercise 50

Lecture One

1. An earthquake is the result of ________________ .
   a. rupture on a fault b. seismic waves c. foreshocks and aftershocks ____
2. __________ are like sound waves.
   a. P Waves b. S Waves c. Tsunami ____
3. ____ earthquakes are felt by people at some place in the world.
   a. All b. Most c. Not all d. No ____
4. The process where pressure waves can turn sediments into water is known as ____________.
   a. earthquake b. fludisation c. tsunami ____
5. The lecturer presents us with a ____________ picture.
   a. scary b. pleasant c. clear d. confusing ____

Lecture two

1 How many reasons does the lecturer offer for your choosing an engineering course?

a. 3 b. 4 c. 5 d. 6 ____

2. How many parameters does the lecture mention?

a. 5 b. 4 c. 3 d. 2 ____

3. Which is the highest need in the hierarchy?

a. Esteem needs b. Living for others

c. Sense of belongingness d. Selfishness ____

4. An example of self-actualisation need is________________.

a. Mother Teresa b. Hitler c. Indira Gandhi ____

5. A title for this lecture can be__________________.

a. A Variety of Needs b. A Variety of Human Needs

c. Why do We Act the Way We Do? d. Why am I lecturing to you? ____

6. The lecturer is __________________.

a. giving you a job b. issuing a threat

c. giving a warning d. blessing you ____

8. Technical Report Writing

8.1 Introduction

You have chosen an engineering career. Your activities as an engineer in an organization will go beyond these engineering ones. You will be, for instance, communicating a lot. In addition to communicating orally, you'll have to be doing a lot of writing, too. Report writing will be one of such writings.

We are reporting to someone when we talk or write about something that the other person does not know anything about. We can report orally or in written form about an accident or incident or event. We make reports again orally or in writing whether a business can be started, the progress a project has made, whether a project should be halted. Reports can be scientific or technical. Reports can be one page long or several pages.

In this Unit, you are going to learn about reports that are well-structured documents, that present information about a study that you have done; or they could be messages of information or proposal that you want to communicate. In other words, you tell what, where, when, why and how something has happened or what, where, when, why and how it should happen (proposal).

8.2 Objectives

- Provide information relevant to a given topic.
- Report an experiment with results/progress.
- Present activities of a given year.
- Make recommendations.
- Document progress (of an on - going activity)
- Present a detailed account of finished work.
- Suggest innovative concepts.
- Record company's growth.

8.3 Report—kinds

Reports can be oral or written. Here we are going to talk about written reports.

Instruction

Report types

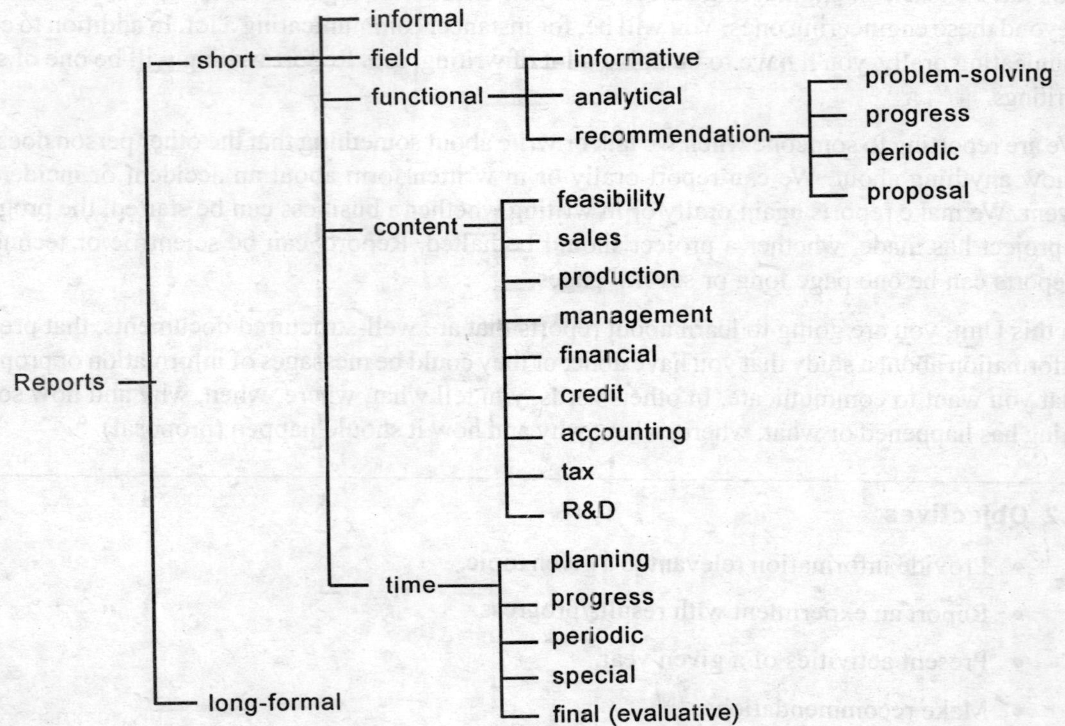

8.4 Formats

Reports can be made in different forms. Most organizations have *printed forms* for routine reports that people make at regular intervals, like inspection reports. Memo [memorandum] is another common format employees use to communicate intra or interdepartmentally. A short report is made in the form of a letter. And long reports are made in the print form, running to hundreds of pages.

The presentation of your report depends on to whom you are writing [whether it is to the top management or to a colleague in another department] and the subject of the report [whether it is just a response to a request for information by another department or a project proposal.]

For instance, if you are reporting to the top management to propose something or to convey the progress of a project it will be a formal report containing several pages with prefatory parts. And if you are writing a report replying to a request for information it need not be formal and it will just contain the needed information in a page or two.

When we talk about being formal or informal we are talking about the structure of the report and not about its language. As all the reports are official documents the language will always be formal.

However, the

tone of the report may be formal, informal
time of reporting may be daily, weekly, monthly
style may be narrative, descriptive, expository, statistical
circulation may be intra or interdepartmental or to another firm or organization.

In formal reports, the structure and subtitles help readers to follow the subject of discussion without difficulty.

Most firms have printed formats where the one reporting fills in information in the spaces provided. These formats are used when the reports are short or informal, and they are usually on small projects, study or investigation.

For instance, a periodic report submitted on a project's progress will look like this:

Sample Report: 1

Firm's Name

Project: ______________________ (identifies the project)

Time Period: ________ to ________ (indicates the duration of assessment)

Name ______________________ (identifies the reporter)

Date	Work Done	Expenses	Any other observation

Sample: 2

If your firm has no such printed form you may use a memorandum or a letter format for your reports.

Memorandum (or) Memo:

Memorandum is an uncomplicated form, which is used within a department or an organization to pass on information. The top portion known as heading contains information on a) who is writing, b) to whom it is written, c) when it is written, and d) what the subject is. The 'To' and 'From' should contain the name of the person or the position of the person addressed; the 'subject' will indicate the subject matter of the report.

To: Dr. Arun, Research – Head, Robotics Division
From: Dr Mark, Principal Investigator, Robotics Division
Date: ____________
Subject: Progress Report on Project Robotic – July 2007

____
____
____
____

Sample Format:

Letter:

You use the letter format when you are writing to someone outside the firm: You may use the formal letter format or any other format your firm may prefer.

Sample Format:
Your Firm's name
Address
Contact details

Date:

Recipient's name/Designation
Firm's name (only if it is addressed to another firm)
Address

(Salutation) (Dear Name)

Content of the report

(Complimentary close) (yours faithfully / truly)
Signature
Name
Designation
Enclosure [encl./enc.] (only if you are enclosing material)
C.C (only if you are sending a copy of the report)

8.5 Pre-writing

This refers to arranging the items in a long report. As the name suggests, this stage precedes your actual writing of the report.

What do you do at this stage?

- Be clear about your purpose and scope.

  Decide the purpose: To improve a system, to rectify an error, to replace an equipment or a system with another? To introduce a new line of thinking or an innovation? To cut costs or to bring profit? To expand or enter new market areas? Only when you know the purpose [=objective of your study] you'll be able to decide the scope [width and depth of your study].

- Know your audience.

  Who is going to read your report? Is your reader a layperson? Then you should use only general English vocabulary and uncomplicated sentence structures. You should use graphics without technical terms. If a technical or professional person, be technical in your report. Or if he is an accountant, deal with the subject in numbers.

  If you feel you should present the reader with your approach, do it. But take care to be totally objective and be flawless in your logic.

- Decide the subject matter.

  Make it as specific as possible. For example, "employee involvement in decision-making" is definitely specific while "employee involvement in management" is vague. "Improvements in personnel selection" is not as specific as "Changes in criteria for selection of skilled workers".

- Use available sources of information

  Jot down related ideas from your experience and your knowledge of the subject. What you know about the subject may not be sufficient, so you may have to get information from outside sources: library research, net browsing, even people-experts, executives, non-specialists, the public-around you will provide a lot of data and information. You can interview these people and get information directly or telephonically and even record it with permission from interviewees. Or you can prepare questionnaires and get feedback from people. You need to select only information that pertains to your area of study and use it effectively.

8.6 Making an outline

An outline helps shape the structure of the report; it helps divide the collected information into a beginning [introduction], a middle[main body], and an end [conclusion]. The middle contains the main ideas derived from the title/subject of the report and sub-topics from the main ideas.

It offers many other benefits:

- Larger and more complex subjects are easy to handle when you break them into manageable parts in the outline.
- You can detect and correct errors in logic .
- You can move parts of an outline around to choose the most effective arrangement of your ideas.

- You can use the outline like a road map and not lose your way.
- You can use the outline to check for coherence and moving from one idea to another and this checking ensures movement of one part smoothly into the next without omitting important details.

Your outline for the report should look like the one you see below:

Title/subject: Note-Making

1.0 introduction [first level heading]

1.1 information explosion [second level heading]

1.1.1 library books [third level heading]

1.1.2 journals

1.1.3 electronic sources

1.1.3.1 television, video cassettes [fourth level heading]

1.1.3.2 computer, CDROMS

1.2 preparation procedure

1.2.1 decide the topic

1.2.2 decide the purpose

1.2.3 select reading material

1.2.4 make notes

1.2.4.1 select relevant information

2.0 steps in the process of note-making

2.1 step 1-why

2.1.1 academic

2.1.2 professional

2.2 step 2-what

2.2.1 selection of reading material

2.2.1.1 reference books

2.2.1.2 journals, newspapers

2.2.1.3 the computer, internet

2.2.2 reading process

2.2.2.1 comprehend sources

2.2.2.1.1 concepts/philosophy

2.2.2.1.2 graphics/statistics

2.3 step 3-how

2.3.1 make notes

2.3.1.1 main titles, subtitles

2.3.1.1.1 content in words, phrases

[quotes, if necessary/desirable]

2.3.1.1.2 list of sources with full details

Note: The above arrangement is based on **decimal system.** But don't go beyond the fourth level because the numbers can get too cumbersome beyond that point.

You can also use the **conventional system:**

1. first level heading
   - A. second level heading, first part
   - B. second level heading, second part
     - 1. third level heading
       - a. fourth level heading
     - 2. third level, second part.
   - C. second level heading, first part

8.7 Structure

Long reports are usually voluminous and so they are bound and presented in a book form. These reports are formal.

All formal reports will contain the following as part of their structure and layout:

1. Title page

   This generally contains: a. the full title b. prepared by c. date of the report d. prepared for.

   The information for a. b. c. and d. is positioned in the centre of the page.

2. Abstract

   This normally follows the title page; it highlights major points of the report in order to enable the reader to decide whether or not to read the entire report.

Title of the Report
Prepared by
(Author's name, Designation, include firm's name, if you are writing to another firm)
date
Prepared for
(Name, Designation, include firm's name, if you are writing to another firm)

3. Letter of Authorization

   A top official of an organization authorizes an individual or an organization to make a report on a particular aspect that is of concern to the organization. Such a request is generally done through a letter. This letter should follow the title page. It names briefly but clearly the problem or a study of a situation in the organization, the scope of operation with limitations, and sometimes even instructions.

4. Letter of Transmittal/Foreword/Preface

This is a letter from an individual or an agency that looks into a problem or conducts a study. Use the layout of the formal letter. The first paragraph begins:

Here is the report on.....

The second paragraph contains comments to the reader on the study made.

The final paragraph expresses gratitude for the job given:

We thank you for this assignment. We are at your service for any further assistance or help.

5. Table of Contents

This has the content divided into chapters or sections with further subdivisions, if any.

Table of Contents	
Content	Page

The Table of Contents lists all the sections - headings, subheadings, illustrations, and also appendices and references, if your report contains them - with their matching page numbers.

6. List of Illustrations

This contains graphics used in the report: all visual material including photographs with titles and page numbers[where they appear].

7. Executive Summary

This is also known as 'summary', 'synopsis', or 'abstract'. It provides briefly but precisely an overview of the aims of the study, the details of the study with data, the analysis of data, results and recommendations, if any.

However, it should **not** go beyond one-eighth of the report length.

8. Actual Report

This contains: introduction, body, closing [summary: major findings, conclusions and recommendations]

Introduction : Reason for reporting, purpose of reporting, scope[boundaries of the problem], history [how the problem started, the need for solution], definitions of terminology used in the report[necessary to understand them], brief description of how the report is being presented

Body	:	This contains detailed information (1) how the investigator went about the job, (2) data collected, (3) data analysis
End of report	:	conclusions-facts emerging from the analysis; recommendations: possible ways of solving or dealing with the problem.
9. Appendices	:	This is necessary only if you have material that cannot form part of the study/investigation like questionnaires, other reports.
10. Bibliography	:	Again this is optional. Here you print a list of books, reports, journals, internet sources that you may have used as references.

Note: Items 1-10 suggested above are normally found in formal reports. **However, if your organization follows a particular structure, use that.**

Footnotes, glossary [technical terms] and index [guide to locate material on a given page] can also form part of the report.

8.8 Writing

You have done all the preparatory work. Now you begin the actual writing. Use titles and subtitles and express the content in paragraphs. Make sure you employ vocabulary and sentence structures that convey your thoughts appropriately. Use words and expressions that link sentences and paragraphs. Take care of spelling, punctuation and grammar. Ensure clarity, logic, coherence. Add visual aids at appropriate places.

Sample 1 Industrial Visit

A Report on a Visit
to the Research and Development Unit of the Hindustan Photo Films, Ootacamund
by
Name, year, Department
To
Designation, Department
Submitted on: Date, Month, Year

Date of Visit: Date, Month, Year
Visit to: Research and Development Unit of the Hindustan Photo Films, Ootacamund . This is a Public Sector Undertaking, under the Department of Heavy Industry. It is the only integrated manufacturer of Photo sensitized goods in the whole of South East Asia and the only company that has the technology for manufacture of Medical X-ray, Graphic Arts and Black and White products of international standards.
Visitors involved: Professor ...., and sixth semester students of .... Department.
Basic purpose of visit:
To learn how the R&D Department troubleshoots and eliminates the different chemical problems that they may encounter and also to know the functioning of the devices and equipment used.

Activities:
The Head of the R&D Mr. X, gave us a warm welcome, briefed us on the role of the Department and also introduced us to his team of researchers. Later his Deputy, Ms. ………, took us on tour.
As she walked with us, she enlightened us about some ongoing research jobs. She gave us a clear picture of the various devices and instruments.

We were enabled to appreciate the role R&D plays in the following areas: Research in Imaging Science and Technology, Photographic Image Reproduction with Silver Halide as well as non-silver Digital systems, New product development, Product and process improvement, Technology Up gradation, Processing Chemistry, Image evaluation, Polymer Research, Fine Chemicals development and Analytical and in-organic Chemistry.

We were also impressed with the facilities such as Pilot bar-Coater with floatation dryers for simultaneous three layer coating and Organic Synthesis Unit.

We could learn about the role of science in and contribution to the working of equipment like Karl Fischer titrator, Falling ball viscometer, Surface interface tensiometer, Ultrasonic cleaner, Densitometer, Conductivity meter, UV-Visible spectrophotometer, Automatic titrator.

Outcomes from Visit:
We found the visit very informative. From the Head of the R & D we also learned that the Department is willing to guide and provide projects for college and university scholars. Hence we take this opportunity to request our Head of the Department to enable us to the benefit of this offer. The highlight of the visit was a group picture taken with the research team.

We thank the Management and the Hindustan Photo Films for providing us this great learning experience.

Sample 2 Accident

Reporting an incident:

When you write a report on an incident – it may be an accident, or an event – you need to present in detail what, when, where it happened, who were involved, and what the impact was (in case of an accident). Present the information in a lucid, concise and coherent manner.

For instance in a report on an accident you need to include:

- ❑ description of the accident – (when, where, how and the impact)
- ❑ elaboration of the cause(s) and consequences
- ❑ description of remedial actions taken
- ❑ suggestions for ensuring safety

However, report only facts and make right inferences. To be able to do this, you need to: a) take a good look at the accident scene, b) make a careful note of the details of damage to machinery and injury to people, c) talk to witnesses to gather details and relevant information, d) also check whether the work procedure or safety measures were followed.

Now put in writing all these in a coherent manner. You may use photographic evidence, if available.

Sample Report on an Accident:

Submitted to
The Principal
(College Name)

Date: (give the date of submission)

Date of Incident: 12 March 2007 Time of Incident: 1.35 p.m.
Place of the Incident: Chemistry Laboratory (Room Number 109)

On the afternoon of 12 March 2007, the first year Chemical Engineering students were working in the Chemistry Laboratory (Room Number 109). Ms. Angelina (roll no. 3), who was working at table 3, spilled concentrated sulphuric acid inadvertently on to her overcoat and her right hand. Hearing a loud cry, Mr. Raj— the Lab Instructor— rushed to her and helped her remove her coat and washed the affected area. The table on which the acid got spilled was neutralized and cleaned.

In the meantime I had called the College Nurse who reached the lab and treated the injured student who was then taken to the College Medical Center for observation and further medical aid.

According to our doctor Angelina's injury is only minor and she is perfectly OK. Students were reminded to follow the safety norms and handle chemicals with utmost care.

Dr. Brindha
Professor- in-charge
Chemistry Laboratory

Or you may use the following format:

Submitted to:

The Principal,
(College Name)

Date: (mention the date of submission)

Date of Incident: 12 March 2007 Time of Incident: 1:35 p.m.

Place of the Incident: Chemistry Laboratory (Room Number 109)

(This may be followed by the report of the accident)

Sample 3 Survey Report

A feasibility report becomes necessary when a firm gets a proposal or wants to start a new business or is interested in introducing a new facility. It would like the new idea or activity to be looked into and assessed so it can decide whether or not to proceed. It will request someone to do this job and present a report. Such a report is known as a Feasibility Report.

For example your firm may want to look into a request from its lady employees to start a crèche for those who would like their babies well taken care of. Before taking a decision it may want to do a feasibility study.

If you are asked to take up this study and submit a report, you first need to decide the scope of the study. You would probably look into factors like

a) the need for a crèche –(Find out the number of women who have babies and also how many of them will be willing to use this facility – through an interview or a questionnaire),
b) Availability of space in your campus – if 'no', how nearer you can have it,
c) the funds needed for starting a crèche (facilities like play area, playthings)
d) number of personnel required and their salaries.

These are some of the general factors you will study and analyze. You may also consider other factors like whether having a crèche will improve the image of the firm. Based on the study and the findings, you draw conclusions and recommend to your firm a particular course of action.

9. Essay Writing

You can use this section gainfully to perform well in **TOEFL**'s Writing Section where you'll have to write a one 30-minute essay. You can use this section gainfully also to organize the 'body' of technical or general reports you may have to write as part of job duties.

9.1 Introduction

It's generally believed that without inspiration, without a magical source, writing is next to impossible. When we see an excellent piece of writing, we tend to attribute that excellence to inspiration or some superhuman guidance. We strongly believe, wrongly of course, that we are not blessed [inspired] and so we will not be able to write. But the truth of the matter is that even inspiration can achieve nothing without sustained perspiration.

It's also generally believed that without an inborn talent, writing is next to impossible. When we see a remarkable piece of writing, we tend to attribute the remarkableness to the innate talent of its writer. We strongly believe, wrongly of course, that we are not blessed [talented] and so we will not be able to write. But the truth of the matter is that even talent can achieve nothing without hard work.

An invisible inspiration there may be, an inborn talent there may be in the case of Shakespeare, T. S. Eliot, Kalidasa, Kambar, Thiruvalluvar, Premchand, Bankim Chatterji, R. K. Narayan. But even they could not have been what they have been to this world and to themselves without sustained motivation and without sustained hard work.

All human beings, including you and me, do possess the ability to communicate. For this ability to blossom, flower and share its fragrance, you should wish to write, start writing, keep writing, check your writing, rewrite, check your writing, rewrite. You may desire to write but do you possess motivation, that is, desire coupled with involvement? To write, you must feel involved, you must feel deeply. You must feel the joy and the pain of others, you must become part of their experience, their pain, their joy. And then put this pain and joy in writing. Keep writing, keep writing, keep writing, keep practising. Revise, edit, write, revise, edit, write. And you will feel satisfied with your writing sooner than later.

Motivation and practice then are **the** requirements for a piece of writing. Inspiration and talent are only supportive. With motivation and practice, it **is** possible to produce good pieces of writing. And with inspiration and talent, it will be possible to produce writing that will stand the test of time.

But first let us become good writers. For this, motivation [=**desire+involvement**] and practice [=**non-stop hard work**] are more than enough. And all of us are capable of being good writers.

Self-doubt is self destructive. Let's have faith in us, let's be motivated, let's practise.

The rest will follow soon enough.

What does writing an essay involve? Let's take a look, shall we?

9.2 Writing Process

steps : 1. select a topic
2. narrow it [making topic as specific as possible]
3. decide the title (this can be done even after completing the essay)
4. gather related thoughts in 'note' form, with the help of
 [a] mind roaming [using knowledge you already have about the topic]
 [b] reading or listening sources [for new, latest knowledge]
5. organise information collected
 [a] convert into main thoughts, major and minor details
 [b] eliminate extra fat—information distracting focus
6. format or organise them into : introduction, body with subtitles, conclusion
7. edit
 [a] self
  remove loose ends: spelling, grammar errors, incomplete sentences
  ensure unity and coherence
 [b] others [friends, relatives]
  tighten thought and expression
  look for further improvements

These are the normal steps when you're penning your thoughts. But in a test or an examination, the topic is given to you. Then use 4 [a], 5, 6 and 7 [a].

9.3 Select a Topic

Let's say you want to write an article for publication. The first step is to select a topic. What are you interested in? Let's say you're interested in education, science, environment, for instance. These three are very broad topics. They are also very vague. They are broad and vague because each one has so many related aspects. It will be difficult to deal with **all** aspects in an essay of a few pages.

9.4 Narrow the Topic

If we want our writing to be **meaningful to readers**, we need to be more specific in defining the topic before we start writing (see also **13** at the end of this section).

education
- in India or overseas?
- school, colleges
- elementary, high school medicine, engineering
- formal /distance education
- govt./self-financing
- processes, problems, causes, solutions

science
- inventions or discoveries?
- medical, engineering, electronic, space
- specific area
- drugs/treatment/products research
- processes, problems, causes, solutions

environment
- in India or the world?
- forests, dams, air, water,
- deforestation, dam height
- pollution: air, land, water
- processes, problems, causes, solutions

While the three titles are too broad for an article or an essay, the expressions that follow below each title help you to narrow down the area of thinking and writing. Most specific would be to look at the titles even from recent activities [at the time of writing] in one of these areas. For instance, 'reservation for women', 'quota on caste basis', 'the death of Prof. Sabarhwal during students' union elections', 'traffic congestion—human and vehicle', 'alarming increase in terrorist activities' and the like are hot topics and most specific in terms of human interest and discussion. 'Yes to Cloning' [see below] is very specific while 'the machine civilisation' and 'the engineer and the society' [see below] are specific enough to write about them.

9.5 Decide the Title

Once you decide the topic, have at least a tentative title. The title should be such that it arouses the interest, curiosity, thinking of readers. This is very important. Unless the title is interesting, the reader may not bother to read. The title, for instance, could be in the form of a question or an assertion as in 'yes to cloning'.

9.6 Gather related thoughts

[a] Next is the 'mind roaming'. That is, you allow your mind to think about the topic, gather together all you know about the topic. Put them on paper as ideas strike you, as thoughts come to you. It doesn't matter, at this stage, whether they are in proper order.

[b] If you think what you know is not enough or if you wish to add latest information, do so by all means, and put them down on paper [in quotes, if necessary, with the name of the source, the date].

> Remember that whatever you put on paper will be or should be in phrases, from which you can later develop full sentences. **At this stage, don't try to write full sentences.**

What does 'mind roaming' mean? Once you know what you want to write about, you start thinking about that. Allow your mind to dwell on that and let your ideas flow. As the thoughts strike you, put them down on paper. There are several ways of putting them down on paper. How you put them down on paper is known as **"invention strategies"**.

'Invention' in this phrase refers to 'mind-roaming'.

strategy one: directed free writing

This is where you start writing straightaway. You focus your mind on the topic and let what you think and know about the topic flow out in the form of sentences and paragraphs. You can go on until you feel you have written enough.

Perhaps you've written only two pages or several. At this stage, pages do not matter. What's important is that you have enough material, sufficient ideas—main ideas, major and minor details in the form of elaborations, explanations and examples. Depending on the length you require, you can add or delete.

strategy two: listing

You can list out your thoughts, think of them as

ideas that will later become topic sentences for paragraphs
ideas that develop these thoughts.

Don't worry about order now. That'll come later.

Here's a possible listing for 'Machine Civilisation':

past civilisation
limbs
implements
animals
industrial revolution
modern civilisation
food production, food preservation
synthetic clothes, fads
walk, animal carts, machines, lazy
oral, birds, runners, stage coaches, radio, TV, Internet
late street plays, stage plays, cinema, home theatre
machine civilisation –good or bad?

strategy three: outlining

man—past civilisation

used limbs	till, walk,
implements	build
animals	clothes

industrial revolution—machines
agriculture – food production, food preservation
textiles – synthetic clothes, fads
transport – walk, animal carts, machines, lazy
communication – oral, birds, runners, stage coaches, radio, TV, Internet
entertainment – late street plays, stage plays, cinema, home theatre
radio, mobile, TV, internet, cinema, video, home theatre
machine civilisation –good or bad?

strategy <u>four</u>: clustering and branching

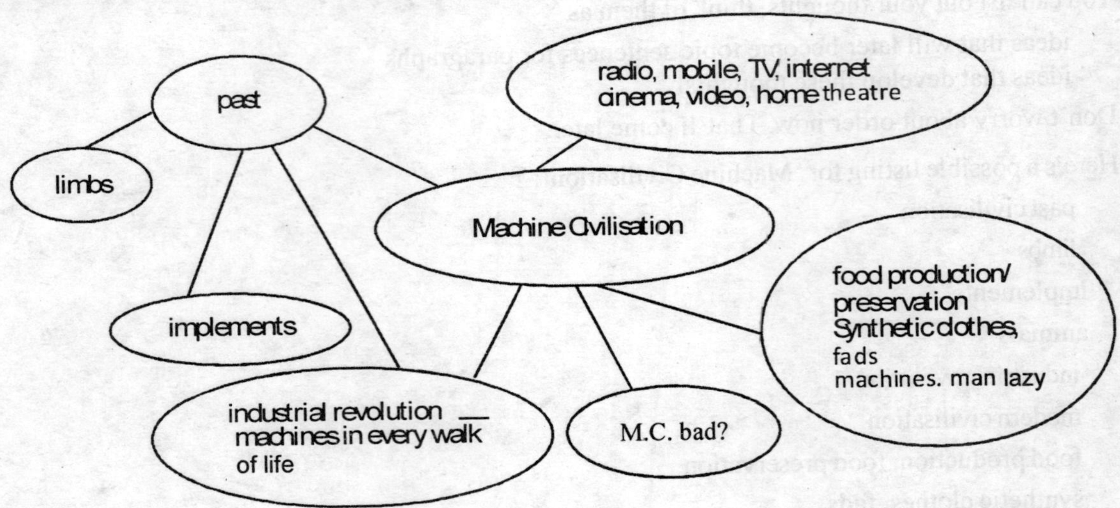

You write the topic in a circle or bubble in the centre and use different bubbles to write down ideas related to the topic. This is known as <u>clustering</u>.

You can gather your ideas also in a <u>branching</u> fashion. You'll put the ideas in squares instead of in circles.

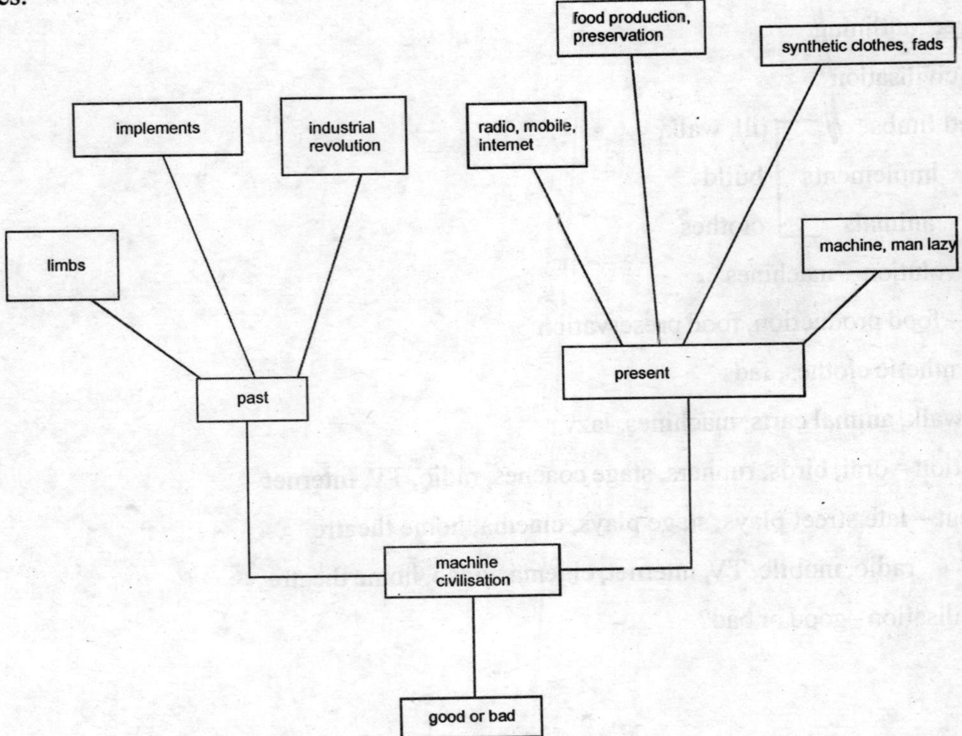

These are the four general ways of organising your ideas that come to you as you think about a chosen topic. You may use any one of these that you are comfortable with.

Here is the full essay:

Machine Civilization

(introduction)

Till about three centuries ago, man lived in small communities closer to each other. Man either walked miles or used animal-drawn carriages. Man ploughed the land, sowed the seeds, reaped the harvest, took it to market to sell. Man made clothes with wooden implements or knitted them with own hands. Man built houses of stone and mud. Hopefully, man was content then and would have continued to be but for certain events that took place in England. These events led to what is now known as the Industrial Revolution, which spread in due course of time to other parts of the world. Though Industrial Revolution stood chiefly for mechanisation of manufacturing and increased production, machines were invented and used in agriculture, clothes-making, transport and other walks of life. And modern civilization, machine civilisation that is, had begun.

(body)

Seeds of change occurred in agriculture and food production. Man tilled, spread seeds, ploughed, kept personal watch and harvested. Women also lent a helping hand. But now you have machines to spread seeds, tractors to till the land, insecticides to keep insects off and artificial manure [chemicals] to nurture crops from factories run by machines.

Changes have occurred in food preservation as well. Oil and salt were the natural preservatives that kept food intact for later use. Now we have all sorts of mass-produced artificial preservatives that harm the body, and refrigerators that pollute. Limbs functioned in the preparation of foods at home. Now you have grinders, mixers, non-sticky pans, mass-produced ready-made powders of all kinds. Man's tastes were simple and elementary but no longer, only to the detriment of health.

Textiles is an area which is most affected by machines. In fact, industrialisation started here. Steam engine-driven factories cropped up. Easy availability of coal and iron hastened mechanisation. Mass-produced cotton clothes gave way to synthetic material clothes which could catch fire far faster than your imagination could conjure up. In the past, man wore clothes that suited the climate and that was within easy reach. Now you wear clothes because they are the fad or the in-thing, however uncomfortable they may be.

Transport witnessed tremendous transformations. Machines dominate. From using legs to animal-driven carts, to simple mechanical vehicles, to machine with oil and power-driven vehicles like buses, cars, trucks, trains, planes. Now, people would not even think of walking a few yards.

Communication is also machine-driven. Messages were exchanged orally in market places. Birds and runners were used to carry urgent messages, later through stagecoaches. From mailbags to telegraphs, to telephones, to radios, to TVs, to mobiles, to satellites, messages move now. The computer with all its accompanying utilities provides the Web, the Internet and the e-mail. Again, machines control.

Entertainment is no exception. Late night dramas or plays were staged in open places; this has given way to closed-door theatres, to silent movies, to talkies, to digital movies. From personal appearance of singers to gramophones, to audiotapes and cassettes, to video cassettes. We have the home theatre too. The computer plays a key role here, too. You witness machine civilisation everywhere, in everything.

(conclusion)

There is no doubt that machine civilisation has brought several boons. But is the modern civilisation free from its banes? The answer is no. Machines are gradually taking control of human life. Man has lost the use of his limbs and he is loaning his brain to machines. They have begun to think for him. And what does the future hold? Only time can tell.

9.7 Organise information

[a] Having done these, it's time to decide whether you want to put in your essay or article everything you've collected. For each main idea, put the related ideas [major and minor details, elaborations, explanations, examples] together.

[b] If you think you have too many ideas, too much of information, then decide how many main ideas you wish to have in your writing. Remember a main idea can be covered even in two paragraphs.

To complete this step, you should know sentences structures and paragraph structures, you should know where and how to use them.

Shall we take a look at good paragraph writing?

9.8 Requisites of good paragraph writing

Introduction

When you write an article or an essay, it will contain a lot of sentences. These sentences develop the topic by breaking it into some or several main thoughts and by breaking each of these main thoughts into several **major and minor details.**

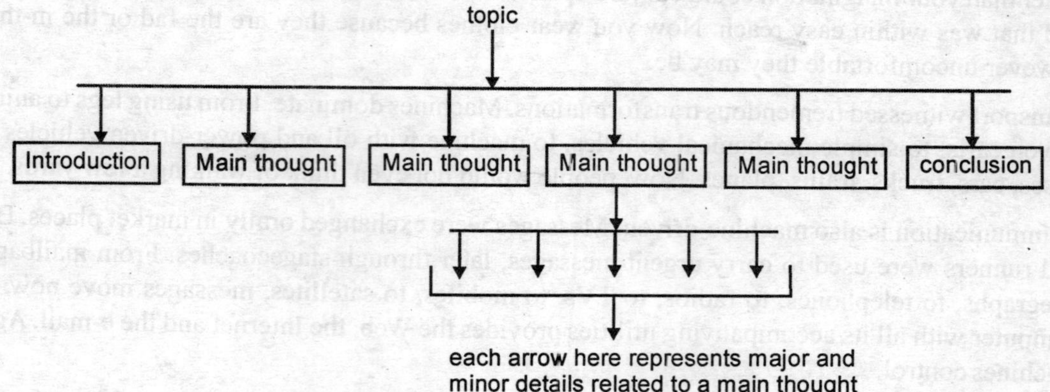

See how the topic 'The Computer' is developed with the help of major and minor details.

The major and minor details are given for your benefit in the next page.

1The computer can become a threat to man. **2** It can endanger his survival and privacy. **3** It also offers excellent encouragement for unethical or criminal activities. **4** It can worsen the unemployment problem as employers prefer the computer and the computer-controlled robots to humans for obvious reasons. **5**The information storage facility the computer provides has led to collection of personal information about individuals and storage of this information in data banks by several employing agencies. **6** If care is not exercised during data gathering, data integrity may suffer. **7**That is, questionable or imperfect methods may be employed; **8** as a result incorrect or incomplete data may be stored, and this may become permanent source and used for any given purpose. **9** Such use of defective information could affect an individual's peace, happiness or career ambitions. **10** Besides, no individual could have private life; **11** his life would be an open book for anyone to read. **12** More importantly, there is this lurking danger that anyone, with the right password, could enter the data bank, add, delete, or change the data to his liking to create false or misleading data. **13** Even money in banks is no longer safe from theft or manipulation. **14** Anyone can add, delete or change monetary transactions and thus erase and rewrite the data; **15** of course, such fraud would be detected but only days after the theft has been committed. **16** If this is criminal, an unethical activity is the unscrupulous piracy of software.**17** It is possible for anyone to make unlawful copying and still escape punishment.

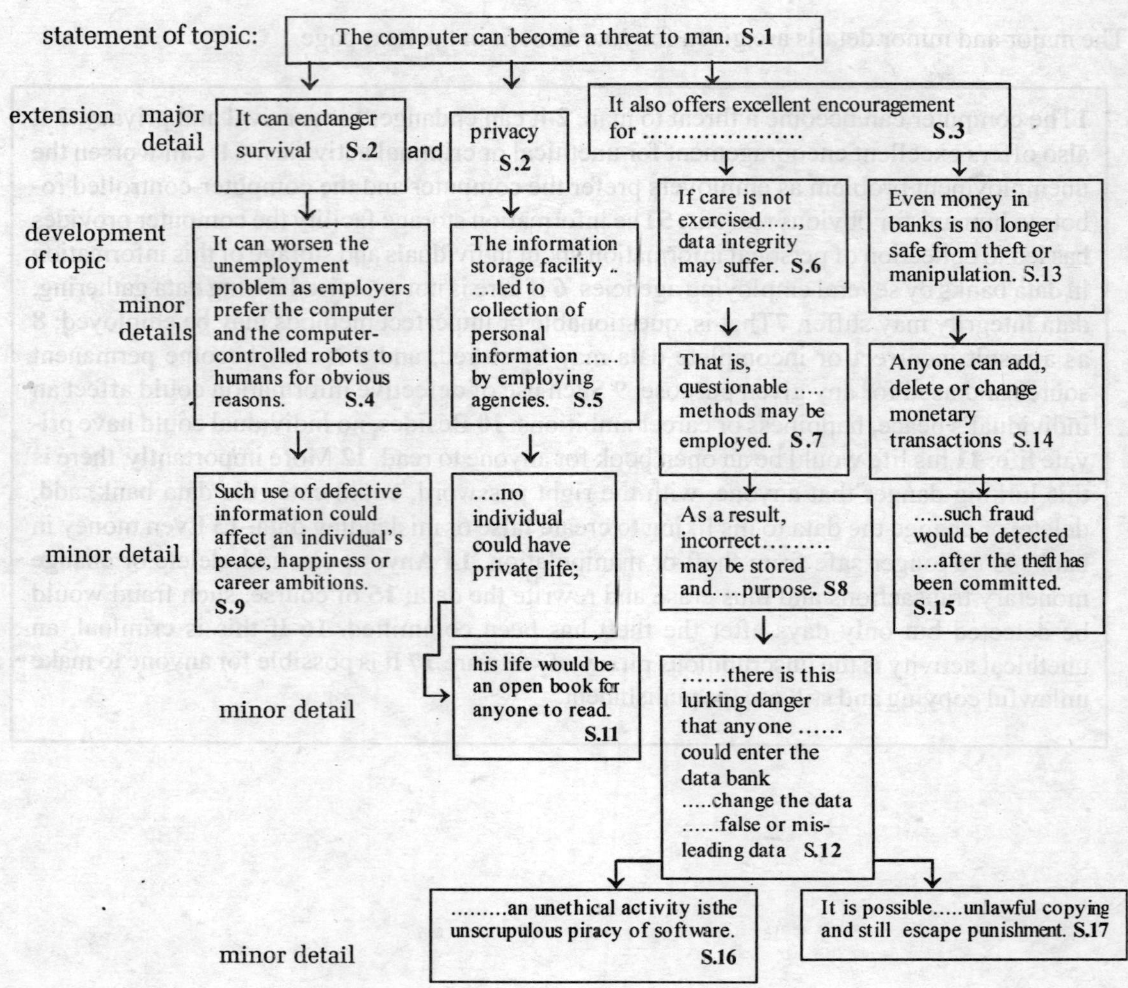

In the paragraph of the previous page, S.2 and S.3 are extensions of S.1. S.4 and S.5 elaborate two parts of S.2. S.9 expands on the kind of danger expressed in S.2. S.10 and S.11 elaborations of the second part of S.2. S.6, S.7, S.8, S.12, S.16, and S.17 expand and elaborate the 'unethical' aspect of S.3. S.13, S.14 and S.15 talk about the 'criminal' aspect of S.3.

Here is another example of how major and minor details help develop a topic sentence.

1There are many different kinds of musical instruments. **2**They are divided into three main classes according to the way they are played. **3**Those that are played by blowing air into them are called wind instruments. **4**These are made of wood, brass and other materials. **5**The family of wood instruments includes the flute, the clarinet, the bassoon, the trumpet, the mouth organ and the bagpipe. **6**The instruments that are played by banging or striking them are known as percussion instruments.**7**An example is the drum. **8**Then there are stringed instruments which are played by plucking the strings or by drawing a bow across the strings. **9**Examples of this are the the guitar, the violin and the cello.

[an adapted version of a passage on p.55 in Michael J. Wallace's Study Skills in English, CUP 1988]

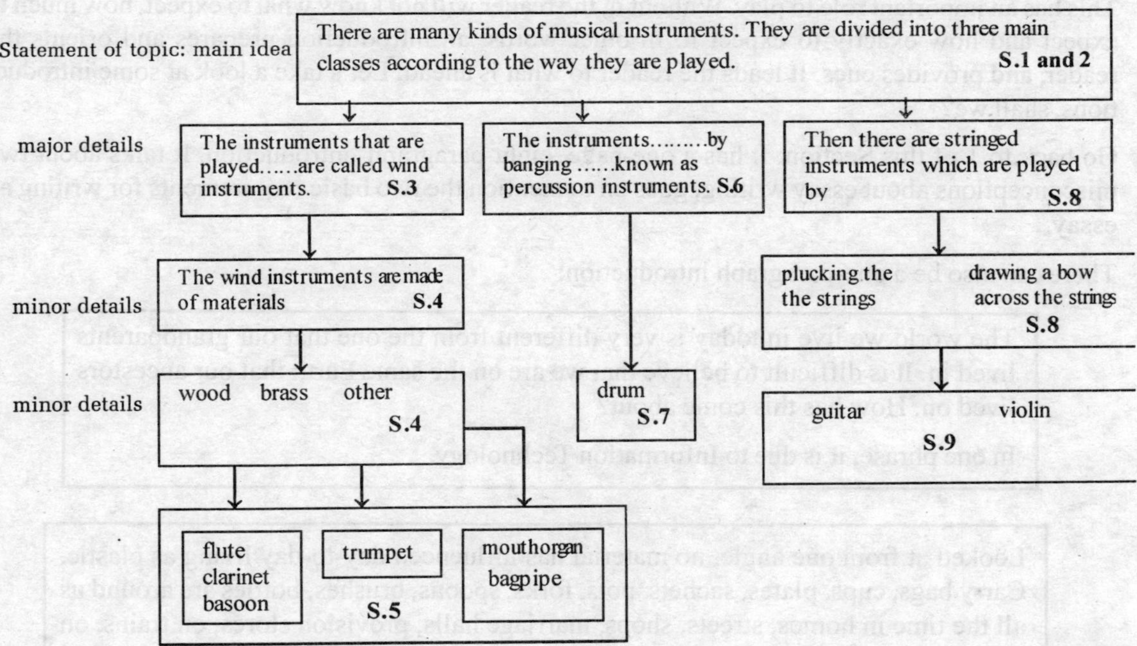

I hope that from these two examples, you've learnt how to support a main idea with major and minor details through expansion, elaboration and examples.

In sum, then,

1. The size of a paragraph should be appropriate to the main thought it is expected to express.
2. A paragraph generally has a topic sentence and a few more sentences related to it.

   A paragraph can have its topic sentence implied in the thought content itself.

   More than one paragraph may be needed to talk about a topic sentence.

3. A paragraph should have sequencing, ideal to the treatment of the topic.
4. A paragraph should have unity of thought. It should develop one aspect of the topic.
5. A paragraph should be coherent. Each thought should be linked logically to others at the thought and structural levels.

9.9 Formatting

introduction, body, conclusion

Any piece of writing should be in three parts. You've seen this in the sample essay on 'machine civilisaiton'. You need to introduce the topic to the reader. This introduction will serve as background or backdrop to the reader. Then comes the 'body'. This contains all the main ideas and their related thoughts in the form of sentences and paragraphs. Finally comes the conclusion. This is where you indicate what and how you want the reader to think in relation to the writing.

Introduction

This has an important role to play. Without it, the reader will not know what to expect, how much to expect and how exactly to expect it. In other words, an introduction prepares and orients the reader, and provides cues. It leads the reader to what is ahead. Let's take a look at some introductions, shall we?

Go back to 1 of this Section. It has a one-page, eight-paragraph introduction. It talks about two misconceptions about essay writing, goes on to mention the two basic requirements for writing an essay.

There can also be a one-paragraph introduction:

> The world we live in today is very different from the one that our grandparents lived in. It is difficult to believe that we are on the same Earth that our ancestors lived on. How has this come about?
>
> In one phrase, it is due to Information Technology.

> Looked at from one angle, no material has influenced day-to-day living as plastic. Carry bags, cups, plates, sachets, pots, forks, spoons, brushes, bottles are around us all the time in homes, streets, shops, marriage halls, provision stores, on trains, on buses. Plastic has brought in the culture of 'use and throw' and this has led to not bothering about its negative implications.

Remember that it's not necessary to begin your essay with an introduction. If you find it difficult to give expression to the main focus of your essay as introduction, it doesn't matter; go on to write what you want to and then come back to this.

You can use quotations, headlines of a newspaper, anecdotes, illustrations; you can even start or end the introduction with a question.

The important thing is you give the reader a bit of your mind in the introduction. Using this, the reader will be able to anticipate, follow and understand what comes in the body.

body

This contains your thoughts, ideas, messages—what you wish to say, what you wish to convey—in the form of paragraphs. There is no limit to the number of paragraphs you may wish to use. The number of paragraphs will depend on the number of main ideas that you'll develop from the topic you've chosen. Sometimes, you may use more than one paragraph to develop one main thought.

Conclusion

It's difficult to imagine an article or essay without a conclusion. Without it, the reader would find it hard to complete in his mind the thought process of the writer. The reader must know what the writer ultimately or finally feels about the topic.

It could be a mere summary of what has been said in the body. It could raise a few questions about the topic that the writer might wish the reader to answer. It could categorically come to certain conclusions or arrive at certain decisions. It could suggest a few steps. It could leave the whole issue very open after highlighting certain vital issues.

> There is no doubt that machine civilisation has brought several boons. But is the modern civilisation free from its banes? The answer is no. Machines are gradually taking control of human life. Man has lost the use of his limbs and he is loaning his brain to machines. They have begun to think for him. And what does the future hold? Only time can tell.

> In essence, JC Bose had a profound vision of the basic unity of life. In his thought and methods, he was a rebel and far ahead of his time. He deliberately rejected offers of patenting his inventions. He was a scientist, not a businessman. That was his strength. A weakness in today's perception?

> We can always argue for and against a proposition, a statement or a thesis. A decision to act or not depends on how strong arguments are either way. In the case of human cloning, the arguments for human cloning are better for the welfare of humanity as a whole.

> When I look at my children lost in their innocent little worlds, when I observe them whiling away their time without any prolonged 'selfish' attachment, when I hear their merry laughter. When I see their eyes twinkling with delight, when I listen to their cheerful, guileless talk I feel I should never have grown. At least not the way I have. I have been childish. How I wish I were child-like!

So when you bring your thoughts from your mind on to paper with these three main parts—introduction, body and conclusion—you get an article or an essay.

9.10 Editing

If all these six steps are important, 'editing' is the most important. No one, I repeat, no one can write a **perfect** essay or article in one attempt.

[a] You need to edit your writing for grammar, spelling, punctuation, unity, coherence, facts and figures [if any]. Also look for more appropriate expressions [words and phrases]; have a good mix of sentence structures; make sure you're using active voice or passive voice appropriately.

[b] If there is time, you can give it to people who are interested in your welfare and growth—be they relatives or friends. They will be able to identify errors that you cannot see.

9.11 Writing an essay as part of a test or an examination

When you seek a job or admission to higher education, you have to sit **a test or an examination in general English**, part of which can be writing an essay on a given topic.

And you may have to write this essay in, say, half an hour and in about 400 words, that is, about two to three pages.

If there are choices, choose the topic you are most comfortable with. If there is only one, you have to answer that, of course.

Steps:

- Spend five minutes to think about the topic and gather four to five main ideas and ideas related to the topic. Put them down on your answer sheet as 'outline'.
- Spend twenty to twenty two minutes to write the essay, developing the main ideas.
- Think of a good introduction. This paragraph need not be long. Even two or three sentences will do. But make sure they introduce the topic in an interesting manner. Here, you can use questions, newspaper items or anecdotes, famous quotations and then say what your essay is going to develop in the 'body'.
- Put each main idea as topic sentence in the very first sentence of each paragraph. Of course, if necessary, you can develop one main idea in two paragraphs. Then put, in a few sentences, major and minor details related to the main idea in the form of elaborations, expansions, examples. Use 'sentence connectors'. Take care of tense, singular/plural, spelling, punctuation. If possible, give subtitles. The sample for 'expository essay' contains subtitles.
- Conclude properly. This paragraph can be a short one. This can serve as a summary of what you've said in the body. And you may raise a few questions about the topic or you may express your own opinions.
- Finally spend three to five minutes to edit. This is a must. The time is short and not enough to make all the improvements, but the time is sufficient to take care of errors in grammar and spelling.

9.12 Kinds of essay

1. narrative
2. .descriptive
3. argumentative
4. expository

Narrative essays contain, as content, sequence of events, incidents. The content may be factual or fictional. All these narrate: short stories, novels, reports, [auto]biography .

Descriptive essays describe; they contain details about a person, a place, action or activity that appeal to the senses. They provide mental images or pictures that come alive as we read. All these describe: diaries, technical, scientific, travel writings, [auto]biography.

Argumentative essays state, create or expect opinions with evidence looking at the pros and cons of an issue, a problem, a behaviour, an event. They try to persuade or influence the reader. They expect the reader to appreciate, and if possible accept, the opinion.

Expository essays explain. They describe, narrate or analyse or also argue; however, their intention is not to convince the reader but just expose information to the reader.

Please remember that

> these four kinds are indicated only for the sake of convenience or for the purpose of focus rather than anything else
>
> and
>
> despite the distinctions brought about in the kinds of essays, no essay or writing will be only narrative, or descriptive, or argumentative, or expository.

Samples

Analytical essay

Read the two essays in the following pages. I consider them excellent samples to show how logic and analysis can be woven into one piece, beautifully, excitingly and tantalizingly.

Sample 1

From **The Fraternity of the Stone** by David Morrell, New English Library[UK edition 1987]

It was autumn again, October, his sixth year in the monastery. The ruddy glow of sunset tinted the brilliant maples on the hill. He heard the rattle of the serving hatch, then the familiar scrape and thump of a cup and bowl being set on the shelf beside his door.

He lowered his axe, the blunt end of which he'd been striking against a metal wedge to split logs for his wood stove, and glanced toward the tiny hole at the base of the workroom wall where Stuart Little suddenly appeared. The mouse sat on his haunches, raising its forearms to brush his whiskers.

All you need is a knife, fork and bib, Drew silently joked, amused at how the rattle of the serving hatch had become Stuart Little's dinner bell.

The mouse scurried over as Drew brought the meal to the workbench. Bread and water; another fast-day. His stomach rumbling, he noticed Stuart trying to climb up his robe, and with a sigh of feigned disgust, he tore off a piece of bread, tossing it down to the mouse. He sat at the bench and bowed his head, pressing his hands, praying.

You know, Stuart, he thought as he finished, you're getting greedy. I ought to make you wait to eat till grace is finished. A little religion wouldn't hurt you. How would you feel about that, huh?

He glanced toward the mouse on the floor.

And frowned. The mouse lay on its side, unmoving.

Drew stared in surprise, not moving either. His chest tensed. Shocked, he held his breath, then blinked and inhaling slowly, bent down to touch Stuart's side.

It remained inert.

Drew gently nudged it, feeling the soft sleek fur, but got no response. His throat seemed lined with sand. As he swallowed painfully, he picked Stuart up. The mouse lay still in his palm. It weighed almost nothing but the weight was dead.

Drew's stomach felt cold. In dismay, he shook his head, baffled. A minute ago, the mouse had practically been dancing for its supper.

Was it old age, he wondered. A heart attack or a stroke? He didn't know much about mice, but he vaguely recalled having read somewhere that they didn't live long. A year or two.

But that was in the wild, exposed to predators, diseases, and cold. What about here, in the cell? He strained to think, telling himself that even with warmth and good care, Stuart Little had been bound to die. There wasn't any way to know how old it had been when it showed up last autumn, but in human terms, by now it might have been ninety.

I shouldn't be surprised. By feeding it, I merely postponed……If it hadn't died today……

Tomorrow.

continued…

He bit his lip, grieving as he set the small corpse back on the floor. And felt guilty because he grieved. A Carthusian was supposed to shut out all worldly distractions. God alone mattered. The mouse had been temptation that he should have resisted. Now God was punishing him, teaching him why he shouldn't become infatuated with transitory creatures.

Death.

Drew shuddered. No. I wouldn't change anything. The mouse was fun to have around. I'm glad I took care of it.

His eyes stung, making him blink repeatedly as he stared down at his lifeless friend. Terrible thoughts occurred to him. What should he do with the body? For sure, he wasn't going to have a custodian brother dispose of it, perhaps even dump it in the trash. The mouse deserved better. The dignity of burial.

But where? Through misted vision, he glanced toward his workroom window. Sunset had turned to dusk, casting his garden into shadow.

A cedar bush grew in a corner of the wall. Yes, Drew thought. He'd bury Stuart Little beneath the shrub. An evergreen, it lived all year. Even in winter, its color would be a remainder.

His throat felt swollen, aching each time he swallowed. Thirsty, he reached for his cup of water, raised it toward his lips, glanced past it toward the thick slab of bread in his bowl.

And paused.

His spine began to tingle.

He peered down at the bread on the floor, the chunk he'd thrown to Stuart Liltle. He stared at the water in the cup he held. And slowly, cautiously, making sure that no liquid spilled over the top, he eased the container back down on the table. Reflexively he wiped his hands on the front of his robe.

No, he thought, it couldn't be.

But what if you're not imagining?

His suspicion filled him with shame. In his sixth stern year of penance, did he still retain the habit of thinking as he had in his former life? Had his training been that effective? Were his instincts that resistant to change?

But just supposing. You know, for the sake of argument. What kind it might be? Did it kill on contact?

Tensing, he stared at his hands. No, he'd touched the mouse. And the bread. Just a minute ago. But the mouse had died quickly. In the time Drew had taken to close his eyes and say grace. If it's poison and it kills on contact, even with my greater size, I ought to be dead now, too.

He breathed.

All right, then, it had to be ingested.

(You've got to stop thinking this way) continued….

Assuming it's poison.

Of course, just assuming. After all, it's still quite possible that Stuart Little died from natural causes.

(But what would you have thought six years ago?)

He struggled to repress his terrible memories. Now God's testing me again. He's using this death to learn if I've truly purged myself. A man of detachment would never think like this.

(But in the old days.......

Yes?

You thought this way all the time.)

He narrowed his vision till all he saw was the unmoving mouse on the floor. Slowly, frowning so hard he felt the beginning of a headache, he raised his eye toward the serving hatch beside his door.

The hatch was closed. But beyond it was a corridor. (No. It makes no sense. Not HERE, not NOW! Who? Why?)

Besides, he was merely guessing. The only way to know for sure if the bread had been poisoned was to....

Taste it? Hardly.

But there was another way. He could investigate the monastery. He stiffened with doubt. The notion repelled him.

But under the circumstances.......

He stared at the door. In the six years he'd been here, he'd left his quarters seldom, only to convene with the other monks for mandatory communal rituals. Those ventures outside had been keenly disturbing to him, nerve-racking intrusions on his peace of mind.

But under the circumstances......

He wiped his sweaty lip. His years of disciplined regimen told him to wait for a short while longer until he normally left for vespers. Yes. The decision calmed him. Avoiding extremes, it appealed to his common sense.

Dusk deepened, shifting to dark. A misty drizzle beaded on his window. He shivered, grieving, too preoccupied to force himself to turn on a light.

The vespers bell stayed silent, but in rhythm with his daily cycle, he knew that it should have been struck by now. He told himself that the mouse's death had disturbed his judgment. Time was passing with exaggerated slowness, that was all. He didn't have a clock in the cell, so how could he be sure when vespers was supposed to occur?

He counted to one hundred. Waited. Started to count again. And stopped.

With a painful sign, he repressed his inhibitions, broke six years of habit, and opened the door.

You liked it, I suppose. Not just for the suspense but the tension that gradually builds up in the mind of Drew as he analyses logically the abrupt death of Stuart Little and what it can mean to him.

Sample 2

From **The Masakado Lesson** by William P. Kennedy, Gold Eagle 1988.

It should be obvious. But it wasn't. They were being used. But he didn't know how and he wasn't sure by whom.

It was time for Toole to begin constructing the pyramids to learn whom he was dealing with and what they were really up to. He was working for John Cobb, a top agent of the secret government involved in the plot of national survival. But who was John Cobb? Was he really part of the U.S. Government, or had Toole committed a cardinal error—believing what he had been told? Cobb had demonstrated his divine authority by opening the gates of a federal prison. And, as Watergate had demonstrated all too clearly, not everyone employed by the government had the country's interests at heart.

Who was Yamagata Fujii? A top computer theorist, of course. But whose side was he on? He was turning over Japan's most closely guarded industrial secrets with no more urging than a transparent threat and no more reward than a suitcase of money. And he could scarcely contain his joy in the process. Was he the victim? Or was he part of the plot?

Then there was this Signet Corporation, described by Cobb as simply a shell that served as a mailing address for stolen information. But who owned Signet? What was its connection to Cobb or to Fujii? And what was it going to do with the computer code that only a dozen or so people in the world could even begin to understand?

He needed answers. He needed to know who was scheming, and who was being victimised. And he needed to know how. Otherwise he was simply one cog in the machine, and cogs tended to heat up and break when the machine was running at top speed.

His gut told him he was being used. But how? As a washing machine to launder money that Signet was paying to Fujii? As a watchman, to keep Karen from inadvertently compromising a scheme she didn't understand? Or as a victim to take the fall if Cobb's house of cards should suddenly become top-heavy and unstable?

Some things seemed clear. From what he had learned on his trip to the United States, it was apparent that Cobb had set him up to be the obvious culprit if the scheme were discovered. The perpetrator of record was not the United States government, but rather Signet Corporation, which had already been caught with its hand in the cookie jar. Cobb had claimed that Signet was nothing more than a mail drop. But the records indicated that it was a legitimate corporation with assets, activities and employees. So if the Japanese were to discover that someone was stealing their computer secrets, they would have to look no further than Toole and Karen. There would be no reason to search Cobb and his secret government associates.

'Fair enough' Toole thought to himself. If the U.S. Government were planning an operation against a friendly country it would be essential that it take steps to cover its tracks. What better cover than to create a much more obvious group of plotters who could shoulder the blame? Who could fault Cobb for not letting him and Karen in on the real reason they had been sent to Japan? Toole had never bothered to brief his marks on the full the nature of the schemes in which he was involving them.

Then there was Fujii. Had he known what Toole was up to the first time they had sat down together at a card table? If he did, then why had he been such a willing victim? Clearly, the Japanese computer expert had no intention of handing over his great invention for money. From Karen's meetings with him, Fujii still thought his supercomputer was going to sink the American fleet of technology. That meant he was certain Karen and Toole were going to be stopped before they could put his secrets to use. But who did he think was going to stop them? It seemed certain that he had inside information on their activities, but where was getting it? How was he managing to spy on them while they thought they were spying on him?

continued....

In fact, he realized painfully, he couldn't even be sure of Karen. She was a legitimate computer expert, a fact that was apparent in their conversations and which he had verified in his trip back to the United States. And she had certainly been recruited by Cobb from an important position with a major American Computer company. But for what mission? The one that Cobb had presented to him of scuttling Japan's new technical wonder? Or perhaps simply to learn as much as she could about Fujii's work? Was the whole plot simply a device to use Toole as a cover for Karen? If it was, did Karen know about it? Had he simply played into a trap by refusing to escape and leave her behind.

Toole kicked the mat and bedding aside to give himself room to pace the floor. Suppose none of them were what they appeared to be? Suppose Cobb had nothing to do with the government. Suppose Cobb and Karen and possibly Fujii were working together to move Japanese technology out of the country for their own private use? Could Toole simply be a cover to protect Fujii? That would explain why handing over his secrets hadn't caused him a moment of anxiety. He would have known that he was simply handing them over to himself. But they had the code months ago. Why would Fujii have waited so long to put the police on Toole's tail? And if they had been watching him, why would they have let him leave the country when they had no reason to think that he planned to return?

Everywhere he looked he found a new maze with convolutions just as puzzling as the heaps of historical data he had left at Karen's house. And yet he was sure there was no obvious answer just as he was sure that Fujii's password was buried somewhere in his long list of names and dates.

This is another masterpiece in logical analysis. Toole's analytical attempt to know what exactly was happening or not happening leads to as many possibilities as he can manage to worry about.

Argumentative essay

In an argumentative essay, you use your reasoning ability and logic to present points with evidence for an issue or a problem that seems to strongly affect the world in general or a society or community, in particular. You may take a stand or position and favour one side of the issue rather than the other. You can reason in three different ways:

[i] use **deductive** reasoning: make a point and use your writing to prove or deduce that point.

[ii] use **inductive** reasoning : first start by laying out some key points and then arrive at a conclusion or the point you wish to make.

[iii] use **persuasive** reasoning: make someone do something or dissuade someone from doing something by giving them good reasons.

The following pages provide samples of these three ways of presenting arguments.

Read them carefully to see how points are presented, what support is provided and how this support is presented.

---

[i] deductive reasoning

Yes to human cloning
outline
introduction
body
  arguments in favour
  arguments against
  their weaknesses
conclusion

sample 3

Yes to Human Cloning

Genetic engineering applies the knowledge obtained from genetic investigations. One of its concerns is improvement of species. Cloning is a procedure in genetic engineering yielding clones. A clone is a group of plants or animals produced artificially from the cell of a single ancestor and therefore containing exactly the same genetic material [same DNA=deoxyribonucleic acid] and RNA [=ribonucleic acid]. Scientists have so far produced animal clones. The next obvious step is cloning humans. Heated debate has been going on for sometime now. I would say yes to human cloning.

Clones form naturally when identical twin or other genetically identical multiple births occur. Single celled organisms, like bacteria, protozoa or yeast, produce, through asexual reproduction, genetically identical offspring which are considered clones. Even in vegetative propagation, a root or stem can generate a new plant that is genetically identical to the donor plant.

Another argument in favour is that couples who are infertile can have children of their own. If this isn't a blessing, what else is it?

Besides, heart transplants and test-tube babies are now accepted. Likewise, in time, clones would receive recognition.

Genetic defects could be identified and removed so healthy children could be produced. Isn't this an opportunity to make healthy beings?

Those who are not for cloning say that doctors might use clones as sources of organs for transplants. But laws could be made to guard against such use.

They say that cloning is against God's will. How sure are they? What evidence is there? In fact, there is evidence to the contrary. Cloning is a process that exists around us. We have come to a stage of human history when cloning can occur in a major way.

Man cannot assume the role of God, they say. But if man is a miniature God, as some of them believe, why not man play the role of God for the good of humanity?

We can always argue for and against a proposition, a statement or a thesis. A decision to act or not depends on how strong arguments are either way. In the case of human cloning, the arguments for human cloning are better for the welfare of humanity as a whole.

[ii] **inductive reasoning**

If only I were a child!

outline
- introduction
- body
  - instance one
  - instance two
  - reflections
- conclusion

sample 4

I was reading a novel. I had been absorbed in the flowing style and the gripping story. Suddenly I heard a piercing cry. The face of my son had a deep cut. I cleaned and dressed the wound. As I did the first aid, my wife told me my neighbour's son had thrown a stone. Without loss of time I gave my neighbour a bit of my mind. In return he warned me of dire consequences if ever my son played with his. Between us, the thread of cordiality snapped and we were no more on talking terms. But to my consternation, I found my son playing with the neighbour's as though nothing had happened between them. My sealed lips and angry stare stopped his explanation: 'But daddy….' He ran home genuinely perplexed.

Another day, my daughter broke the flower vase to pieces while attempting to tuck a rose in. The vase, besides being an expensive one, was dear to me. It was one of those pieces that reflected my artistic turn of mind. And when it broke I felt my heart broke too. It was too much to bear. I beat up my daughter, and she was laid up for a week.

The silent sobbing in her slumber, the jerky fall and rise of her chest set me thinking. All past events rushed to occupy my mind. I, a professor, was no better than my children. I, an educated man, worried for trifles while my children behaved better. I, a civilized man, was 'smaller' and 'meaner'. A sense of shame crept in me.

"Child is the father of man!" How right Wordsworth was! I had so much to learn from my little ones. I had the haughtiness to think that my child was a gem while others' weren't whereas he didn't. I had the cheekiness to keep 'my artistic' loss foremost in my thoughts whereas my daughter's act was only well-intentioned. I forgot my education and fought with my neighbour while my son continued his relation with his playmate. How vain I've been!

The child has little part in the human melodrama enacted with a plethora of exaggerated emotions—jealousy, hatred, ambition or revenge. He takes no event to heart. Of course, he quarrels, fights, feels jealous. But he doesn't make much of petty emotions. He forgets. He never drags the past into the present or future.

When I look at my children lost in their innocent little worlds, when I observe them whiling away their time without any prolonged 'selfish' attachment, when I hear their merry laughter, when I see their eyes twinkling with delight, when I listen to their cheerful, guileless talk I feel I should never have grown. At least not the way I have. I have been childish. How I wish I were child-like!

In the previous essay, the writer makes a statement at the beginning and supports it with arguments in a compare and contrast mode. In this essay, the writer leads us with examples to his conclusion about himself and the implied general comment on grownups.

[iii] persuasive reasoning

Here are two letters that persuade and dissuade. The first one provides arguments for doing something, and the second one for **not** doing something.

sample 5

Dear Kumar

Congrats! You're employed now.

Your dad tells me you're not too happy about it. You must have your reasons. I can understand.

But think about this. You won't have to trouble your parents for your needs. Your getting a job must be some relief to them, and to you, too.

Think of the unemployed. Aren't you better placed?

Yes, it's a small firm. But, remember, it's a growing concern. You can grow along with it. In a larger firm, your growth will not be as fast.

No, the money isn't much. But then, your salary will be yours alone. Your family won't require it.

Yes, for your talents, you deserved a better chance. But in a larger company, you'd have more competition and naturally, tension would go with it. Here, use your talents and you'll rise quickly. Because there'll be less jealousy, less backbiting.

More importantly, your team leader is a good person. You're in good hands. You can learn the trick of the trade from a veteran.

Besides, too much money too early in a career can have adverse effect!

All said and done, whatever you may be feeling, enjoy yourself. Emotions are important, yes, but growth is more important. You'll think about, won't you?

With love

Uncle Ramu

note: This sample is a letter but it follows the pattern for a persuasive essay:
introduction: sentence1 introduces the topic, assertion: paragraph 2 makes a statement indirectly.
concession and rebuttal: paragraph 2 understands the stand taken by Kumaran and the rest of the letter accepts the logic behind Kumaran's feelings but provides rebuttal [=counterarguments] for Kumaran's consideration. Proof follows Uncle Ramu's arguments. The last paragraph provides the conclusion: need for Kumaran to rethink.

note: This letter follows a 'linear' arrangement of ideas: introduction, point 1, point 2, point 3 and so on.

Dissuading

Sample 6

Dear Manju

Raju rang me up last night asking me to intervene on his behalf.

Thought I'd give a call but on second thoughts, I decided to write because I thought I could say more here.

Why do you have to insist on Raju joining the medical course? It seems to me you're thrusting your dreams on to your son. Is that fair? Also, Raju is entitled to his dreams about his future, wouldn't you agree? Normally you would, I know. But in your eagerness to provide a safe future, you're brushing aside his objections.

What are they? One, you can't afford the course, given your financial position. You'd have to borrow very heavily. Do you want Raju to start his career as a borrower?

Second, Raju has always been creative. And he has proved it in school days. Why not let him pursue a course which will help him flower as a creator? After all, you want him happy, don't you? Why make him unhappy, and in the process, feel unhappy?

Third, Raju is your only child, and a delicate one at that. He might finally agree. But that's no reason to make your dreams come true through him, is it? Let your only child do what he wants and let him bear the burden of his decision.

Otherwise, he could fault you until you lived; he'd accuse you, and you'd accuse him. Why torment yourselves? Happiness, ultimately is of the mind, not of the world. Think about it.

Lots of love

Renuka

note: This sample is a letter that dissuades. It follows the pattern for a persuasive essay: introduction: sentence1 introduces the topic, assertion: paragraph 3 makes a direct assertion. concession and rebuttal: paragraph 3 understands the stand taken by Manju and the rest of the letter accepts the logic behind Manju's feelings but provides rebuttal [=counterarguments] for Renuka's consideration. Proof follows Renuka's arguments. The last paragraph provides the conclusion: need for Renuka to rethink.

note: This letter follows a 'linear' arrangement of ideas: introduction, point 1, point 2, point 3 and so on.

A persuasive essay

Sample 7

A Case for Indian English

English, the language of England, is also the language of other nationalities. The English have theirs, the Americans, theirs, the Australians, theirs and the New Zealanders, theirs. The rest of the world use British English or American English as their model to educate themselves in the use of English. Formal learning in India follows the British model. However, shouldn't we have an English of our own?

Formal learning tells me I'm wrong when I say 'she described about her bizarre experiences', when I say, 'did you discuss about my promotion?', when I ask, 'what's your good name, please?', when I pronounce 'walked' as 'walk**ed**', when I enquire, 'he went, no?' or 'he saw you, isn't it?' I get corrected, I get a lesson, or my teacher may look at me pityingly. The Indian and/or the White experts term these as errors and patiently explain them as 'mother tongue interferences'. They go a step further and suggest a method or two to get rid of such 'bad habits'. But are they?

Do the same experts react similarly when they hear some educated English persons pronounce **cut** as /kut/, when they hear the educated British and the Americans pronounce 'laboratory' differently, when they know the former use 'meet' without 'with' and the latter use 'meet' with 'with', when they see the educated British write 'interfere between' and the Americans write 'interfere with', when the former write 'different from' while the latter write 'different than'? No, they don't. Is it because being English they are privileged to pronounce words as they please? Is it right that the Americans, the Australians, the New Zealanders please themselves by differing from the English? If it is, why is it wrong for Indians to differ? By what logic? If the three nationalities decided on their own to be different from the English, can't we Indians decide on our own to be different and have our own English? Should we borrow when we need not?

Neither the English nor the Americans can proclaim that English is their sole property. Isn't English as much ours as it is theirs? History has seen to that, hasn't it? This is not a tall claim, only a tall fact. In this shrinking world, nobody really owns anything.

The Americans, the Australians and the New Zealanders are as much multilingual as we are. In their case, unilingualism with flavours different from the British English happened as a matter of history. Our case is slightly different, English with a distinct flavour can happen and hence should happen as a matter of intent. Americans roll their r's and the English silence them. Why can't we pronounce them? Shouldn't we put our heads together and come up with an Indian model?

The English of each of these four nations appropriately contains and carries with it its distinctive 'thinking' and cultures. Isn't it appropriate for us to think about an Indian English that will contain and carry with it our distinctive 'thinking' and culture?

The thought of a distinctive Indian English may seem like madness. If we think for a moment, we will find this unusual thought not so unusual. Adopting or adapting a culture or a habit as part of our lives has been a common enough activity with us, hasn't it? Can adapting English to suit our thinking and needs be unthinkable then? Come, let's make English our own, let's add another jewel to the Indian 'body', let's add another medium to the Indian 'mind and spirit'. Or shouldn't we at least set the ball rolling and let posterity decide?

9.13 Topic specificity

Reasons for specificity

It's possible that writers may focus on how to impress their readers but they may not succeed because they may choose a topic too general or broad. As a result, they may fail in two ways: readers will not know where they are going and will not know how to respond, and two, writers may not be able to do justice to the topic, they may not be able to talk about the topic sufficiently enough to create interest in their readers.

You write because you want others to know your thoughts, feelings, reactions; also because, if possible, you want others to think like you do, to do as you wish them to. It's not enough if you have a wish. As you translate this wish into action, you need to do two things: choose a topic that will interest others, and two, make it as specific as possible or focus on a specific area of the topic so that your readers are able to appreciate your efforts.

Writing: the process and the parts

The process:

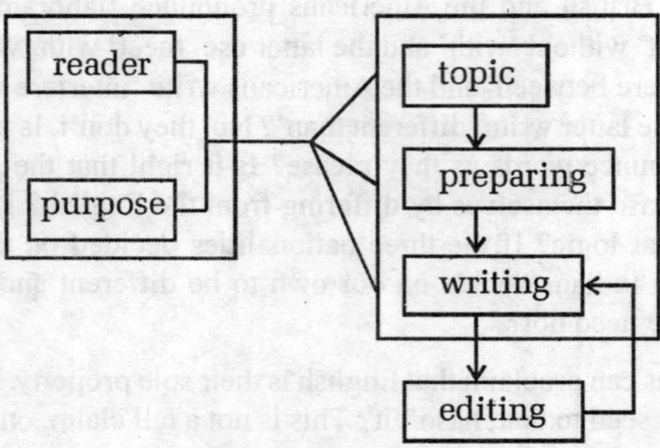

The parts

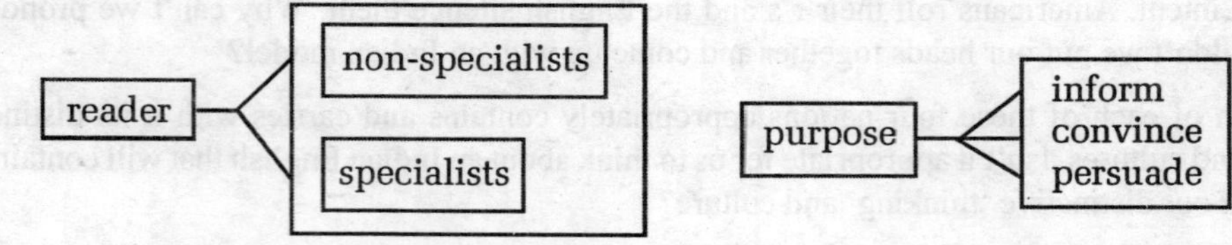

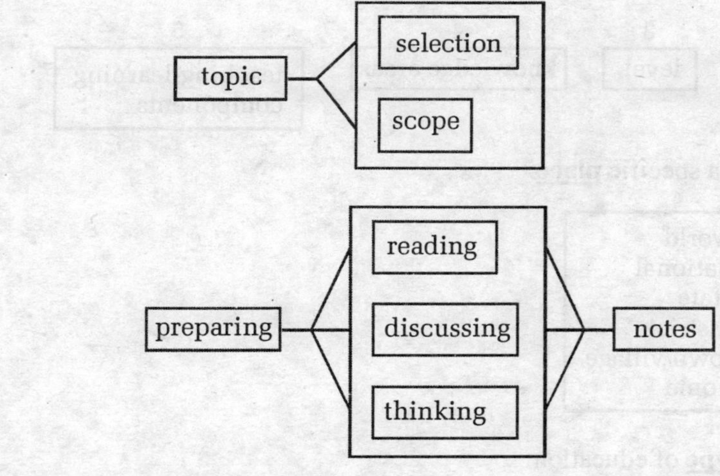

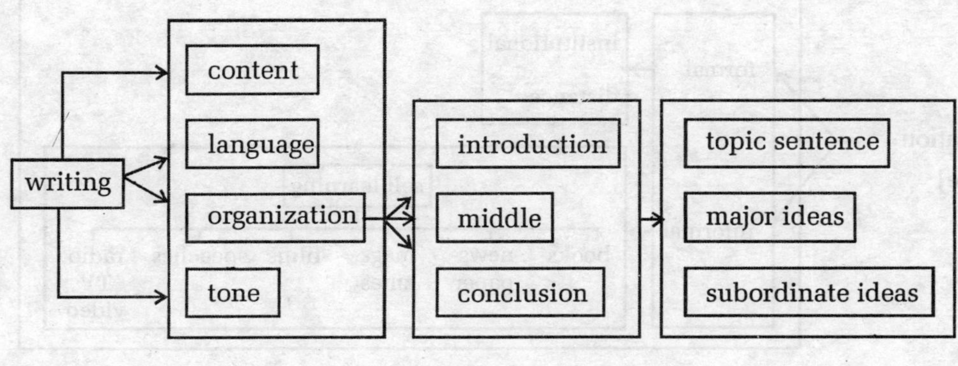

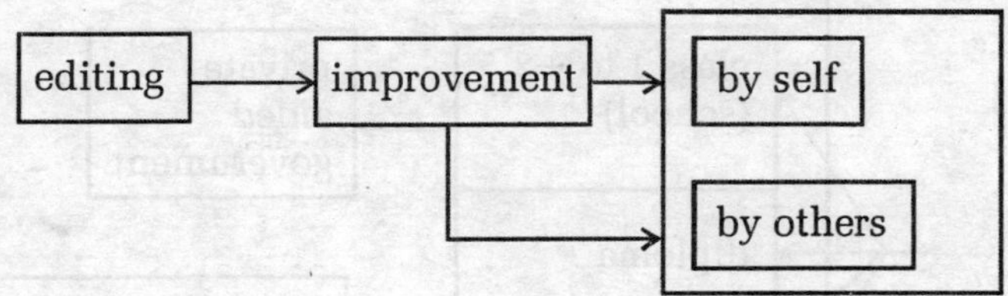

The visuals in the previous two pages picture in a nutshell the process of writing an article for publication, a paper for presentation, an essay in an examination or a contest.

From general to specific

As I said in 4.109, the topic you choose to write about should be limited in its scope; in other words, you need to contextualize it or lend it specificity. How do you do this? Well, let's look at an example. Let's take 'education'. You decide to write about 'education'.

You can think about it in several ways:

You have to give it a location—a specific **place**:

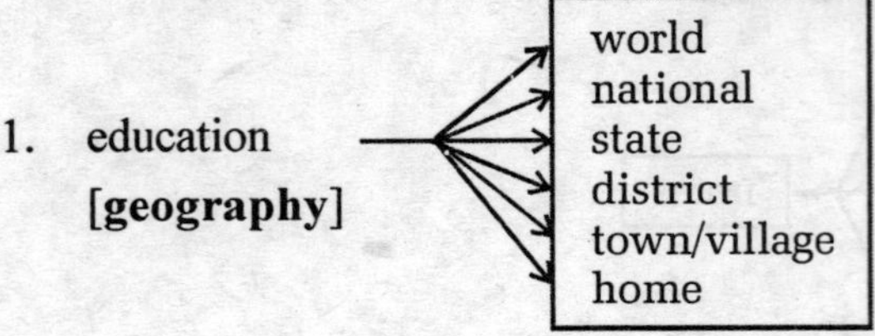

Now you have to think of the **type** of education:

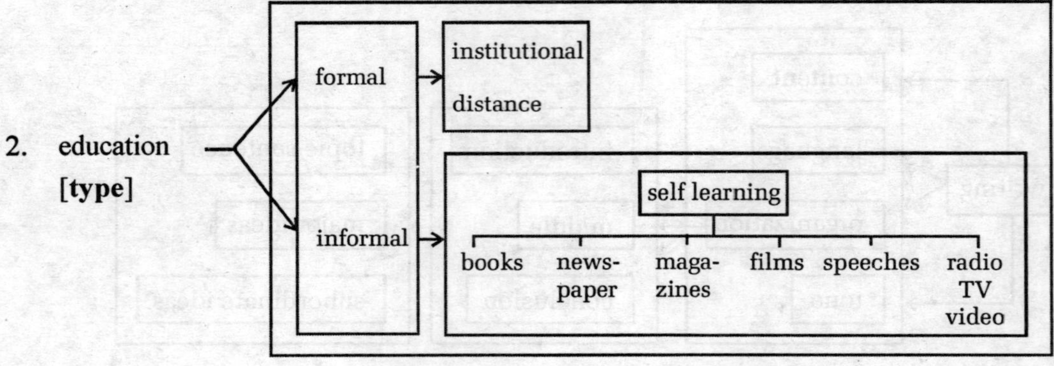

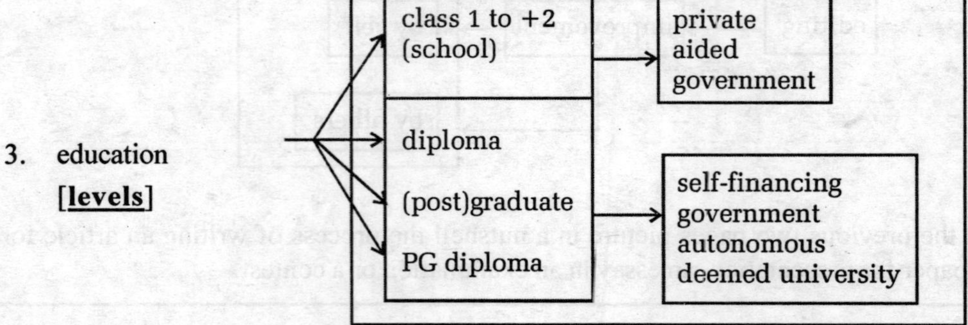

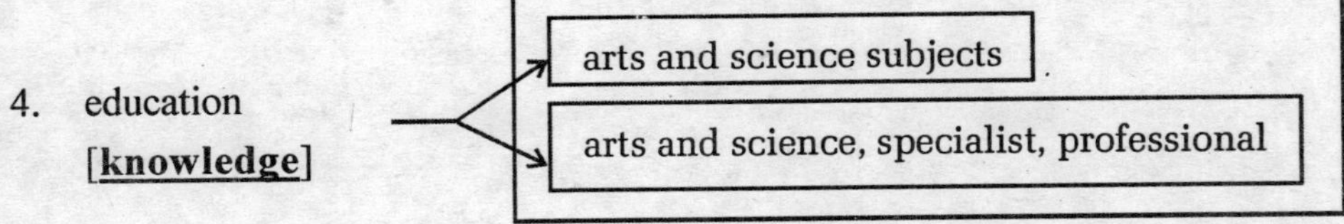

5. education [**related components**]

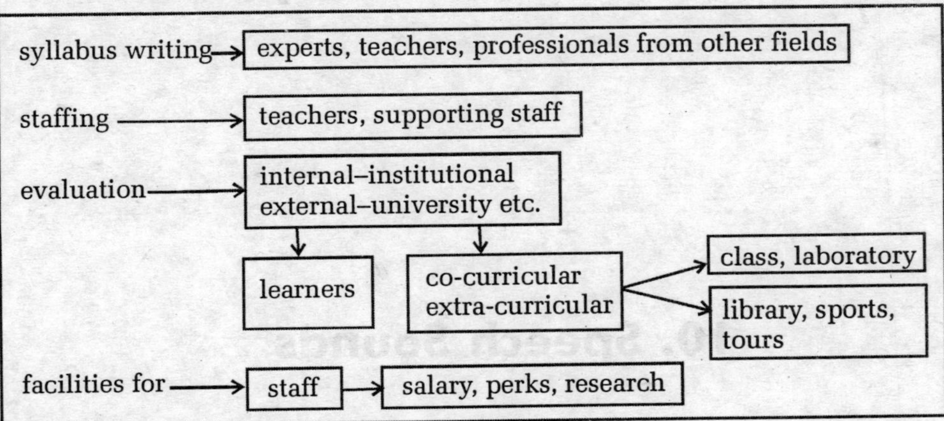

Note: The scope, the range and the depth as presented above are not exhaustive. The attempt is only to indicate how you can achieve topic specificity. Depending on your readers and purpose, you can generate [think of] any number of topics

10. Speech Sounds

10.1 Introduction

Speech sounds? What's that? Well, well, don't panic! I know you're not a student of linguistics. I'll not bother you with technical details. But since you'll soon be entering and staying in a professional multinational environment where you'll have to speak and listen to English a lot of the time, you'll need to learn to pronounce English sounds, articulate them by themselves, in pairs and in groups, with accent, intonation and pitch movement. To learn all these, you'll need some related technical information. This is what this Section does. It introduces you to their use in communicating thoughts and their roles in the comprehension process. As you come to the end of this Section, you'll know I've kept my promise!

10.2 English Sounds

Every language is a set of sounds produced with the air that we breathe out. Different sounds are produced as different parts of the mouth and the throat take different positions and as the air (breath) comes out through these positions.

There are several languages in the world. No two languages may have the same set of sounds, though there may be more similarities than differences. For example, the ' వి in విధాతా of Thelugu is not the same as 'v' in 'very' of English. Again, the ట in నాటకం of Thelugu is not the same as 't' in 'ticks' of English. Certain sounds may be available in one language while they may not in another language. For instance ణ in ప్రాణం of Thelugu and ళ in ప్రళయం of Thelugu do not exist in English.

When we speak the English language we use the tongue, the lips, the teeth in different positions and the throat and the nose in different ways to produce

12 vowel 8 diphthong 23 consonant	sounds.

These sounds are represented in writing in two ways:

(i) the English alphabet with 26 letters in different combinations to form words: for accuracy in spelling
psychology debt think then

(ii) International Phonetic Alphabet for phonetic transcription: for accuracy in pronunciation
/saɪkɒlədʒɪ/ /det/ /θɪŋk/ /ðen/

The examples in (ii) are written in a phonetic script according to what is known as Received Pronounciation (RP) which has been accepted for the purpose of teaching pronunciation. The American pronunciation of the English sounds is slightly different from RP with regard to certain sounds. The 'sch' in 'schedule' is pronounced /ʃe/ in RP and /ske/ in American. We in India generally hear or learn and use RP.

To be able to know the right pronunciation and to use it, you'll need to learn to read the **phonetic symbols** which you'll find in between slashes: /   /, which is no effort at all, I assure you.

10.3 Pure vowels

Listen to Track 11 on your CD for the first four vowels.

The tongue positions while pronouncing the vowels:

1. /i:/

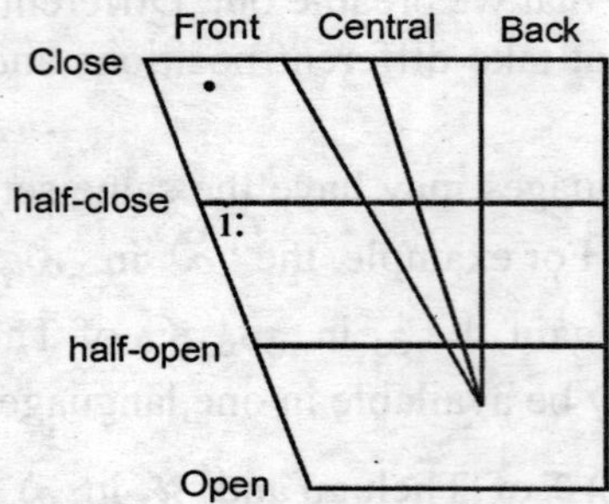

Articulation

The front of the tongue is raised in the direction of the hard palate to an almost close position. The lips are spread. The tongue is tense.

free / fri: /	complete / kəm'pli:t /	seat / si:t /	field / fi:ld /	receive / rɪ'si:v /
key / ki: /	marine /mə'ri:n /	quay / ki: /	people / 'pi:pl /	these / ði:z /
tree / tri: /	fee / fi: /	canteen / kæn'ti:n /	cream / kri:m /	reason / ri:zn /
sea / si: /	chief / tʃi:f /	piece / pi:s /	perceive / pə'si:v /	
seize / si:z /	machine / mə'ʃi:n /	police / pə'li:s /	prestige / pres'ti:ʒ /	

2. /ɪ/

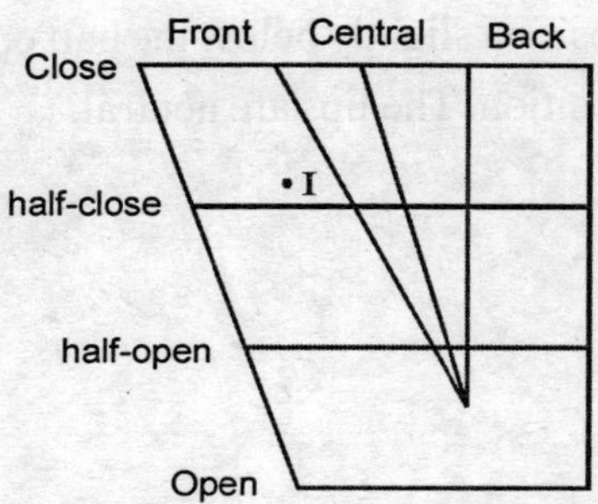

Articulation

The hinder part of the front of the tongue is raised in the direction of hard palate to a position between close and half close position. The lips are loosely spread. The tongue is lax.

miss /mɪs /
coffee / ˈkɒfɪ /
bit / bɪt /
whip / wɪp /
except / ɪkˈsept /
city / ˈsɪtɪ /
village / ˈvɪlɪdʒ /
cities / ˈsɪtɪz /
women / ˈwɪmɪn /
perfect (adj) / ˈpɜ:fɪkt /

many / menɪ /
journey / ˈdʒɜ:nɪ /
cliff / klɪf /
begin / bɪˈgɪn /
exam / ɪgˈzæm /
mystery / ˈmɪstrɪ /
baggage / ˈbægɪdʒ /
carries / ˈkærɪz /
circuit / ˈsɜ:kɪt /
symbol / ˈsɪmbl /

started / ˈstɑ:tɪd /
build / bɪld /
silk / sɪlk /
reduce / rɪˈdju:s /
catches / ˈkætʃɪz /
rhythm / ˈrɪðəm /
surface / ˈsɜ:fɪs /
money / mʌnɪ /
minute (n) / ˈmɪnɪt /
carriage / ˈkærɪdʒ /

---

3. /e/

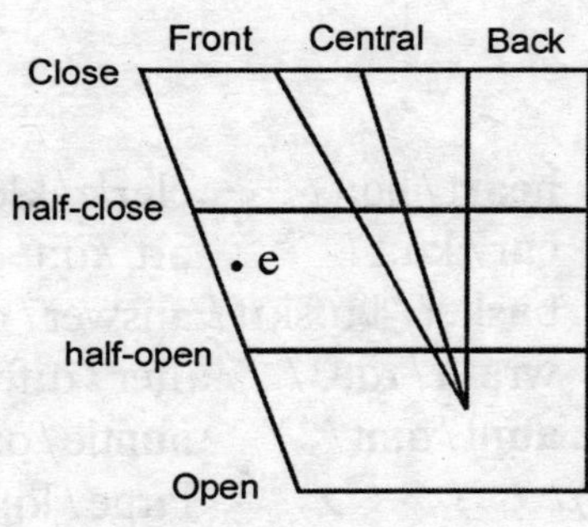

Articulation

The front of the tongue is raised in the direction of hard palate to a position between half-close and half-open. The lips are loosely spread and are slightly wider apart than for / i /. The tongue may have more tension than in the case of / i /.

kettle / ketl /
bed / bed /
measure /ˈmeʒə (r) /
leisure / ˈleʒə (r) /

health / helθ /
net / net /
any / enɪ /
perfect (v) / pəˈfekt /

many / menɪ /
set / set /
said / sed /
feather / ˈfeðə (r) /

friend / frend /
dead /ded /
ate / et /
again / əˈgen /

4. /æ/

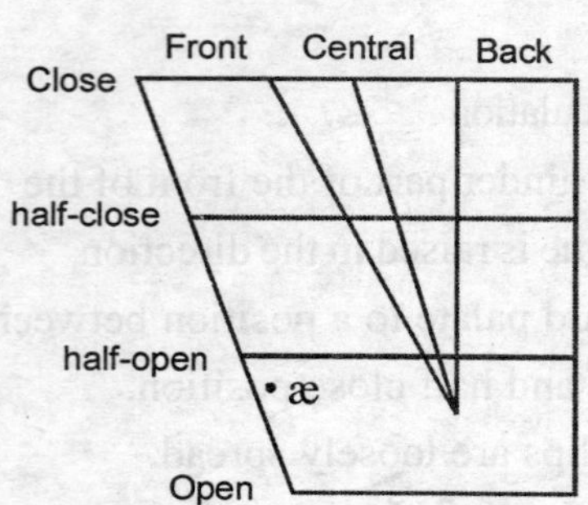

Articulation

The front of the tongue is raised to a position slightly below the half open position. The lips are neutral.

bad / bæd / **fan** / fæn / **tax** / tæks / **mass** /mæs/
can / kæn / **plait** / plæt / **plaid** / plæd / **man** / mæn /

Listen to Track 12 on your CD for 5, 6, 7, 8.

5. /ɑ:/

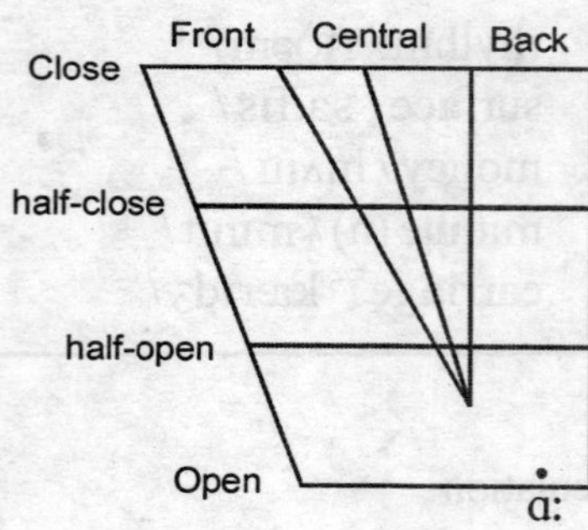

Articulation

The back of the tongue is in the fully open position. The lips are neutral.

cart / kɑ:t / **class** / klɑ:s / **park** / pɑ:k / **heart** / hɑ:t / **clerk** / klɑ:k /
palm / pɑ:m/ **tomato** / təˈmɑ:təʊ / **vase** / vɑ:s / **car** / kɑ:t / **art** / ɑ:t/
march / mɑ:tʃ / **ask** / sɑ:k / **castle** / kɑ:sl / **basket** / ˈbɑ:skɪt / **answer** / ˈɑ:nsə(r)/
branch / brɑ:ntʃ / **dance** / dɑ:ns / **bath** / bɑ:θ / **wrath** / rɑ:θ / **after** / ɑ:ftə(r) /
calm / kɑ:m / **half** / hɑ:f / **palm** / pɑ:m / **aunt** / ɑ:nt / **auntie** / ɑ:ntɪ /
laugh / lɑ:f / **drama** / ˈdrɑ:mə / **father** / fɑ:ðə(r) / **large** / lɑ:dʒ /
sergeant / ˈsɑ:dʒənt / **hearth** / hɑ:θ /

---

6. /ɒ/

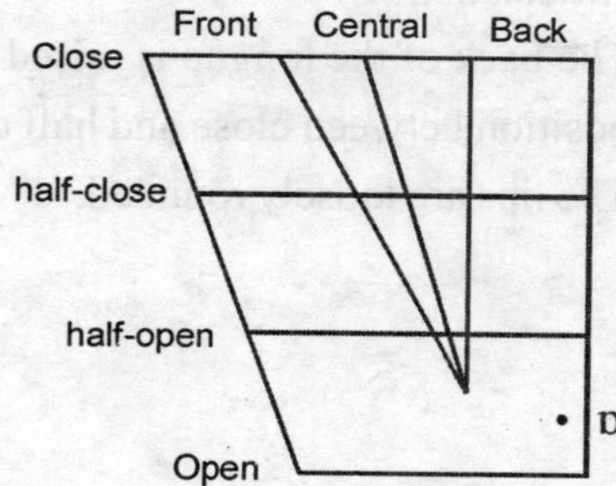

Articulation

The back of the tongue is raised in the direction of soft palate and it is in the fully open position. The lips are rounded.

cot / kɒt /
quantity / 'kwɒntətɪ /
b**o**rrow / 'bɒrəʊ /
wh**a**t / wɒt /
l**au**rel / 'lɒrəl /
g**o**ne / gɒn /
s**au**sage / 'sɒsɪdʒ /
d**o**g / dɒg /
m**o**ral / 'mɒrəl /
qu**a**lity / 'kwɒlətɪ /
tr**ough** / trɒf /
w**a**s / wɒz / (strong form) / wəz / (weak form)
c**ough** / kɒf /
b**o**ttle / 'bɒtl /
st**o**ry / 'stɒrɪ /
bec**au**se / bɪk'ɒz / (or) / 'bɪkəz /
y**a**cht / yɒt /
kn**ow**ledge / 'nɒlɪdʒ /
r**o**b / rɒb /
c**au**liflower / 'kɒlɪflɑʊə(r) /
h**o**nour / 'ɒnə (r) /

---

7. /ɔ:/

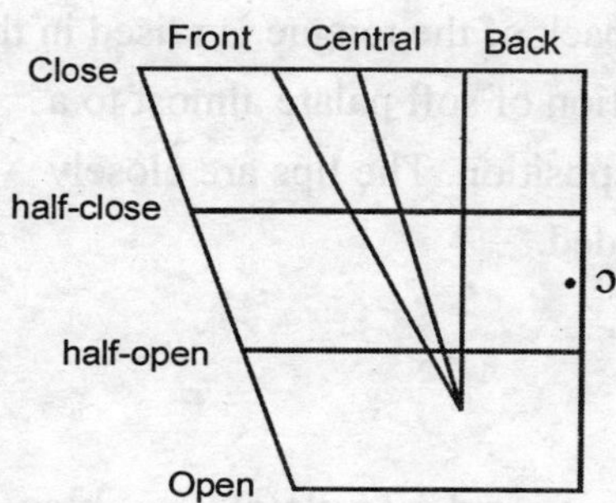

Articulation

The back of the tongue is raised in the direction of the soft palate to a height between half close and half open. The lips are rounded.

Most of us tend to pronounce this sound as / /.

c**augh**t / kɔ:t /
t**a**lk / tɔ:k /
w**a**ll / wɔ:l /
w**a**r / wɔ:(r) /
p**ou**r / pɔ:(r) /
b**ough**t / bɔ:t /
f**au**lt / fɔ:lt /
s**a**lt / sɔ:lt /
p**aw** / pɔ: /
bef**o**re / bɪ'fɔ:(r) /
c**o**rn / kɔ:n /
f**ou**r / fɔ:(r) /
c**ou**rt / kɔ:t /
f**ough**t / fɔ:t /
awkward / 'ɔ:kwəd /
w**a**ter / wɔ:tə(r) /
s**o**rt / sɔ:t /
d**oo**r / dɔ:(r) /
h**o**rse / hɔ:s /
t**ou**r / tɔ:(r) /
all / ɔ:l /
th**ough**t / θɔ:t /
w**a**rm / wɔ:m /
b**ough**t / bɔ:t /
b**oa**rd / bɔ:d /
m**o**rning / 'mɔ:nɪŋ /
b**o**rn / bɔ:n /
d**augh**ter / 'dɔ:tə(r) /
fl**oo**r / flɔ:(r) /
s**aw** / sɔ: /
qu**a**rter / kwɔ:tə(r) /
abr**oa**d / ə'brɔ:d /
c**a**ll / kɔ:l /
n**o**r / nɔ:(r) /
p**o**rt / pɔ:t /
l**aw** / lɔ: /
c**au**se / kɔ:z /
d**aw**n / dɔ:n /
for / fɔ:(r) / (strong form) / fə(r) / (weak form)

8. /ʊ/

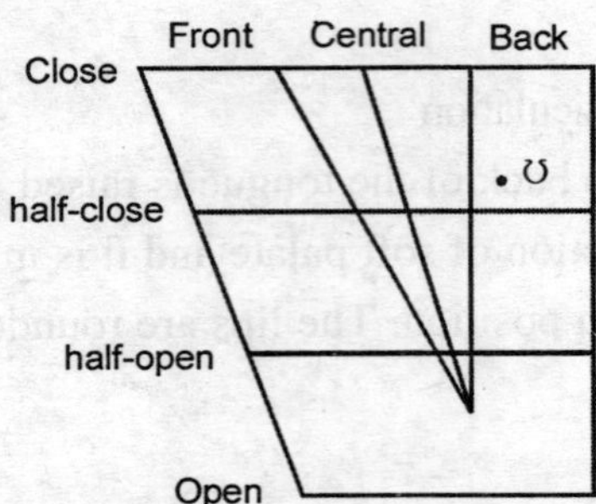

Articulation

The back of the tongue is raised to a position between close and half close. The lips are loosely rounded.

fu**ll** / fʊl /	**w**o**lf** / wʊlf /	**look** / lʊk /	**should** / ʃʊd /	**woman** / wʊmən /
bush / bʊʃ /	**Ju**ly / dʒʊlaɪ /	**book** / bʊk /	**foot** / fʊt /	**wood** / wʊd /
could / kʊd /	**would** / wʊd /	**courier** / ˈkʊrɪə(r) /		

Listen to Track 13 on your CD for 9, 10, 11, 12.

9. /u:/

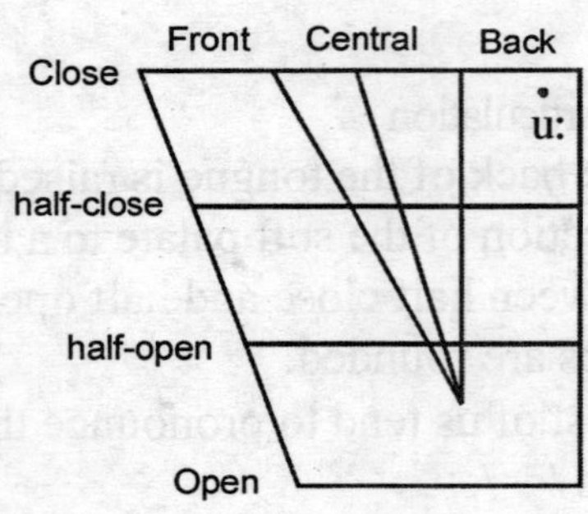

Articulation

The back of the tongue is raised in the direction of soft palate almost to a close position. The lips are closely rounded.

fool / fu:l /	**prove** / pru:v /	**soup** / su:p /	**ru**ler / ru:lə(r) /	**blew** / blu: /
blue / blu: /	**food** / fu:d /	**ju**ice / dʒu:s /	**shoe** / ʃu: /	**ru**de / ru:d /
June / dʒu:n /	**du**ty / dju:tɪ /	**u**nion / ˈju:nnɪə /	**mu**sic / ˈmjˈu:zɪk /	**choose** / tʃu:z /
loose / lu:s /	**noon** / nu:n /	**lose** / lu:z /	**who** / hu: /	**move** / mu:v /
group / gru:p /	**you** / ju: /	**wound** / wu:nd /	**fruit** / fru:t /	**new** / nju: /
mew / mju: /	**chew** / tʃu: /	**two** / tu: /	**true** / tru: /	**beau**ty / bju:tɪ/
nuisance / ˈnju:sns /		**minute** (adj) / maɪˈnju:t /		

10. /ʌ/

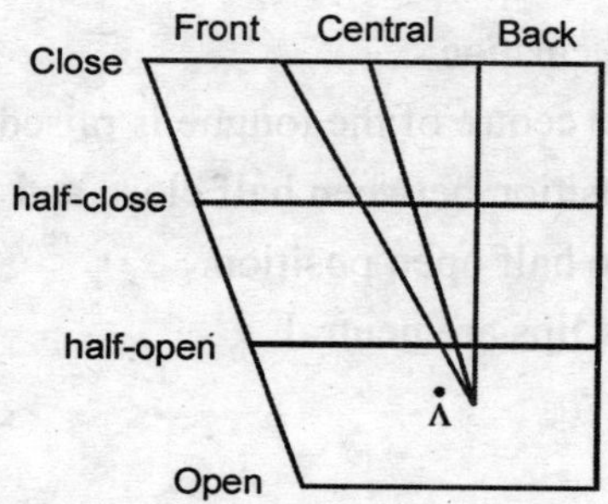

Articulation

The centre of the tongue is raised to a position between open and half open. The lips are neutral.

c**u**t / kʌt /	c**o**me / kʌm /	bl**oo**d / bʌld /	d**oe**s / dʌz /	c**u**p / kʌp /
uncle / ˈʌŋkl /	g**u**n / gʌn /	g**o**vern / ˈgʌvn /	w**o**rry / wʌrɪ /	fl**oo**d / flʌd /
c**ou**ntry / ˈkʌntrɪ /	en**ou**gh / ˈɪnʌf /	d**ou**ble / ˈdʌbl /		

---

11. /ɜ:/

Articulation

The centre of the tongue is raised in the direction of the roof of the mouth to a position between half close and half open. The lips are neutral.

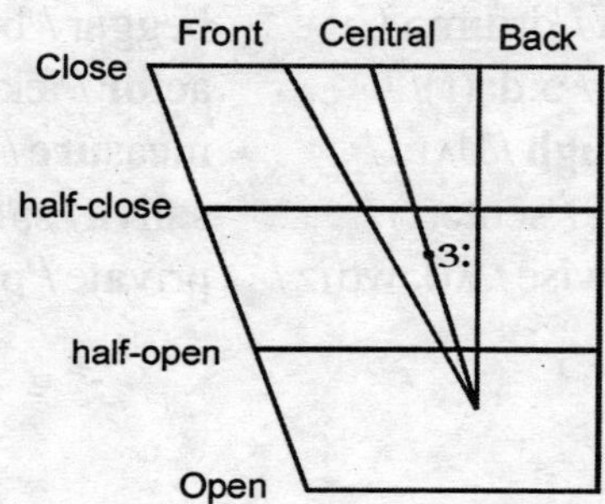

b**ir**d / bɜ:d /	m**yr**tle / mɜ:tl /	ins**er**t / ɪnˈsɜ:t /	**ear**th / ɜ:θ /	w**or**k / wɜ:k /
t**ur**n / tɜ:n /	c**olo**nel / ˈkɜ:nl /	s**er**ve / sɜ:v /	t**er**m / tɜ:m /	h**er** / hɜ: /
th**ir**st / θɜ:st /	c**ir**cle / ˈsɜ:kl /	f**ir**m / fɜ:m /	b**ur**n / bɜ:n /	c**ur**l / kɜ:l /
m**ur**der / ˈmɜ:də(r)/	s**ur**face / ˈsɜ:fɪs /	w**or**d / wɜ:d /	w**or**se / wɜ:s /	c**our**tesy / ˈkɜ:təsɪ /
h**ear**d / hɜ:d /	**ear**ly / ɜ:lɪ /	l**ear**n / lɜ:n /	s**ear**ch / sɜ:tʃ /	

---

12. /ə/

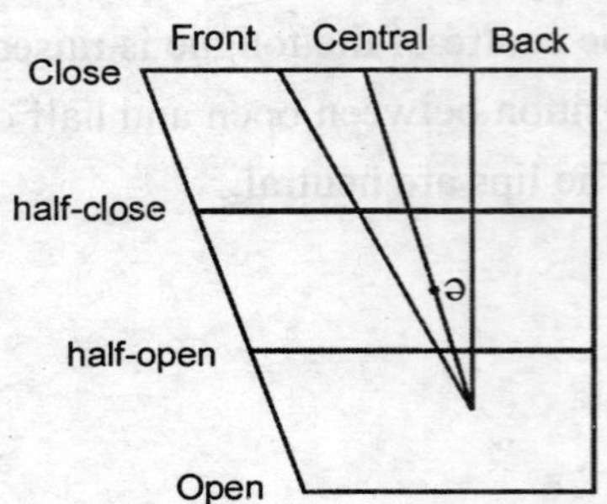

Articulation

The centre of the tongue is raised to a

i. position between half close and half open

ii.the half open position.

The lips are neutral.

possi**ble** / 'pɒsəbl /
col**umn** / 'kɒləm /
col**our** / 'kʌlə(r) /
wom**an** / 'wʊmən /
probl**em** / 'prɒbləm /
for**eign** / 'fɒrən /
observe / əb'zɜ:v /
eff**or**t / 'efət /
s**u**cceed / sək'si:d /
doll**ar** / 'dɒlə(r) /
doct**or** / 'dɒktə(r) /
creat**ure** / 'kri:tʃə(r) /
advertisement / əd'vɜ:tɪsmənt /

gentlem**en** / 'dʒentlmən /
backw**ar**d / 'bækwəd /
fig**ure** / 'fɪgə(r) /
subst**an**ce / 'sʌbstəns /
sent**e**nce / 'sentəns /
terr**i**ble / 'terəbl /
pr**o**duce(v) / prə'dju:s/
contin**uou**s / kən'tɪnʊəs /
s**ur**prise / sə'praɪz /
bigg**er** / 'bɪgə(r) /
hon**our** / 'ɒnə(r) /

alone / ə'ləʊn /
moth**er** / 'mʌðə(r) /
about / ə'baʊt /
p**ar**ticul**ar** / pə'tɪkjələ(r) /
ent**er**tain / entə'teɪn /
horr**i**ble / 'hɒrəbl /
lov**a**ble / 'lʌvəbl /
theat**re** / 'θɪətə(r) /
dram**a** / 'drɑ:mə /
ord**er** / 'ɔ:də(r)/
thor**ough** / 'θʌrə /
cent**re** / 'sentə(r) /
oth**er**wise / 'ʌðəwaɪz /

oblige / əb'laɪdʒ /
thor**ough** / 'θʌrə /
breakf**a**st / 'breɪkfəst /
stand**a**rd / 'stændəd /
lib**er**ty / 'lɪbətɪ /
condition / kən'dɪʃn /
horr**or** / 'hɒrə(r) /
fam**ou**s / 'feɪməs /
begg**ar** / 'begə(r) /
act**or** / 'æktə(r) /
meas**ure** / 'meʒə(r) /
s**a**liva / sə'laɪvə /
priv**a**te / 'praɪvət /

Learn to distinguish these sounds from one another – Listen to Track 14 on your CD.

a.

/iː/	/ɪ/
bead	bid
beat	bit
feet	fit
deed	did
field	filled
peep	pip
read	rid
reap	rip
leap	lip
leave	live
seep	sip
seek	sick
sleep	slip

b.

/iː/	/ɪ/	/e/
bead	bid	bed
neat	knit	net
seat	sit	set
deed	did	dead
field	filled	fed
peep	pip	pep
read	rid	red
reap	rip	rep

c.

/iː/	/ɪ/	/e/	/æ/
beat	bit	bet	bat
reap	rip	rep	rap
deed	did	dead	dad
field	filled	fed	fad

d.

/æ/	/ɑː/
mat	mart
batter	barter
lad	lard
hat	heart
am	arm
matter	martyr
ban	barn

e.

/ɑː/	/ɒ/
cart	cot
cast	cost
last	lost
large	lodge
part	pot
clerk	clock

f.

/ɑː/	/ɒ/	/ɔː/
cart	cot	caught
part	pot	port
barn	bon	born
hark	hock	hawk
cart	cot	court
card	cod	cord

g. /ɑː/ /ɔː/ /ɜː/

/ɑː/	/ɔː/	/ɜː/
bard	board	bird
parch	porch	perch
park	pork	perk
part	port	pert
card	cord	curd

10.4 Diphthongs

Listen to Track 15 on your CD.

Diphthongs are two vowels pronounced in a few combinations.

There are eight diphthongs:

/eɪ/ /ɑɪ/ /ɔɪ/ /əʊ/ /aʊ/ /ɪə/ /ɛə/ /ʊə/

1. /eɪ/ date, rain, today, eight, prey, great, debris

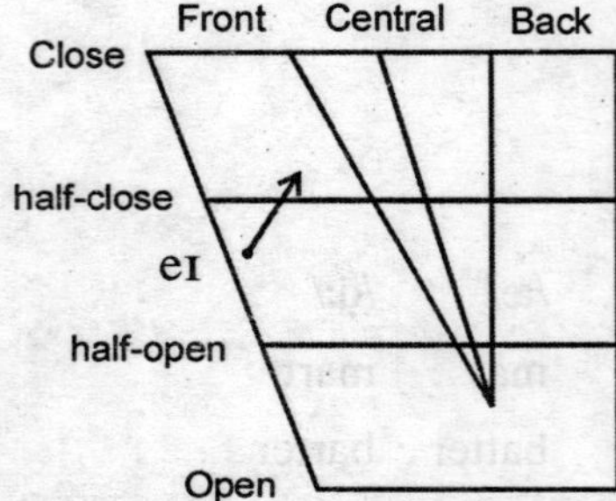

2. /ɑɪ/ time, dry, high, height, die, dye, either, aisle, eye, buy

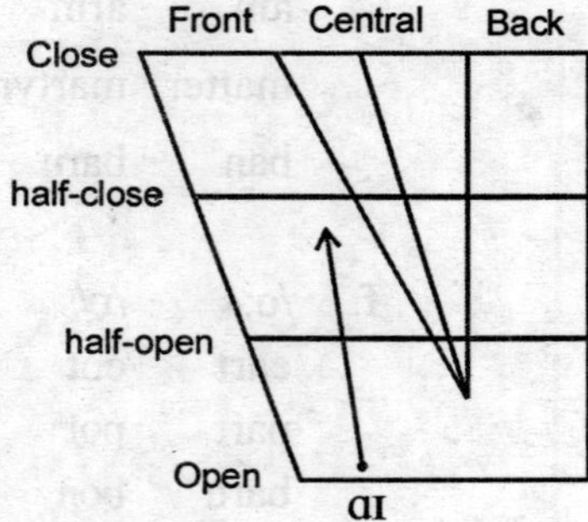

3. /ɔɪ/ loiter, boy, void, employ

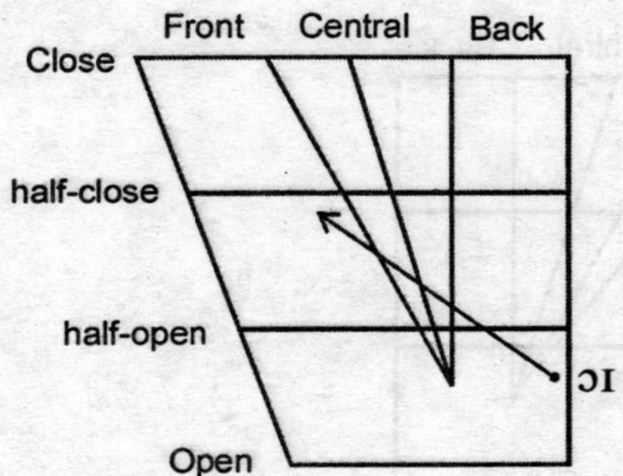

4. /əʊ/ go, road, foe, soul, know

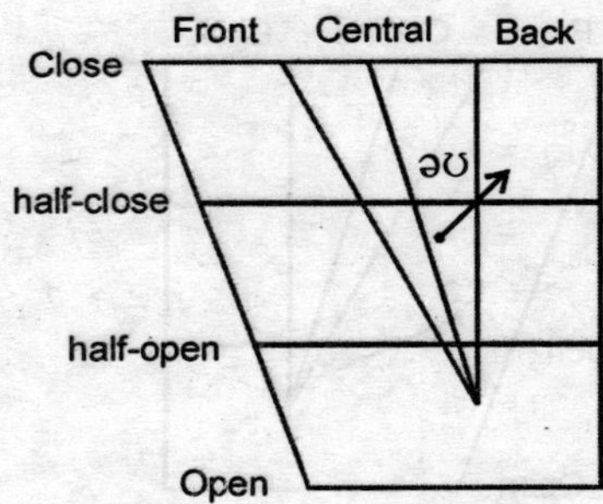

5. /ɑʊ/ house, loud, allow, town

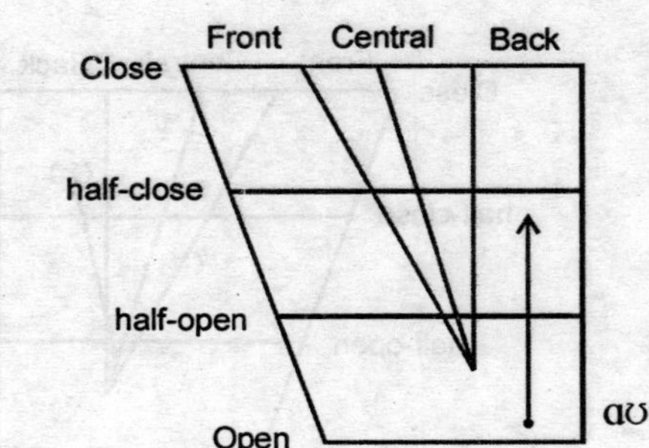

6. /ɪə/ deer, dear, mere, weird, fierce, idea, museum, theory, curious, here

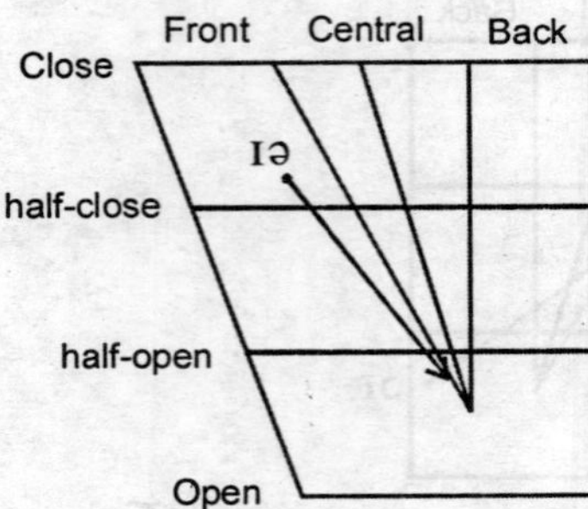

7. /ɛə/ there, chair, dared, aeroplane, bear, heir, scarce

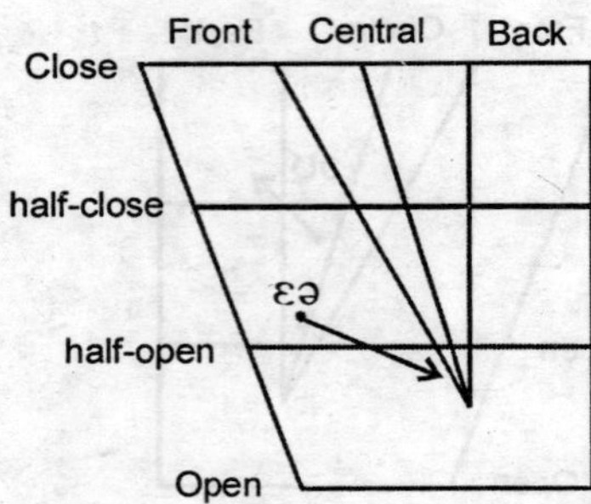

8. /ʊə/ fluent, newer, sure, tour, poor, curious, jewel, truant

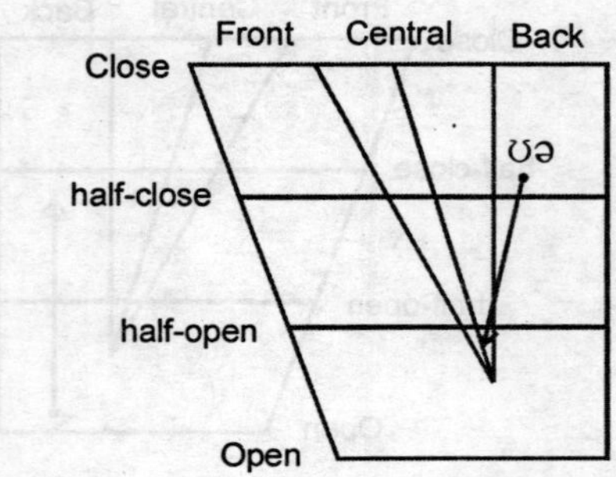

10.5 The tongue positions of all RP monophthongs and RP diphthongs:

RP monophthongs:

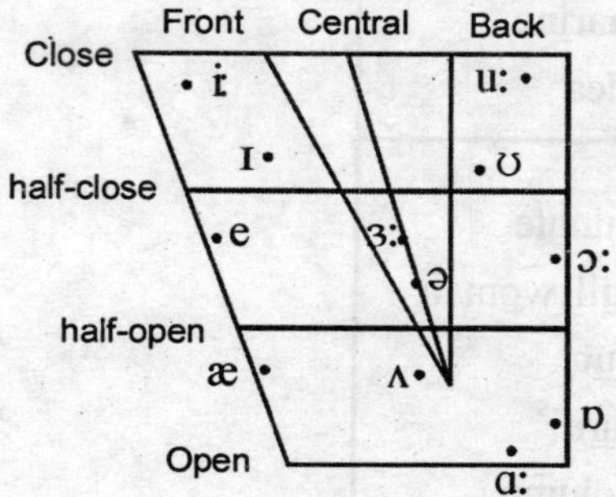

RP diphthongs:

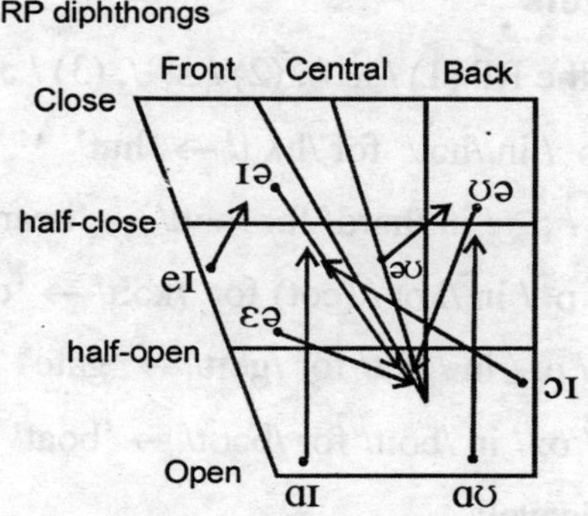

10.6 "a, e, i, o, u" and the sounds they represent

As you have seen, *a, e, i, o, u* are five letters of the alphabet that represent in writing *12 vowel sounds* alone or in combination. We have seen in phonetic script what these vowel sounds are and what spellings stand for these sounds. Now let's take a look at the vowel sounds that each of a, e, i, o, u letters represents.

letter	sound	word	letter	sound	word
1. **a**	/æ/	man	2. **e**	/e/	kettle
	/e/	many		/i:/	complete
	/ɑ:/	palm		/ɑ:/	clerk
	/ɒ/	what		/ə/	mother
	/ə/	abide		/ɪ/	refer
	/ɪ/	advocate		/ɜ:/	refer
	/ɔ:/	albeit		/eɪ/	elite
	/eɪ/	date		/ɪə/	hero, mere

3. i	/ɪ/	miss	
	/i:/	marine	
	/aɪ/	idea	
5. u	/ɪ/	minute	
	/ʊ/	full, woman	
	/ʌ/	cut	
	/ɜ:/	turn	
	/ə/	column	
	/u:/	pollution	

4. o	/ɒ/	cot
	/ʊ/	wolf
	/u:/	prove
	/ʌ/	come
	/ɜ:/	colonel
	/ə/	doctor
	/əʊ/	go
	/aʊ/	owl
	/ɪ/	women

10.7 A final word about vowels

We Indians have problems with the RP (1) / ʌ /, (2) / ɜ: /, (3) / ɔ: /, (4) / eɪ /, (5) / əʊ /.

We pronounce the RP / ʌ / as / ə / in /hət/ for /hʌ t/ → 'hut'

/ ɜ: / as / ə / in /hərd/ for /hɜd/ → 'heard'

/ ɔ: / as / ɒ / in /kɒt / (cot) for /kɔ:t/ → 'caught'

/ eɪ / as / e: / in /ge:t/ for /geɪt/ → 'gate'

/ əʊ / as / o: / in /bo:t/ for /bəʊt/ → 'boat'

So, please practise the RP vowels well.

10.8 Commonly mispronounced words—1

Listen to these on Track 16 on your CD.

The list below contain some ***very common*** words which we Indians tend to pronounce very differently from the generally accepted manner—known as RP. They are not difficult to learn to pronounce if you make the effort.

Listen to them on your CD and practise them in your lab and also at home. They are not difficult to learn. The maximum benefit from this practice is you'll be able to pronounce them well. Thc least benefit will be you'll find it easy to recognize and understand them when you come into contact with people who use RP.

abdomen	/ ˈæbdəmən /	able	/ ˈeɪbl/
ability	/ əˈbɪlɪtɪ /	about	/ əˈbaʊt /
above	/ əˈbʌv /	absurd	/ əbˈsɜ:d /
account	/ əˈkaʊnt /	advantage	/ ədˈvɑ:ntɪdʒ /
advertise	/ ˈædvətaɪz /	advertisement	/ ədˈvɜ:tɪsmənt /
alibi	/ ˈælɪbaɪ /	amateur	/ ˈæmtə(r) /
animal	/ ˈænɪml /	apparatus	/ æpəˈreɪtəs /
atmosphere	/ ˈætməsfɪə(r) /	attack	/ əˈtæk /
avoid	/ əˈvɔɪd /	award	/ əˈwɔ:d /
baggage	/ ˈbægɪdʒ /	balcony	/ ˈbælkənɪ /
ball	/ bɔ:l /	banana	/ bəˈnɑ:nə /
bargain	/ ˈbɑ:gən /	basket	/ ˈbɑ:skɪt /
binoculars	/ bɪˈnɒəkjələz /	biology	/ baɪˈɒlədʒɪ /
geology	/ dʒɪˈɒlədʒɪ /	ideology	/ aɪdɪˈɒlədʒɪ /
psychology	/ saɪˈkɒlədʒɪ /	technology	/ teknˈɒlədʒɪ /
biscuit	/ ˈbɪskɪt /	bottle	/ ˈbɒtl /
bridge	/ brɪdʒ /	casino	/ kəˈsi:nəʊ /
cassette	/ kəˈset /	caste	/ kɑ:st /
certainly	/ ˈsɜ:tnlɪ /	cinema	/ ˈsɪnəmə /
charisma	/ kəˈrɪzmə /	choir	/ ˈkwaɪə(r) /
class	/ klɑ:s /	colleague	/ ˈkɒli:g /
colloquial	/ kəˈləvkwɪəl /	college	/ ˈkɒlɪdʒ /
collusion	/ kəˈlu:zn /	command	/ kəˈmɑ:nd /
commercial	/ kəˈmɜ:ʃl /	comparable	/ ˈkɒəmprəbl /
competition	/ ˌkɒmpəˈtɪʃn /	competitor	/ kəmˈpetɪtə(r) /
competitive	/ kəmˈpetɪtɪv /	compulsory	/ kəmˈpʌlsərɪ /
conclusion	/ kənˈklu:ʒn /	condition	/ kənˈdɪʃn /
confusion	/ kənˈfju:ʒn /	consult	/ kənˈsʌlt /
corrupt	/ kəˈrʌpt /	cotton	/ ˈkɒtn /
coupon	/ ˈku:pɒn /	courier	/ ˈkʊrɪə(r) /

career / kə'rɪə(r) /
cousin / 'kʌzn /
cruel / 'kru:əl /
curious / 'kjʊərɪəs /
debris / 'debri: /
debut / 'deɪbju: /
decision / dɪ'sɪʒn /
delegate / 'delɪgət /
demand / dɪ'mɑ:nd /
develop / dɪ'veləp /
dictionary / 'dɪkʃənrɪ /
disease / dɪ'zi:z /
divorce / dɪ'vɔ:s /
economical / ˌi:kə'nɒmɪkl /
every / 'evrɪ /
except / ɪk'sept /
expertise / ˌekspɜ:'ti:z /
fanatic / fə'nætɪk /
fasten / 'fɑ:sn /
finale / fɪ'nɑ:lɪ /
garbage / 'gɑ:bɪdʒ /
generally / 'dʒenrəlɪ /
geography / dʒɪ'ɒgrəfɪ /
lithography / lɪθ'ɒgrəfɪ /
philosophy / fə'lɒsəfɪ /
gesture / 'dʒestʃə(r) /
goodbye / ˌgʊ'dbaɪ /
honest / 'ɒnɪst /
hook / huk /
hour / 'ɑʊə(r) /

carrier / 'kærɪə(r) /
crucial / 'kru:ʃl /
cucumber / 'kju:kʌmbə(r) /
dance / dɑ:ns /
debt / det /
decay / dɪ'keɪ /
decisive / dɪ'sɑɪsɪv /
delete / dɪ'li:t /
deposit / dɪ'pɒzɪt /
devotee / devə'ti: /
dinner / 'dɪnə(r) /
dissolve / dɪ'zɒlv /
document / 'dɒkjumənt /
elect / ɪ'lekt /
exam / ɪg'zæm /
executive / ɪg'zekjətɪv /
extempore / ek'stempərɪ /
fantastic / fæn'tæstɪk /
film / fɪlm / not / fɪlɪm /
food / fu:d /
Gemini / 'dʒemɪnaɪ /
gentleman/men / 'dʒentlmən /
biography / bɑɪ'ɒgrəfɪ /
photography / fət'ɒgrəfɪ /
geometry / dʒɪ'ɒmətrɪ /
glove / glʌv /
guava / 'gwɑ:və /
honour / 'ɒnə(r) /
hotel / həʊ'tel /
idea / ɑɪ'dɪə /

idle	/ ˈaɪdl /	illegal	/ ɪˈli:gl /
January	/ ˈdʒænjrʊərɪ /	February	/ ˈfebrʊərɪ /
July	/ dʒʊˈlaɪ /	October	/ ɒkˈtəʊbə(r) /
November	/ nəʊˈvembə(r) /	Wednesday	/ ˈwenzdeɪ /
listen	/ ˈlɪsn /	lower	/ ləʊə(r) /
machine	/ məˈʃi:n /	machinery	/ məˈʃi:nərɪ /
madam	/ ˈmædəm /	menu	/ ˈmenju: /
middle	/ ˈmɪdl /	modern	/ ˈmɒdn /
mosquito	/ məˈski:təʊ /	movement	/ ˈmu:vmənt /
Mrs	/ mɪsɪz /	Ms	/ mɪz /
naïve	/ naɪˈi:v /	one	/ wʌn /
onion	/ ˈʌnjən /	opponent	/ əˈpəʊnənt /
oven	/ ˈʌvn /	photograph	/ ˈfəʊtəgrɑ:f /
photographer	/ fəʊˈtɒgrəfə(r) /	photography	/ fəˈtɒgrəfɪ /
plumb	/ plʌm /	pollution	/ pəˈlu:ʃn /
possess	/ pəˈzes /	population	/ pɒpjuˈleɪʃn /
potato	/ pəˈteɪtəʊ /	product	/ ˈprɒdʌkt /
profession	/ prəˈfeʃn /	professor	/ prəˈfesə(r) /
pure	/ pjʊə(r) /	sure	/ ʃʊə(r) /
quality	/ ˈkwɒlətɪ /	question	/ ˈkwestʃən /
quote	/ kwəʊt /	receipt	/ rɪˈsi:t /
regular	/ ˈregjələ(r) /	ridiculous	/ rɪˈdɪkjələs /
robot	/ ˈrəʊbɒt /	salute	/ səˈlu:t /
sample	/ ˈsɑ:mpl /	science	/ ˈsaɪəns /
separate	/ ˈseprət /	society	/ səˈsaɪtɪ /
social	/ ˈsəʊʃl /	solution	/ səˈlu:ʃn /
souvenir	/ ˌsu:vəˈnɪə(r) /	student	/ ˈstju:dnt /
suggestion	/ səˈdʒestʃən /	taboo	/ təˈbu: /
technique	/ tekˈni:k /	thumb	/ θʌm /
tomato	/ təˈmɑ:təʊ /	tomb	/ tu:m /

twenty	/ ˈtwentɪ /	vehicle	/ ˈvi:kəl /
video	/ ˈvɪdɪəʊ /	woman	/ ˈwʊmən /
women	/ ˈwɪmɪn /	elevan	/ ɪˈlevn/
twelve	/ twelv /	stupid	/ ˈstju:pɪd /
garage	/ ˈgærɑ:ʒ / (or) / ˈgærɑ:dʒ /	bouquet	/ bʊˈkeɪ /
buffet	/ ˈbʊfeɪ / (or) / ˈbʌfeɪ /	restaurant	/ ˈrestrɒnt /

10.9 Commonly mispronounced words—2

Here are a few pairs that we use very frequently but make mistakes in pronouncing them. Each word in each pair should be pronounced properly to distinguish between the roles they play in sentences.

Listen to them on Track 17 on your CD and practise them in your lab and also at home. They are not difficult to learn.

1.	conduct (verb)	/ kənˈdʌkt /	11.	object (verb)	/ əbˈdʒekt /
	conduct (noun)	/ ˈkɒndʌkt /		object (noun)	/ ˈɒbdʒɪkt /
2.	conflict (verb)	/ kənˈflɪkt /	12.	perfect (verb)	/ pəˈfekt /
	conflict (noun)	/ ˈkɒnflɪkt /		perfect (adjective)	/ ˈpɜ:fɪkt /
3.	content (noun)	/ ˈkɒntent /	13.	permit (verb)	/ pəˈmɪt /
	content (adjective)	/ kənˈtent /		permit (noun)	/ ˈpɜ:mɪt /
4.	contest (noun)	/ ˈkɒntest /	14.	present (verb)	/ prɪˈzent /
	contest (verb)	/ kənˈtest /		present (noun/adj)	/ ˈpreznt /
5.	contract (verb)	/ kənˈtrækt /	15.	produce (verb)	/ prəˈdju:s /
	contract (noun)	/ ˈkɒntrækt /		produce (noun)	/ ˈprɒdju:s /
6.	contrast (verb)	/ kənˈtrɑ:st /	16.	progress(verb)	/ prəˈgres /
	contrast (noun)	/ ˈkɒntrɑ:st /		progress (noun)	/ ˈprɒgres /
7.	converse (verb)	/ kənˈvɜ:s /	17.	project (verb)	/ prəˈdʒekt/
	converse (noun/adj)	/ ˈkɒnvɜ:s /		project (noun)	/ ˈprɒdʒekt/
8.	convert (verb)	/ kənˈvɜ:t /	18.	prospect (verb)	/ prəˈspekt /
	convert (noun)	/ ˈkɒnvɜ:t /		prospect (noun)	/ ˈprɒspekt /
9.	convict (verb)	/ kənˈvɪkt /	19.	protest (verb)	/ prəˈtest /
	convict (noun)	/ ˈkɒnvɪkt /		protest (noun)	/ ˈprəʊtest /
10.	import (verb)	/ ɪmˈpɔ:t /	20.	subject (verb)	/ səbˈdʒekt /
	import (noun)	/ ˈɪmpɔ:t /		subject (noun)	/ ˈsʌbdʒekt /

10.10 Consonants

Vowels are *sounds* that are produced as the air escapes through the mouth freely and continuously without any audible friction (=stop). The lips are open.

When we utter consonants, the free *flow* of air out of the lungs is *impeded* (= obstructed) by the lower lip and the tongue. Also, the vocal cords are held either wide apart (without vibration = buzzing sound) or loosely together and vibrate (with buzzing sound).

[p, t, k, t ʃ, f, θ, s, ʃ, h] are voiceless consonants and

[b, d, g, dʒ, v, ð, z, ʒ, m, n, ŋ, l, r, j, w] are voiced. Consonants are voiceless when there is no vibration. They are voiced when there is a vibration.

Try this:

Cover your ears with your palms. Say this one by one: b, d, g, dʒ, v, ð, z, ʒ, m, n, ŋ, l, r, j, w. Each time you'll here a buzz in your ears. So they are all **voiced** consonants. Say these one by one: p, t, k, t ʃ, f, θ, s, ʃ, h. Each time you'll here no such buzz. So they are **voiceless** consonants.

letters	words	sounds	letters	words	sounds
b	bed	/bed/	r	rat	/ræt/
c,(k)	cat	/kæt/	s	sick	/sɪk/
c,(s)	cell	/sel/	t	tea	/ti:/
	chloride	/'klɔ:raɪd /	v	very	/verɪ/
d	dog	/dɒg/	w	one	/wʌn/
f	fat	/fæt/		wife	/waɪf/
g	give	/gɪv/	x	fax	/fæks/
	gentle	/'dʒentl/		xerox	/'zɪərɒks/
h	hat	/hæt/		exact	/ig'zækt/
j	jam	/dʒæm/	y	many	/menɪ/
k	kill	/kɪl /		yes	/jes/
	quay	/ki:/	z	zinc	/zɪŋk/
l	lamb	/læm/	tʃ	chain	/tʃeɪn/
m	man	/mæn/	θ	think	/θɪŋk/
n	nib	/nɪb/	ð	then	/ðen/
p	pin	/pɪn/	ʃ	sheep	/ʃi:p/
q	quick	/kwɪk/	ʒ	measure	/meʒə/
	queue	/kju:/	ŋ	single	/'sɪŋgl/
	curious	/'kjuərɪəs/	ŋ	sink	/sɪŋk/

Voiceless	Production	Voiced
	plosives	
	air stopped by	
p	lower lip against upper lip	b
t *1	tongue against teeth-ridge	d *1
k	back of tongue against roof of mouth	g
	fricatives	
	air passage narrowed between	
f	lower lip and upper teeth	v *2
θ*3	tip of tongue and upper teeth	ð *3
s	tip of tongue and teeth ridge	z *4
ʃ*5	front of tongue and back of teeth ridge	ʒ *5
	with wider opening than for (s, z)	
	affricates	
tʃ	like (S, “) but tip of tongue touching	dʒ
	teeth-ridge to make a complete stop at first.	
	nasals	
	nasal passage open and	
	mouth stopped as for (b)	m
	mouth stopped as for (d)	n
	mouth stopped as for (g)	ŋ
	semi vowels	
	lips are rounded and the tongue and	
	the lips move quickly to the position	w *2
	of next vowel like very short [I]	j *6
	vowel-like in its articulation	r *7
	lateral	
	tip of tongue touching teeth or teeth	
	ridge, air escapes from the sides of	*l*
	the tongue	
	glottal fricative	
h	air escapes through a narrow glottis	

We, Indians, do not pronounce / t /, / d /, / ʃ /, / v /, / θ /, / ð /, / s /, / z /, / ʃ /, / ʒ /, / w /, / j /, / r / properly. It's not difficult to learn to pronounce these consonants. You'll now listen to these on Track 18 on your CD.

*1. / t / and / d /

You should pronounce these sounds by placing the tip and the blade of your tongue against your teeth ridge, that is, your tongue touching the part of the mouth behind your upper front teeth. (Don't let your tongue curve and touch the roof of your mouth.)

For every word, listen to me, press pause, repeat.

teak, tick, technique, tack, task, top, talk, tool, tuck, turn

deed, did, dead, dad, dance, dog, door, doom, dug, dirt

*2. /v/ and /w/

Many of us pronounce /v/ without friction by placing our lower lip on our upper front teeth. We shouldn't do this but only bring our lower lip very close to the edge of our upper teeth, so that there is a narrow open space. When we pronounce /v/ this way, the air passes through the narrow space with friction.

Listen to the pronunciation of these words, press pause, repeat:

vaccine, vacuum, valid, value, vanity, variety, vegetable, very, victim, video

We pronounce / w/ like / v / without friction. Pronounce /w/ with rounded lips. That is, form your lips like a circle to produce / w /. Listen to these words, press pause, repeat:

wage, waist, walk, wander, warning, weapon, week, wedding, wheel, which, work

Listen carefully to the pronunciation of each pair, press pause, repeat:

verse	worse	veal	wheel	vine	wine	vile	while
veil	wail	avail	away	vary	wary		

*3. / θ / and / ð /

Many of us pronounce these two sounds by placing the tip of the tongue behind your upper front teeth. But the tip of the tongue should make a light contact with the upper front teeth.

For each of these words, listen, press pause, repeat:

thank, think, theme, thought, thousand, throat, thumb

than, then, there, thus, they, this, that

*4. / z /

Pronounce / z / by bringing the tip and the blade of your tongue very close to the part of the mouth behind your upper front teeth. Don't pronounce / z / like /   / as in 'judge'.

For each of these words, listen, press pause, repeat:

zero, zinc, zip, zone, zoo, zoom

*5./ ʃ / and / ʒ /

Pronounce these by (1) raising the front of the tongue towards the roof and (2) bringing the tip and the blade of the tongue very close to the teeth ridge.

For each of these words, listen, press pause, repeat:

ship, sheep, shirk, shrunk, shun, shoe, shape, shut

pleasure, measure, treasure, usual

*6. / w / / j / Semi-vowels

These are classified as consonants because they do not form the nucleus of a syllable. Only a vowel can occur in the nuclear position in a syllable: cat, howl, prove, alive, wave, young, very, but

*7. [r] This is pronounced only before a vowel sound. This is pronounced as

butter	/'bʌtə/
butter and jam	/ 'bʌtər ən dʒæm/
father	/ 'fɑ:ðə /
father ate the bread	/fɑ:ðər eit ðə bred

8. In the following words, the underlined consonants are not pronounced:

debt", dumb, thumb, comb, receipt, judge, bouquet, handsome, handkerchief, grandmother, cupboard, coup, adjust, adjective, often, subtle, sachet, farm, charter, palm, calm, island, oven

9. consonants mispronounced

The sound represented by "z" is mispronounced as "j": zero

The sound represented by "s" is to be pronounced as "z", not as 'j': thousand

The sound represented by "s" is to be pronounced as "z", not as "s": news

The sound represented by "w" is mispronounced as "o": twelve twenty

The sound represented by "w" is mispronounced as "v": when, wet, water

The sound represented by "qu" is to be pronounced as "kw": colloquial, quote

The sound represented by "u" is to be pronounced as "oo": pollution,

The sound represented by "f" is to be pronounced as "v": of

10. The sound represented by the letters "sh" is mispronounced as "s":

    she, **ship**, **shoe**, **shun**

11. The sound represented by the letters "su" is mispronounced as

    "z" : mea**su**re   trea**su**re

    [or]

    "sh" : mea**su**re   trea**su**re

12. There is a tendency to not pronounce the sound for "w" in

    won't   **w**ool

13. There is a tendency to begin with "i" to words like:

    i**s**tart   i**s**chool   i**s**creen

10.11 Tongue twisters

Practise these and have fun!

1. A skunk sat on a stump and thunk the stump stunk,
   but the stump thunk the skunk stunk.

2. Peter Piper picked a peck of pickled peppers.
   Did Peter Piper pick a peck of pickled peppers?
   If Peter Piper picked a peck of pickled peppers,
   where's the peck of pickled peppers Peter Piper picked?

3. Red lorry, yellow lorry, red lorry, yellow lorry.

4. Betty Botter had some butter,
   "But," she said, "this butter's bitter.
   If I bake this bitter butter,
   it would make my batter bitter.
   But a bit of better butter—
   that would make my batter better."
   So she bought a bit of butter,
   better than her bitter butter,
   and she baked it in her batter,
   and the batter was not bitter.
   So 'twas better Betty Botter
   bought a bit of better butter.

5. A big black bug bit a big black bear,
   made the big black bear bleed blood.

6. She sells sea shells by the sea shore.
The shells she sells are surely seashells.
So if she sells shells on the seashore,
I'm sure she sells seashore shells.

7. Shy Shelly says she shall sew sheets

8. Which wristwatches are Swiss wristwatches?

9. Lesser leather never weathered wetter weather better

10. How much wood would a woodchuck chuck
if a woodchuck could chuck wood?
He would chuck, he would, as much as he could,
and chuck as much wood as a woodchuck would
if a woodchuck could chuck wood.

11. We surely shall see the sun shine soon

12. Which witch wished which wicked wish?

13. Twelve twins twirled twelve twigs

14. Truly rural

15. The blue bluebird blinks

16. Ed had edited it

17. Freshly fried fresh flesh.

18. What time does the wristwatch strap shop shut?

19. Mix, Miss Mix

20. Selfish shellfish

21. Upper roller, lower roller

22. Red lorry, yelow lorry

23. Which wristwatch are Switch wristwatches?

24. Tragedy strategy

10.12 Accent

When we pronounce one part of an English word more than the other parts, it's known as *accent*. In other words, we pronounce one or more parts of a word with less force and another part with more force. The parts of a word are known as syllables.

A syllable is made up of one or more speech sounds with a vowel in it. There can be no syllable without a vowel in it. Words can have one syllable or more than one syllable.

We must remember that we produce sounds in groups to form words and that words may have several letters. So there can be a difference between how we pronounce sounds in groups and how we write them with the letters of the alphabet:

Look at these words:

one syllable words	:	go, eat, feel, field, screen, straight
two syllable words	:	a|bove, in|fant, per|mit, free|dom,
three syllable words	:	e|du|cate, po|si|tion, no|mi|nate
four syllable words	:	ex|cel|lent|ly, cor|res|pond|ence
five syllable words	:	ac|com|mo|da|tion, ac|cu|mu|la|tion

note: The vertical bars indicate the number of syllables. We mark the accent with a **vertical bar** ['] on that syllable of a word which is heard more than other syllables:

(i) There is <u>no</u> need to mark the accent if the word is of <u>one</u> syllable.

view see leap kept quick large teeth next child straight

(ii) When there is more than one syllable, the syllable that is heard more than the other is marked as shown below:

a'go a'bove fa'ther sai'lor no'tice per'mit re'lease
'educate 'advertise 'citizen 'nobody con'nection
ac'celerate recog'nition recon'struction eligi'bility
accommo'dation accumu'lation

The following guidelines will help you decide where to put the accent with the help of the vertical bar [as shown above]:

1. words with <u>weak prefixes</u> receive the accent on the <u>root</u>:

a 'broad a'lone a'cross a'head be'come be'neath be'low

2. The accent of the root words applies to words derived with suffixes [added at the end of root words] like **–s, -es, -ed, -ing, -age, -ance, -en, -er, -y, -ess, -ful, -hood, -ice, -ish, -ive, -less, -ly, -ment, -ness, -or, -ship, -ter, -ure, -zen:**

   ˈvillage —ˈvillage**s** ˈmango—ˈmango**es** reˈpeat—reˈpeat**ed**

   beˈgin—beˈginn**ing** ˈmarry—ˈmarri**age** ˈenter—ˈentr**ance** ˈbeauty—ˈbeauti**ful**

   ˈactor— ˈactr**ess** reˈlation—reˈlation**ship** ˈbitter—ˈbitter**ness** ˈlaugh—ˈlaugh**ter**

   ˈbroad—ˈbroad**en**—ˈbroad**er** ˈwidow—ˈwidow**hood** ˈcoward—ˈcoward**ice**

   ˈstyle—ˈstyl**ish** cogˈn**ition**—cogˈnit**ive** apˈpoint—appoint**ment** ˈact—ˈactor

   ˈactual—ˈactual**ly** ˈmeaning—ˈmeaning**less** reˈgret—reˈgret**ful** ˈcity—ˈciti**zen**

3. words ending **-ion** have the accent on the syllable previous to it:

   examiˈnat**ion** appliˈcation determiˈnation deterioˈration legisˈlation defaˈmation globaliˈsation recommenˈdation

4. words ending in **–ic, -ical, -ically-, -ious, -ial, -ially**, have the accent on the syllable previous to it:

   eˈlectric eˈlectrical ˈradically cereˈmonious confiˈdential confiˈdentially

5. word ending in **–ity**, have the accent on the third syllable from the end:

   reˈliability geneˈrosity deˈpendability

6. word ending in **–al, -ally** shift their accent:

   ˈresident resiˈdential ˈorigin oˈriginal ˈincident inciˈdental

Here is a list of some **very common words** with accent marked (Listen to Track 19 on your CD):

ˈabsent	absenˈtee	abˈsorb	ˈaccent	acˈcept	adˈvance
exˈample	acˈcount	adˈdition	adˈmire	ˈadvertise	iˈmagine
toˈbacco	inˈdustry	comˈplete	hoˈrizon	sucˈceed	sugˈgest
aˈbroad	beˈfore	supˈport	preˈpare	atˈtack	beˈtween
oˈpinion	interˈrupt	opˈpose	umˈbrella	transˈlate	perˈmission
aˈgree	agˈreement	emˈployee	deˈfend	ˈrecognise	ˈpolitics
poˈlitical	poliˈtician	forˈget	deˈgree	uniˈversity	diˈgest
ˈkitchen	ˈhistory	hisˈtoric	efˈfect	deˈvelop	caˈdet
reˈceipt	poˈlice	ˈexpert	experˈtise	reˈject	poˈtato
casˈsette	ˈrobot	adˈvertisement	comˈparison	ˈphotograph	phoˈtographer
photoˈgraphic					

Listen to these words on Track 19 on your CD.

Place the **accent** mark ['] at the right place in the following words:

1. defeat	2. contamination	3. conduct [as verb]	4. teaching
5. certain	6. examination	7. produce [as noun]	8. consist
9. affect	10. release	11. female	12. editorial
13. bottom	14. delay	15. avoid	16. factual
17. revelation	18. exhibition	19. psychology	20. geography
21. environment	22. individuality	23. parapsychology	24. computerisation
25. rigid	26. availability	27. development	28. conservation
29. intricate	30. appeal	31. massage	32. economic
33. commercial	34. advantageous	35. convert [v]	36. convert [n]
37. convict [v]	38. convict [n]	39. survey [v]	40. survey [n]
41. permit [v]	42. permit [n]	43. atmosphere	44. photograph
45. photographer	46. electricity	47. pollution	48. community
49. commercial	50. commerce	51.pioneering	52. location
53. post	54. academic	55. decline	56. academy
57. academician	58. correct	59. simplicity	60. equality
61. afternoon	62. morality	63. moral	64. morale
65. English	66. originality	67. memorial	68. scientific
69.action	70. employ	72. engineer	73. doctor
74. precede	75. technology	76. persuade	77. production

10.13 Intonation—1 (Listen to Track 20 on your CD)

A

English is a language very different from a language like, say, Thelugu. When you speak a word in Thelugu, you pronounce equally every sound it contains and your friend hears every sound pronounced equally. For instance when you say 'abhiprayam', you pronounce all the seven sounds equally and your friend hears all the seven sounds equally. So when you speak words in Thelugu, your voice doesn't rise and fall, it's at the same level from the first sound to the last.

But when you say 'opinion', you should not speak all the sounds equally but pronounce 'p' louder than the other sounds and your friend will hear 'p' louder than others.

Another example. When you say 'bhugolam', you pronounce all the sounds equally and your friend hears all the sounds pronounced equally. That is, your voice doesn't rise and fall. But when you say 'geography', you should say 'o' louder than others and your friend will hear 'o' louder than others.

You should realize the importance of this difference between saying words in Thelugu and English. And you should bring out this difference when you utter words in English.

In the previous track, you learnt to say certain sounds in words louder than others.

B

The same difference applies also when we speak sentences. When I say this Thelugu sentence '*meerakkdikelle loga athanelli pothe*?', I pronounce the sounds equally. That is, my voice moves at the same level at which it began. There is no rise-fall, fall-rise. Only at the end, there is a rising tone, which of course indicates I asked a question. Now I say this: '*What if he left before you reached there*?' Did you hear my voice rise and fall? No because I spoke the English question sentence the same way I spoke the Thelugu question sentence. This is how Indians normally say sentences in English.

Sentences in English are not said with a level voice. Now listen to this: *What if he left before you reached there*? You heard me, didn't you, pronouncing 'w' in 'what', 'l' in 'left', 'f' in 'before', 'r' in 'reached' louder than others. I said the other sounds at the same level.

Whatifhi **l**eft be**f**oreyou **r**eachedthere?

This is known as 'rhythm'.

Shall we practise this 'level-rise-fall-level-rise-fall-level? Listen to each sentence carefully, press pause and repeat until you get it right each time:

She wanted me to meet her this evening.

He came late to class.

When he reached home, he found the door locked.

What do you think you're doing?

Did you watch yesterday's game?

Turn to the right at the end of the street.

That's not what I wanted to ask you about.

It would have better if he hadn't taken her seriously for she wasn't worth his attention.

I'm sure you now have a very good idea of how to speak sentences in English. Practise at home with other sentences until you're comfortable with the 'rise and fall'.

10.14 Intonation – 2

(i) The nucleus / tonic syllable is that one which receives the pitch movement. Generally speaking the tonic syllable is the primary syllable of the last important word in a given group of words

He's a `teacher.

I 'hear your 'son 'married a `widow.

My 'brother has ar`rived. / He's pre'senting a 'paper in the `conference. "Teacher", "widow", "conference" are the last important words: the primary syllables "tea", "wi" and "con" indicate the pitch movement and are known as tonic syllables.

(ii) It's also possible to change the pitch movement to syllables in the earlier words depending on the meaning we want to convey: (Listen to these sentences on Track 21 on your CD.)

I 'love `coffee. (I may not like tea.)

I `love 'coffee. (Emphasis is on the act of loving.)

`I love 'coffee. (not my wife)

I love coffee.

I love coffee.

I love coffee.

I love coffee.

The sentence is repeated four times. But they don't convey the same meaning. Because the way I said each of them.

I 'love `coffee.

This is an ordinary statement which indicates your liking for something.

I 'love `coffee.

I `love 'coffee.

`I love 'coffee.

The way I said these three sentences, you must've understood they give messages in addition to the message when I said it the first time.

I 'love `coffee. The additional message is: I may not like tea. [depending on the context]

I `love 'coffee. The additional message is: I just don't drink it, I enjoy it.

`I 'love 'coffee. The additional message is: My wife doesn't. [depending on the context]

Here is another example to indicate different messages through pitch movement:

I spoke to him yesterday on my way home.

Normally, when someone says this to us, we hear 'spoke', 'yesterday' and 'home' louder than 'I', 'to' or 'on my way' because in English we **don't** utter **all** the words with equal force like we do in Indian languages. This is known as 'stress' pattern.

But when we want to give special focus to a particular word, we speak that word with more force than the other words: (Listen to track 21 on your CD)

ˋI *spoke to him yesterday on my way home.*

The stress on 'I' means 'it's I, not anybody else' who spoke to him.

I ˋspoke *to him yesterday on my way home.*

The stress on 'spoke' means 'I spoke to him, not hit him'.

I spoke to ˋhim *yesterday on my way home.*

The stress on 'him' means 'I spoke to him, not anybody else'.

I spoke to him ˋyesterday *on my way home.*

The stress on 'yesterday' means 'I spoke to him yesterday, not today'.

I spoke to him yesterday ˋon way home.

The stress on 'on my way home' means

'I spoke to him yesterday on my way home, not 'anywhere else'.

Such stress on different parts of a sentence helps us communicate different **messages.**

10.15 Intonation – 3

Listen to Track 22 on your CD.

There are three basic intonation tunes:

(a)the falling tone (b) the rising tone (c) the rising and the falling tone

1. When we speak statements, the voice (the tone) **falls** on the last content word:

   Listen to each sentence carefully, press pause and repeat:

   I'll ˈspeak toˋhim.

   The ˈaged ˈProfessor ˈwent on adˈvising without ˈbothering about the ˈsentiments of the ˋaudience.

   He ˈleft lastˋnight.

   They ˈcome and ˈgo as theyˋwish.

2. When we command or exclaim, the voice (the tone) **falls** on the last content word:

   ˋSit down! Don't ˈleave theˋroom! ˋGive it to me. ˈDo it toˋday. ˈClose the ˋwindows!

   ˈWhat aˋsunset! ˈWhat aˋgoal! ˈWhat a ˈbeautiful ˋflower! ˈHow aˋnnoying!

3. When we ask 'wh' questions, the voice (the tone) **falls** on the last content word:

   ˈWhen will they ˈreachˋDelhi?

   ˈWho's ˈgoing to ˈwin theˋcontest?

   ˈWhy did youˋgo there?

   ˈWhat will you do ˋnow?

   ˈWhich of these do you ˋwant?

(b) When we begin sentences with **a single word**, **a phrase** or **a clause**, the tone **rises** on the last content word:

(i) incomplete expressions (appended words, phrases, clauses)

ˏLuckily, / I was ˈable to ˈmake it to the ˋinterview.

It's eight O' ˏclock/ and the ˈnewspaper hasn't ˋcome yet.

ˈWhen I ˈread the ˏletter / I was ˋshocked.

(ii) yes - no questions

ˈDid you acˈcept the proˏposal ?

ˈHaven't you ˏseen it yet ?

ˈIsn't the news ˏtrue?

(iii) wh-questions enquiring in a warm and friendly manner.

ˈHow d'you ˈfeel ˏnow?

ˈWhat is the ˏmatter?

ˈWhy did you ˏgo there?

(iv) polite requests or invitations

ˈDo ˈcome ˏin.

ˈplease ˈshut the ˏdoor.

(c) falling and rising tone

When we imply there's something more that what we say :

ˈShe's ᵛclever (= she's clever but cannot keep secrets)

The ᵛcoffee was good (= but the service was not)

The college has ᵛfine buildings(= but teaching is poor)

You had no problem practicing these, did you? That's because you have all these tones in Thelugu.

PART TWO

This part deals with the Syllabus topics listed under 'train2success.com':

1. Preparing for being Interviewed
2. Interviewing Skills

These two topics have already been dealt with under 4 in **PART ONE.**

3. Telephone Skills

3.1 A description—factors affecting communication

So far, we've dealt with face-to-face pair communication. Let's see how we should communicate through the telephone. Since communication takes place between two faceless persons it will not be possible to use body language to interact effectively or to repair any damage occurring from poor use of language. Besides, words can be missed or misheard because of the noise around, because of the poor acoustic quality of the telephone link or because of poor articulation. Therefore it's essential to use appropriate tone, accurate articulation and right loudness of voice. The person on the other side can be very impatient or irritating, to add another problem. Hence, there's a great need to exercise patience and control over emotions. Moreover, the other person should not be left to make guesses about what is being said. The information to be provided should be complete; the other caller should not be made to ask several questions to understand what is being sought or asked for. Similarly, every attempt should be made to receive accurately the information being given. But the major controlling factor is the relationship between the pair. Care should be taken in the use of language and tone if the other person is a stranger, a customer, an official or a superior.

3.2 Sample conversations: (You've already practised 1, 2, 3, 4, 5, 6, 8, 9, 11. You can, if you wish, play these roles again. But 7, 10, 12, 13, 14 are new. Practise them in class)

1.

The telephone rings
"Hello!"
"Is Sundar there?"
"Which Sundar?"
"What do you mean?"
"There's no Sundar here."
"How come? Oh, isn't that 2627 5533?"
"Wrong number!" (idiot!)

2.

Hello!
Isn't that 2627 5335?
No.
Sorry I bothered you!
No problem. (That's okay.)

3.

Hello!
Can I speak to Sundar?
Which number do you want?
Isn't that 2627 5335?
No.
I'm sorry to have troubled you.
It's OK.

4.

"Hello!"
"Is that 2627 5533?"
"Yes."
"Can I speak to Sundar?"
"Who do I say is calling?"
"Kapil, a friend of Sundar's."
"Please hold on. Sundar, a call for you."

5.

"Hello!"
"Is that 2627 5533?"
"Yes."
"Can I speak to Sundar? I'm Kapil, a friend of Sundar's."
"Please hold on. Sundar, a call for you."

In 1, both the speakers are ignorant of telephone etiquette. Neither is courteous. Besides, they've wasted time and money. In 2, both are knowledgeable and courteous. Dialling a number wrongly is not uncommon. In 3, a little time is wasted because the caller assumes he has dialed the correct number. 4 and 5 are good examples of telephone use except that in 4 Sundar's friend identified himself only after being asked and thus wasted a few seconds.

A few **conversations**: formal and informal

6.

```
"Mr Kumar's residence."*1
"Could I speak to Mr
  Kumar?"*2
"May I know who is
  speaking?"*3
"I'm Raghavan*4, a friend
  of Mr Kumar's."
"Will you please hold on?"
"Yes, thank you."
```

Other possible ways of saying 1,2, 3 and 4:

*1 This is 2649 1222./Kumar here./ Kumar speaking.

*2 Is Mr Kumar in?/I'd like to speak to Mr Kumar.

*3 Who may I say is calling?/Who do I say is calling?/Who should I say is calling?

*4 My name is Raghavan.

7.

"Sundaram here."
" Good morning, Mr Sundaram. Sorry to bother you. [It's okay.] My name is Narayanan. I have an appointment with you tomorrow at 11 a.m. I'm sorry I won't be able to make it."
"I see. Thank you for calling."
"Could I possibly see you same time Thursday instead?"
"I'm not too sure. You may contact my P.A. later in the day

8.

"This is double two three six seven nine O." [2236790]
"Good morning. Is Mr Narasimhan in?"
"I'm his mother. He's gone to keep an appointment."
"Oh. Is he likely to be back soon?"
"Are you by any chance Mr Murugan,?"
"Yes, Mam."
"He said he had already put in a word to Mrs ……… and you could meet her the day after tomorrow at 3.30 p.m."
"Thank you, mam."
"You're welcome."
"Please convey my regards to Narasimhan."

9.

"This is double two three six seven nine O." [2236790]
"Good morning. Is Mr Narasimhan in?"
"I'm his mother. He's gone to keep an appointment."
"Oh. Is he likely to be back soon?"
" ….I don't really know. May I know your name so I can inform my son.?"
"Rajan, a colleague of his."
"I see. I can take a message."
"Thank you, Mam [Not at all.] but I'll call again around five. If he comes earlier, ask him to give me a call,"
"Okay."

6, 7, 8, 9 are formal but personal calls.

10.

"Good afternoon, British council."
"Could you connect me to Mr Jones?"
"Who may I say is calling?"
"I'm Reuben. I'd like to invite him for our College Day."
"Just a moment, sir……………. "Yes, Gita!" "Sir, a Mr Reuben is on the line." "I'll speak to him." "Mr Reuben, Mr Jones is on the line."
"Thank you. Hi, James!"
"Hello, Jack. How are you?"
"Fine. How's Stella? And Grace?"
"They're fine. How about your family?"
"They are all right. Our College Day is next Thursday at 2 p.m. Are you free to chat with our PG literature students?"
" Just a sec. Let me check my diary…..Yes, I am."
" Don't worry about the transport. Will send an official request tomorrow. Bye."

11.

"Good afternoon, TVS."
" I'd like to speak to the service engineer."
"Just a moment, please….. Excuse me, the service engineer is unavailable. Will anyone else do?"
"Yes, thank you……….Am I speaking to the deputy service engineer?"
"Yes, sir. What can we do for you?"[How can we help?/Can I be of help?]
"I'm Gopalarathinam, Professor at IIT. My car was supposed to be ready last evening. Its registration number is TN—01 Y3254."
"Just a moment, sir……I'm afraid it's not ready yet. You may collect it tomorrow at 10a.m."
"But……"
"Sorry to interrupt you, Prof. We ran out of stock of one spare part. In fact, yours is one of the cars being attended to right now."
"Couldn't I have it later in the day?"
"Much as we are eager to oblige you, it's being driven out for the last leg of servicing."
"Last leg of servicing?"
"Yes, Dr Gopalarathinam. It'll be driven through the streets to check its fitness state. Should there be any problem, we'll need time to attend to it. Hence the delivery tomorrow."
"You've made me happy. Thank you for your time and explanation."
"The pleasure is ours, Prof."
"Good night, Mr……"
"Thomson, Joe Thomson."
"Thank you very much, Mr Thomson."

12. Here's another formal and official conversation, besides 10 and 11.

"Good morning, FRS!"
"Good morning. I'm GM—Purchases, C&C Services. I wish to speak to your GM—Sales."
"I'm afraid he's out of town; he will be back only Monday next."
"Oh, no!"
"The Deputy GM is available, sir, if you wish to speak to her."
"Okay………………….Am I speaking to Deputy GM—Sales?"
"Yes, sir. How can I help you?"
"We received a thousand watches the day before. According to our Inspection Department, half of them are not in working condition. They were meant to be Deepavali gifts to our workers."
"I'm very sorry to hear that, sir. But though I don't have the authority to do what I'm going to do, if you will send someone with proper authorization and identification, I'll arrange for 500 watches in perfect condition."
"Am I relieved! Thank you Ms……."
"Hemalatha Chandrasekar."
"Ms Hemalatha, I won't forget your timely help, I assure you. And I'm Raghavan."
"This is no help but serving a valuable customer. You may please return the defective ones through your agent."
"Of course. Thank you once again, Ms Hemalatha. Good-bye."

Here are two informal conversations:

13.

"Good afternoon, FRS!"
"Good afternoon! I'm Badrinath, GM—Purchases, ABC Services. I'd like a word with your Deputy GM—Sales, if he is available. Isn't he Mr Ravindran?"
"Yes, Mr Raghavan. In a moment, please. "Sir, Mr Raghavan, GM—Purchases, ABC Services wishes to speak to you." "Put him through, please." "Yes, sir." Sir, Mr Ravindran is on the line."
"Thank you. Hello, Ravi!"
"How are you, Raghav?"
"Not fine! You people have dropped 500 useless watches in my lap. They were to be Deepavali gifts. What a mess you've put me into!"
"Sorry. Raghav. These things do happen, you know."
"Don't you imagine I'm getting soft! I want 500 new watches in perfect condition by this evening."
"I can understand your position. But my boss isn't coming for another two days."
"Oh, God…. But…"
" Just wait, will you? ……..All right. I'm exceeding my authority. I'll have 500 watches sent first thing in the morning."
"Thanks a lot, Ravi."
"I've put trust in your report. What else, Raghav?"
"Well, why don't you drop by, this weekend?"
"Mm, if God wills it, yes. Bye."

14.

"Somasundaram speaking."
"Any news, Somu?"
"Looks as if you phoned up only to know if there's any news."
"Normally there is, isn't there? Well, what gives?"
"Heard about Raju?"
"Yes, can you believe it! He's gone out of his mind, don't you think?"
"Because he's married a lady fifteen years older?"
"A lady? Say a hag."
"Why so vehement? Seen her?"
"A lady fifteen years older and not a hag? How crazy can he get!"
" I doubt it... May be the money did the trick. Or may be he's just being clever!"
"Is she rich?"
"Rich? Stinkingly rich she is! But Raju never had any respect for the money god, did he?"
"Oh, people do change, don't they?"

3.3 Telephone etiquette

In the absence of face-to-face communication, the telephone is one link to the outside world. It's not always possible to meet someone in person, nor will it be necessary to speak directly to someone. In the past, letters were written. Today, the telephone comes in handy. Though it is one of the most popular tools for personal or business purposes, we don't make the best use of it.

Every human social behaviour depends on the context in which it takes place—whether we communicate in person or over the phone. We need to maintain a certain level of formality where it is necessary. So, it makes no difference if we are answering the phone or making calls. When we use a language and a tone appropriate to the caller or the receiver, when we are fully prepared to receive information or to give information without wasting time, conversation through the telephone becomes a pleasant experience for both the participants.

However, what happens in reality is generally not pleasant at all. Here are some possible reactions:

- "The telephone seems to ring endlessly and dies."
- "They place me on hold for hours together, it seems."
- "The line remains engaged for hours, it appears."
- "It seems I keep talking for ages only to realize that I've been speaking to a wrong person."
- "When someone other than the one I want to speak to receives the call, they are not helpful."
- "They transfer me to a wrong person."
- "They tell me to call back without giving me a name or number or division to ask for."

- "The receiver says, 'Wait', but takes a long time to come back on the phone."
- " Sometimes, I seem to get the impression that I'm disrupting their work."

Relationships, personal or business, are not meant to break. But they will if our communication is casual, indifferent, aggressive or even rude.
It's not difficult to avoid a breakdown. Make sure your voice, language, tone and information are **receiver-friendly.**

Remember the following while making or receiving calls:

1. Answer calls within three or four rings.
2. Switch off TV/radio or minimize the volume when calling or taking calls.
3. Have a pen and a pad ready to note important information.
4. Have someone take messages in your absence.
5. Greet the caller appropriately. [See 2.18 on a later page.]
6. Always identify yourself when you answer the phone: "This is ……..", "Surendar speaking." When you call someone and they answer the phone, identify ourselves: "This is …..", "Akila calling."
7. while on the phone, avoid
   - talking to people nearby (if we do, we can't hear what's being said).
   - typing or shuffling papers (it suggests we're not listening).
   - munching food or chewing gum (it reflects lack of respect or indicates poor manners).
8. Put down the phone gently, after the call is over.
9. Speak directly into the receiver.
10. Apologize if you dial a wrong number. [Don't just hang up.]
11. Do one of these, if someone walks in to talk to you while you are on the phone and if you're talking to your:
    - boss, use body language to make the other person quiet
    - friend or someone from home and the person entering is our superior, tell the caller we'll call later or with the caller's permission [if it's a stranger] depress the HOLD button and place the handset on the cradle
    - customer and the person entering is our superior, apologize to the caller and promise to call later.
12. Don't just hang up if you've dialed a wrong number; apologize: "I'm sorry. I must have pressed the wrong numbers", "I'm sorry for bothering you" or "I'm sorry for the interruption."
13. Make the call you promised. If you didn't call at the given time, your friend/relative might understand but strangers or customers or officials would have a poor opinion of you and this might affect relations in the future. In case you know you'll not be able to make the call, inform

the person concerned and also say when you'll be able to make the call. If you didn't leave a number/message for someone to call you back, it won't be fair to get upset or angry if they are not available when you call again.

14. Speak clearly at a moderate pace with sufficient loudness.
15. Spell out vital information: names, addresses, figures, date/day, time. To make doubly sure, repeat the information with something polite like: If you don't mind, let me repeat it.
16. Be specific in your information. Say: "…….will be available between 3 and 4 p.m." instead of "………will be available in the afternoon."
17. Keep calls as short as possible.
18. Listen carefully, repeat the other's request to make sure you've got the message.
19. Inform your contacts any change in the contact number[s]; request them to inform you of any change in their contact numbers.
20. Avoid saying "He's in conference"/"She's in a meeting"/ "He's out for lunch"/ "She's out for coffee", "I don't know where he is", for the simple reason many don't believe it. A better approach would be to say "He/She is unavailable at the moment. I can take a message/You may call at……….." If it's a message, take down the caller's name [ask the caller to spell] and number with extension, if necessary and the message.
21. Use expressions such as "thank you" and "please", "would you mind…..", "if I may suggest…." "I'm sorry to interrupt…..", "Just a moment, please". The caller will be happy to hear such responses.

---

4. Positive Thinking

A pessimist sees difficulty in every opportunity, an optimist sees opportunity in every difficulty.'

Winston Churchill

'A man is but the product of his thoughts; what he thinks, he becomes.'

Mahathma Gandhi

'When you put faith, hope and love together, you can raise positive kids in a negative world.'

Zig Zigar

'If you think about disaster, you will get it. Brood about death and you hasten your demise. Think positively and masterfully, with confidence and faith, and life becomes more secure, more fraught with action, richer in achievement and experience.'

Swami Vivekananda

4.1 Introduction

Read the following situations and see how you may react to them, that is, what and how you think:

Situation one:

Imagine you're waiting for a friend. You wait, you wait, and you wait; yet, there's no sign of him (or her?!).

reaction one

As time passes, you become anxious, then you get tensed up, then you work yourself up—stress yourself, curse your friend, yourself, and everything under the sun! You try his mobile and fail. So you grimly decide to give a piece of your mind when you meet him next.

reaction two

As time passes, you start wondering about the delay, then you start looking for reasons—probably you had not made yourself clear about the meeting, probably he's caught in a traffic jam, or his mobile is low on battery, probably he couldn't get out of office. You're not unduly worried.

Situation two:

Imagine you asked your friend for a loan. He said he'd try to help. After a day or two, he says 'Sorry.'

reaction one

You blame your friend for not helping, you accuse him of not being frank, of robbing your chance of asking another. Your relationship with him may become strained. For no fault of your friend!

reaction two

You accept your friend's inability to help. You understand the reason(s) he offers. So you continue to be friends with him.

Situation three:

Imagine you've been called for a job interview. You're fresh out of college and you know you're not good at using English.

reaction one

Your imagination runs riot now—you're almost sure they won't consider you, the interviewer(s) may even look down upon you, the interview may just be an eyewash. And now, you may even be thinking if you should attend the interview at all. Then you decide to go. You begin to feel they're asking the most difficult questions, they're exposing your ignorance, your inadequacy. You can't find your voice, or you stutter, you mumble and you feel miserable. And you blame them for this.

reaction two

You know your limitations. You begin to plan how best you can present yourself—to go early, to wear a smile as you enter, to request, if necessary, for repetition of a question, to say what you know without worrying about your faulty constructions, to say 'I don't know' when you really don't, to thank with a smile before leaving.

In these three situations, how do you find yourself reacting? Be true to yourself. If your reaction is similar to 'one', your thinking is negative, and if it is similar to 'two', it is positive. Thinking negatively doesn't help you— it weakens your confidence in yourself, it adds problems, it makes the situations worse than they are, and finally it results in failure. If you continue to think negatively, you are likely to add stress to your body and mind, you're more likely to fail than succeed. You are likely to blame your failures on others rather on yourself. And you may end up a failure. On the other hand, thinking positively helps you—it strengthens your confidence in yourself, it lessens problems, it improves the situations and it can result in success. If you continue to think positively, you are likely to minimize stress to your body and mind, you're more likely to succeed than fail. And you're likely to blame your failures on yourself rather than others. And you may end up a success.

4.2 Thinking

Now, a few thoughts about how we think, how we act or react.

'***I think, therefore I am.***'

There can't be two opinions on this: the mind is the driver, the body—the five senses—, the vehicle. The mind gives directions, issues orders, and the body obeys. The body may hear, the mind may not listen, the body may see, the mind may not notice or watch, the body may sensate, the mind may not register. Sounds reach our ears, but we don't 'know' what is said. Pages are open, but we don't 'know' what we are reading. A fly may perch on our body but we don't 'feel' it. At sometime or the other, all of us have had such experiences. Hearing, talking, reading, writing, seeing, acting, feeling, emoting, as responding or initiating acts or activities, depend *entirely* on what and how the mind frames and intends. What does the mind frame and intend? Thoughts (ideas, opinions, conclusions, decisions, sensations, feelings/ emotions)—initiating or responding.

In other words, it's <u>what</u> and <u>how</u> the mind **thinks** that forms the source action, inaction or non-action, for friendship or enmity, for joy or sorrow, for pain or pleasure, for peace or war, for heaven or hell on this earth. If this duality of experience emanates from ***thinking***, it then stands to reason that we must do something about this thinking of ours *if* we want success, *if* we want friendship, *if* we want peace, *if* we want joy, *if* we want pleasure. Surely, we want all these, but <u>only for us or more for us than for others</u>. Surely, we want all these in our private lives or in public life—as individuals or as members of a family, a group, a society, a community, a nation. Surely, at **any** cost, to some who then wage war on individuals, tradition or society. At **some** cost, to several who try and fail and hence live cursing. At **no** cost, to several others who never even try and thus live in agony and make hell for others, intentionally or otherwise. Our lives and life around us abound with live everyday samples of 'at any cost', 'at some cost', 'at no cost'.

In fact, this warring, this cursing, this living in agony and this making hell is considered 'the man thing'! But we **could** <u>avoid</u> warring, cursing, living in agony and making hell if only we set our minds to it. This implies changing our way of thinking, changing how we perceive (see) others and ourselves, changing our attitude or outlook.

That is, **convert negative thinking into positive thinking**. It's easier said than done, yes, but try we must, for the other alternative is wishing or thrusting hell on others and us.

4.3 What happens when we don't change or when we change?

Negative thinking	Positive thinking
• makes you think of your weaknesses	• makes you think of your strengths
• reduces your self-confidence	• improves your self-confidence
• erodes your self-esteem	• strengthens your self-esteem
• worsens your communication	• improves your communication
• makes you see only 'bad' in others	• makes you appreciate the 'good' in others
• blame others for your failures	• pinpoints you as source for your failure
• makes you miserable	• makes you happy
• forces you to make others miserable	• helps you to make others happy
• increases 'stress' on body and mind (deteriorates physical and mental health=) (reduces immunity of the body and mind)	• minimizes 'stress' on body and mind (keeps body and mind healthy=) (increases immunity of body and mind)
• accept 'defeat' as a fact of life	• look at failures as stepping stones
• prevents you from playing your role as son/daughter, as a friend, as wife/ husband, as a parent, as a neighbour, as a member of society, as a citizen.	• encourages you to play your role as son/daughter, as a friend, as wife/ husband, as a parent, as a neighbour, as a member of society, as a citizen.

4.4 What is positive thinking?

As a positive person, you

- believe in yourself as an achiever,
- develop only the 'good' in yourself and others,
- see a new situation as 'an opportunity to learn',
- look at a complicated situation as a source of inspiration,
- look for new sources when known ones fail you,
- take on an impossible-looking situation as a challenge,
- welcome breaks from tradition,
- discover new channels when the usual ones aren't adequate,
- see the positive side of dear and near, of strangers, of colleagues, of subordinates, of superiors,
- encourage the young and support the elderly,
- are not deterred by failure but remain motivated to continue to strive.

4.5 How can you make your thinking 'positive'?

1. Thinking, generally speaking, is contagious. We affect others and others affect us—consciously or unconsciously, with or without our knowledge. This can happen also instinctively and subconsciously. So, avoid 'negative' people and choose to make friends with those who are 'positive' in thinking and action.

2. Think 'I can' even when the situation or the person is very difficult.

3. Make 'failures' part of learning and growing. Don't lose heart, don't give up, don't be bitter, for success does not come easily. Analyze failures and learn from them—identify what went wrong or where you went wrong, make corrections or ask your 'positive' friends, change your perception (how you see yourself, people and situations), improve your attitude so you don't repeat your mistakes. To say the least, you've done your best trying and by continuing to try. This is the beginning of success.

4. Praise the efforts of others, be gentle with their errors—say they've just slipped, not fallen, say it's only a bruise, not a wound, get them to think and try again. If you exhibit positive thinking, it will rub off on others over a period of time. Your efforts to make others 'positive' will ensure your remaining positive because you cannot ask them to do what you yourself don't practise!

---

5. Time Management

Time is what we want most, but what we use worst.

William Penn

Better three hours too soon, than one minute too late.

William Shakespeare

The key is in not spending time, but in investing it.

Stephen R. Covey

Take care of the minutes and the hours will take care of themselves.

Lord Chesterfield

One thing you can't recycle is wasted time.

Author Unknown

Time is at once the most valuable and the most perishable of all our possessions.

John Randolph

In truth, people can generally make time for what they choose to do; it is not really the time but the will that is lacking.

Sir John Lubbock

5.1 Value of 'time'

Time and (time) again, haven't we heard '(there is) no time like the present' (=now is the time to do something, not in the future), 'time flies' (=time seems to pass very quickly), 'time is money' (=time is valuable and should not be wasted), 'a stitch in time saves nine' (=it's better to do something now because if you wait, it may become worse or more difficult and cause extra work)?

'Time and tide wait for no man', 'Strike when the iron is hot' are two other popular sayings that strikingly highlight the importance of 'time' in our lives, of how we should use the 'time' available to us. 'Time' keeps moving on and doesn't wait until we are ready for it. We all know only too well about the sense of 'timing', which is another way of referring to the skill of 'doing something exactly at the right time'. The second saying refers to this skill, for the iron can be given shape only when it is hot.

5.2 How we treat 'time'

Yet, quite a few of us have difficulty in managing 'time':

Students say:

'Travel to and fro college eats up most of my time.'

'Travel makes me so tired I can't think of doing any serious reading.'

'Submission of time-bound 'assignments' and writing of 'records' leave little time for little else.'

'My friends manage to get good grades even though they study only as the university exams approach. So, why not me?'

'I'm out of my depth in certain portions of 'theory' of a subject or two.'

Office workers say:

'Getting ready to leave for office is tension-ridden.'

'Commuting to and from home is an ordeal.'

' Commuting makes me so tired I can't think of attending to files.'

' Superiors and co-workers add to **already** stress-ridden mind.'

These statements are reasons or excuses cited by students and employees for not making adequate use of available time. But how valid/acceptable are they? It seems we concentrate on putting the blame only on factors <u>outside</u> of us, and we seem to declare: 'well, if I don't manage my time well, it's not my fault.' It cannot be denied that these statements are facts but by citing them we declare ourselves to be weaklings, willing (forever!) to be in the grip of external factors. But we are little aware we are buying, free of cost, maximum stress and its attendant ills, both of body and mind, (and of course, we pay heavily for such free-of-cost purchase! But we don't seem to realize this.)

Are we ready to realize passing the buck isn't going to help us in anyway? Are we ready to realize it's likely to result in ill health? Are we ready to realize the only solution to all these is learning to manage our time?

If we are to survive, if we are to progress in our personal and professional lives, it becomes imperative to learn to manage time.

5.3 Time Management as a professional concept

Well before this concept wore its 'professional look', humans used the sun's movement across the sky to do their jobs, to complete tasks, to perform their duties. Then came the sundial, grandfather clock, wall clock, alarm clock.

Experts enumerate the emergence of 'time management' as a concept that developed over a period of time. Clocks and watches were probably the first devices people used to remind themselves of tasks/jobs to be done at a given time and thus to manage their time. The complexity of managing time as a result of today's interlocking of human enterprise activities led to the use of calendar and appointment books as part of setting goals, planning related activities and preparing for action. The complexity was made more sophisticated by prioritizing goals on a daily basis. It has been further refined with 'importance over urgency' as in the words attributed to Dwight D. Eisenhower: *What is important is seldom urgent and what is urgent is seldom important.*

5.4 What is time management?

There are only 24 hours in your day, just the same as in everybody else's. The good news is that provided you use time economically, there is enough time for all the things—the routine ones, the short-term ones and the long-term ones.

You use time economically when you have an exact idea of all the things you need to do—from waking to going to bed and when you apportion time appropriate to each activity—five minutes for bath and, say, twenty to go over your notes for an 'internal' test. You're not economical if you turn the other way when your mother says, "Gokul, wake up, it's time!' You're not economical if you silence the alarm and go back to sleep. You're not economical if you wake up and laze away in bed. You're not economical if, for whatever reason, you pick a fight with your sister/brother when you should be having your bath or pressing/ironing your dress for the day, if you bathe a little longer than necessary, if you thought you'd have enough time before leaving home to give final touches to your assignment but don't find time to do it or can't locate the assignment, and so on.

You're not economical if you forget a purchase list at home and spend office time looking for it, turning everything upside down, if you curse your wife for not reminding you. You're not economical if you're not able to locate a file or a paper your superior wants for immediate reference, if you have to search for the 'rules' book, if gossip eats up your time and you have to face an irate superior, and so on.

If you're not economical, you cannot be efficient and so cannot be effective. If you spend time *without a focus*, without bearing in mind all that you have to do, you **waste** time because the result is neither efficient nor productive. If you spend time *with a focus*, bearing in mind all that you have to do, you perform tasks in less time than previously, and you **save** time. If you spend time to *plan* managing time or to undergo *training*, you **invest** time so that you can use future time more efficiently for long-term activities.

5.5 Why do you manage time poorly?

Because your priorities are wrong. In other words, you give importance to and spend more time than necessary on:

- sending, reading, forwarding SMS on the mobile,
- chatting on the net,
- going through websites not directly connected to a main activity,
- TV,
- being with friends,
- reading and forwarding emails,
- gossip,
- plotting against someone, and so on.

Except for the last one in the list, it's no great sin to indulge in these activities. They have their own uses in your lifestyle and growth and definitely your sources for relaxation. They become time wasters when the indulgence goes to a point where more important activities get stagnated.

In addition to these, you could be under the influence of

- procrastination

  If you say, 'One more day/Another hour won't make any difference' or if you say, 'I work best under pressure', you're delaying, you're procrastinating.

- indifference

  You're probably not interested, for whatever reason, in doing what you must be doing. This is a perception problem that has negative impact on your attitude and motivation and on time management.

- defiance

  Again, for whatever reason, you refuse to perform the tasks expected of you.

- willful neglect

  You choose, for whatever reason, to ignore your responsibilities.

  You won't find it difficult to understand now why you manage your time poorly. Of course, the above discussion may not be news to you, and you may already know you ARE mismanaging your time. And if you're bent upon mismanaging time, this discussion will be of little meaning and use to you. But if you know now the cause(s) **and *if you wish to improve the situation***, you definitely can do something positive about it.

Take a look below.

Obviously, you have to design a plan and a method of executing the plan. If you're a student, try this:

- Prepare a general 'to-do' list.

  Put here all you need to do everyday—making the bed, brushing your teeth, having coffee/tea, attending to call of nature, bathing, dressing, breakfasting, journeying to and fro college, having light refreshments, watching the TV, studying, having supper, continuing, studying, sleeping.

- Prepare a general 'to-do' list for weekends.

  You can probably spend a considerable portion for relaxation or entertainment, visits, short trips, and of course, not an inconsiderable portion for studying/revising/record-writing/completing assignments or projects.

- Now decide how much time you normally spend on routine activities and 'studying'.

- Take away a few minutes from each of the routine activities, total it up and add it to your time for studying. You may be surprised to see you've gained an hour or two for everyday study time.

- Now divide this increased time into convenient zones for re-reading, revising, preparing and writing assignments, doing extra reading, putting down on paper what you've comprehended, what you have not.

The intention here is not to recommend rigid compliance but rather to give you a direction so that you see the need to plan in order to maximize academic output.

Now the method or the technique. Time-tabling has its definitive advantages. This can be complemented with **prioritizing**. Arrange your activities in terms of importance or urgency or both.

Now you'll have three lists:

- activities that you see as urgent and important,
- activities that you see as important but not urgent,
- activities that you see as neither important nor urgent.

Take a good look at the listed activities under each of these heads, see if they are properly placed, and if they're not, rearrange them. ***Now there is clarity in your thinking, purpose in your planning, focus in your execution. This is time management.***

5.6 Checklists

These are helpful in managing your time for **specific tasks**.

Whenever we want to do something, most usually we check mentally the what, the when, the where, the how of that activity, if it is somewhat important. Once we do this, we feel we're ready for that activity. But we may not be completely ready for it.

Let's say a circular was read out to you. You have to pay your tuition fees within the week. You inform your father and he gives you a DD (Demand Draft) for Rs.30600. You go the bank but the clerk returns the DD saying you've forgotten to add the late fee and the commission amount because it is a DD from another bank.

This problem wouldn't have been there if you had written down these items as a list and checked them like this:

		Rs.	Put a tick
1.	**What** the amount:		
	a. tuition fees	29250	
	b. commission	250	
	c. late fee	1100	
		30600	Yes ☐ No ☐
2.	**When** on or before 28/12/2002		Yes ☐ No ☐
	you're paying on 30/12/2002		Yes ☐ No ☐
3.	**How** a DD from a bank		Yes ☐ No ☐
	other than Indian Bank (where)		Yes ☐ No ☐

2 and 3 are linked to 1c and 1b. You put a tick (a) in the appropriate box. Preparation such as this will help you avoid embarrassment (= feel awkward or ashamed).

So it's good to make a checklist where you write down **all that you require to do and all that you have to do**. This will tell you what you have and what you don't have or what you've done and what you have to do.

Let's say you're planning a trip with your family by train to Palani to visit Lord Muruga. Let's also say you request a travelling agency to make the arrangements.

To know whether the agency has done what you wanted, let's prepare a check list:

		Put a tick	
1.	train journe		
	onward		
	15.06.2003	Yes ☐	No ☐
	Madurai Express	Yes ☐	No ☐
	II class A/C	Yes ☐	No ☐
	5 adults	Yes ☐	No ☐
	1 child	Yes ☐	No ☐
	Dindigul – Palani – taxi with A/C	Yes ☐	No ☐
	taxi agency name	Yes ☐	No ☐
	taxi registration number	Yes ☐	No ☐
	return		
	17.06.2003	Yes ☐	No ☐
	same as for onward	Yes ☐	No ☐
2.	stay in Palani		
	Hotel name	Yes ☐	No ☐
	Two family rooms with A/C	Yes ☐	No ☐
	hot water shower bath	Yes ☐	No ☐
	veg. meal, chilli free, spice – free	Yes ☐	No ☐
	communication from hotel	Yes ☐	No ☐
3.	Darshan		
	person to contact		
	at the hotel	Yes ☐	No ☐
	or at the Devasthanam	Yes ☐	No ☐
	confirmation letters	Yes ☐	No ☐

If there is any 'no', you know what to do. Without such a list a you might run into problems.

Sample 2

Checklist for a meeting with VIP

i) introduce yourself

   a) your name (without Mr. and initials e.g. I am Swaminathan)

   b) your position (Gen. Sec./ President of Students' Association/ACE/IEEE/AME, etc.)

   c) name of the College, its location (place)

ii) state the purpose of inviting him

   a) Inauguration

   b) Annual day

   c) Sports day

   d) Valedictory function

iii) mention date, time, place

iv) suggest a theme or topic for addressing you (as a general audience) or request him to speak on a specific topic for addressing you as a discipline audience (say, ECE or Chemical)

v) talk about your arrangements for transport (by car / rail / plane) or if he so wishes agree to his own arrangements (indicate meeting expenses) depending on the distance between his residence and your Institution or Organisation.

vi) request him to play any additional role, if you wish

vii) a) find out if he's available for the date

   b) or if he is not free, ask if he is free for another date.

viii) express your happiness about his acceptance or say you will contact him later to confirm his acceptance.

Sample 3

Payments

Middle – class salaried people usually make regular payments to individuals and/or organizations. Delayed payments or payments forgotten to be made will attract unpleasantness from individuals and or/ added interest etc. So it's good to make a check list that will help payments in time.

1. Loans
    - a) LIC premium date(s). — monthly (every 8th)
        - quarterly (every 10th)
        - half yearly (every 1st)
    - b) House Loan — dates
    - c) bank loan (s) — date(s)
        - TV
        - Fridge
    - d) Personal loan(s)
        - individual name(s)
            1.
            2.
            3.
2. Electricity bill (date)
3. Telephone bill (date)
4. Water charge (date)
5. House tax (date)

Another type

First Aid kit at home

1. Dettol 2. Cotton rolls 3. Bandage roll of different sizes
4. Bandage – plastic strips – assorted sizes. 5. Burnol
6. approved pain killer 7. ear drops 8.eye drops
9. cough syrups 10. sore throat menthols

Note: Remember the expiry dates. Buy fresh stock.

Note: If there is time, someone can suggest a situation or two, and you can write checklists for them.

Exercise 51

You're planning to travel to Bangalore in your car with your family. You want to get the car ready for the journey. Make a **check list** for this purpose.

6. Team Building

Together

Everyone

Achieves

More

—Author unknown

Coming together is a beginning.
Keeping together is progress.
Working together is success.

Henry Ford

No one can whistle a symphony. It takes an orchestra to play it.

H.E. Luccock

Teamwork: Simply stated, it is less me and more we.

Unknown

It's easy to get good players. Getting them to play together, that's the hard part.

Casey Stengel

"We must all hang together, or assuredly, we shall all hang separately."

Benjamin Franklin

"Behind every able man, there are always other able men."

Chinese Proverb

"Strength lies in differences, not in similarities."

Stephen Covey

6.1 Introduction

'Two is company, three is crowd' is a saying that we all know too well.

When there are more than two,

perceptions—seeing/understanding things, people, activities—may not be uniform,

attitudes—likes and dislikes—can and do affect discussion and decision-making, **motivation**—interest in performing—can and does dip,

divergence of opinion can and does increase,

egos—sense of superiority or inferiority—can and do emerge,

personalities—sense of being able to handle issues or situations—can and do clash,

conflict, as a result of different 'leanings', can and does occur,

consensus can and does become difficult;

as corollaries, gossip, jealousy, selfishness, bitterness, pain, enmity, harm, can and do result.

From another perspective, 'crowd' implies 'mob behaviour', which further implies 'people can and do go berserk', 'emotions can and do become volatile', 'senselessness and violence rule behaviour' and all these give way to destruction of relationships.

However, team building has always been one of the primary goals of humans, ever since they realized the need to stay in groups: if only to fight the predators, if only to exploit 'nature', if only to live in a rule-governed system to achieve progress, prosperity. Civilizations and nations are examples of team building. Today's concept of 'global village' reflects the significance of team building.

As human history reveals abundantly clearly, despite failures in human efforts, despite disappearances of civilizations, humans have persisted with the concept of team building for the simple reason they've understood that they cannot survive, act, live, grow as separate individuals. Thus, civilizations and nations on a larger scale and companies, firms, associations, clubs on a lesser scale continue to form, to exist and to work together.

6.2 What is team building?

Team formation is one thing; team building is quite another. When more than two individuals come together or brought together for a purpose or goal common to them, a team gets formed. A family is a team formed. A resident welfare association is a team formed. A company or firm is a team formed. A council of ministers is a team formed. A group of workers is a team formed. A group of friends is a team formed.

Teams form either naturally or intentionally. When like-minded individuals come together, a team forms naturally. They may not initially have any specific purpose in mind other than being together, moving together, enjoying life together. They are, for all purposes, informal in intent, each other but stick together in crisis.

When individuals, like-minded or not, are brought together, a team forms intentionally. They are formed into a group because they are believed to possess the competence, focus, capacity to bring a task to fruition. They are, for all purposes, formal in intent, thought and action. (Of course, a certain level of informality may develop as time passes.) They have a set of rules to abide by, a set of directions to follow, a specific time-bound goal to reach.

But such teams and others, formed through individuals coming together, can be termed as **team building** *only when* individuals in these teams

- willingly accept the team's goal(s) as theirs
  or, if there is a choice, modify, improve or reshape the goal(s)
  without hurting others,
- work purposefully towards realizing the goal(s),
- perceive the team's progress as more important than theirs as individuals,
- practise positive attitude to working together through thick and thin,
- continue to maintain their motivation levels high,
- help support other members in times of stress or uncertainty,
- make such contributions that will ensure goal realization,
- communicate intelligibly, intelligently, carefully

  Avoid : We should do A, not B
  Say : What if we did A, instead of B?
  Avoid : We must take a vote now.
  Say : It's time for a vote now, I think.
  Don't you? / What do you say?

- respect differing views or approaches by patient listening,
- convince or be ready to be convinced,
- constantly remember that their partners are as important as they are,
  if not more than them,
- keep emotions in check,
- avoid interrupting, offending, belittling, condescending, intimidating,
- don't use 'status' as a weapon,
- ask for guidance without feeling shy,
- accept, in principle and practice, the leader assigned to the team
  or participate meaningfully in (s)electing a leader,
- understand, accept, move in the direction sought by their leader,
- maintain the pace of progress so the time-bound goal(s) can be achieved,
- share the joy of success or analyze failures to improve future performance.

Leadership

"We lead by being human. We do not lead by being corporate, professional, or institutional."

Paul G. Hawken, founder, Smith and Hawken

The greatest leader isn't necessarily the one who does the greatest things. The greatest leader is the one who gets the people to do the greatest things.

Ronald Reagan

To lead the people, walk behind them.

Lao-tzu

Leadership is influence.

John C. Maxwell

Leadership is an action, not a position.

Donald H. McGannon

6.3 Need for a leader

'Too many cooks spoil the broth' is a saying that by implication underlines and emphasizes the need for a team to have a leader, a captain for a ship, a general for an army, a prime minister for a council of ministers. No group can complete its task within a time frame without a leader—an informal or formal one.

Of the many messages implied in the saying, the three most important ones are: there must be someone to *coordinate*, to *oversee*, to *focus*.

6.4 Deciding a leader

In an informal group, there may not be a leader in the formal sense of the word. Still, a particular member, when a need arises, may charge a specific member with a specific task, suggest ways to carry it out, check the progress. And this may become a pattern over a period of time, and that member becomes the undeclared leader. On the other hand, in a formal group, leadership may be assigned to a particular individual on the basis of seniority, experience, expertise or some other criterion. Or a leader may be chosen first and may be asked to select individuals with knowledge, experience or expertise in specific areas intimately linked to a chosen task/goal.

A leader is one who is clear about the task and what it entails. A leader is one who is constantly conscious of the time limit set to complete the task. A leader is one who can keep expenses within the budget allocated but has the courage and ability to ask for more, if need be. A leader is one who can, when asked to do so, identify the right people for the right tasks. A leader is one who knows, through the dossiers given to him, the strengths and weaknesses of every member. A leader is one who can design a plan for the task. A leader is one who assigns sub-tasks with a time schedule. A leader is one who can locate and gather the necessary resources. A leader is one who frames a time schedule and meets each member individually or as a group for reports, feedback, consultation. A leader is one who is willing to allow, consider and accept suggestions each member may put forward. A leader is one who identifies with the members. A leader is one who leads by example. A leader is one who inspires.

A leader is an able thinker, a bold planner, a capable organizer, a willing listener, a competent communicator, an expert guide, a sympathetic critic, a firm controller, a respecter, a developer.

---

7. Decision Making

If you chase two rabbits, both will escape.

Author unknown

Indecision is debilitating; it feeds upon itself; it is, one might almost say, habit-forming. Not only that, but it is contagious; it transmits itself to others.

H.A.Hopf

Take time to deliberate, but when the time for action has arrived, stop thinking and go in.

Napoleon Bonaparte

There is no more miserable human being than one in whom nothing is habitual but indecision.

William James

If you put off everything 'till you're sure of it, you'll get nothing done.

Norman Vincent Peale

By failing to prepare, you are preparing to fail.

Benjamin Franklin

7.1 Introduction

When we react to a situation, we can/we'll possibly behave in three ways:

• action • inaction • non-action

Action is a 'process of doing something to make something happen'; inaction is 'lack of action/ not doing something about a situation'; non-action is 'absence of action'. There is an element of involvement in 'action' or 'inaction'— performing or not performing. Whereas non-action, by its very nature, is a non-involvement one; when we see two persons fighting, we either go our way or simply watch; we don't wish to embroil (=involve) ourselves.

An action or act is 'a thing someone does'. This may or may not involve **decision-making**. We perform certain acts at *subconscious* level:

- reflexive act— which is performed without conscious thought
- instinctive act— which is a natural tendency to behave in a particular way using knowledge and abilities we're born with
- impulsive—which is a strong urge/desire to act (without thinking).

There is no decision-making occurring in these subconscious acts. We say, 'Ouch!' in pain when we stumble or trip over a stone. We recoil in fear when we see a snake. Both are reflexive acts. If I'm accused of embezzlement, I instinctively deny it. When we see a child weep, we impulsively take her in our arms, saying, 'Now, now, don't cry, there's a good girl!'

There are situations where we take ***quick*** decisions. Practically, there is no process of decision-making. Here we are governed by

- emotions—love, magnanimity, sympathy, anger, jealously, hatred, disgust shape our decisions.
- confidence—intelligence, experience, knowledge helps us decide.

As against this, there are situations where we do***n't*** take decisions at all. Practically there is no process of decision-making. Here we are governed by

- indifference—no interest in (not)taking a decision
- inertia __no desire to (not) take a decision
- no motivation—no reason to (not) take a decision.

When we don't take a decision either way, we are **drifting**.

But there are acts that occur at conscious level and therefore involve decision-making. Decision-making automatically implies **choices** from which we select one. We look at a situation, we think about it—what it implies, what is expected of us, what choices we have, what results are definite, probable or possible—desirable or not desirable, whether, if these are desirable, how desirable they are, how they would impinge on others, us and/or the future. We think, analyze, we argue for and against, we weigh, we judge and then decide to take action or not to take action.

Let's quickly summarize:

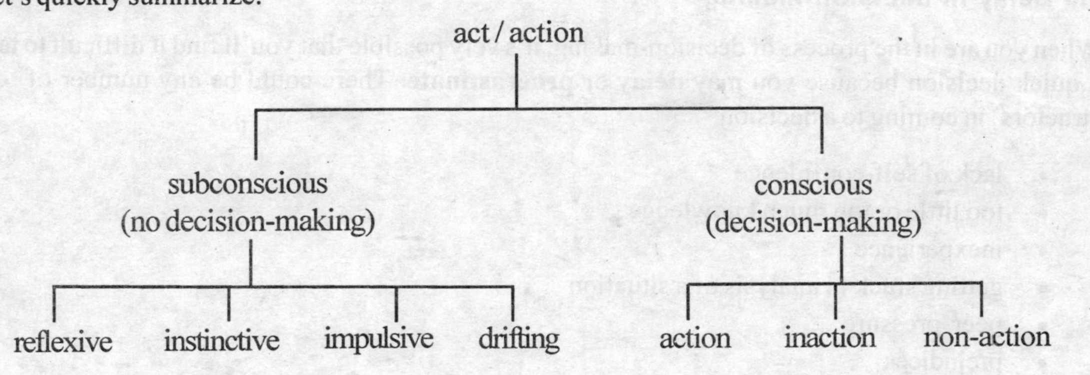

7.2 Decision-making and what it implies

Now that we've got an overall background picture, let's move on to 'decision-making'.

A decision emerges from engagement of heart alone, of mind alone, of both mind and heart. It indicates a final choice from a given number of choices/options.

As an individual, you take decisions in two capacities:

- as an individual
- as a member of a group.

As a individual, you initiate the process of decision-making in areas that affect you personally—habits, manners, education, use of free time, job, hobbies. Now, you are either *subjective* or *objective*. You are subjective when you're influenced by your feelings, tastes, opinions and ignore hard facts or evidence to decide whether to act or not. You are objective when you're not influenced by your feelings, tastes, opinions but when you analyze and weigh hard facts and evidence to decided whether to act or not.

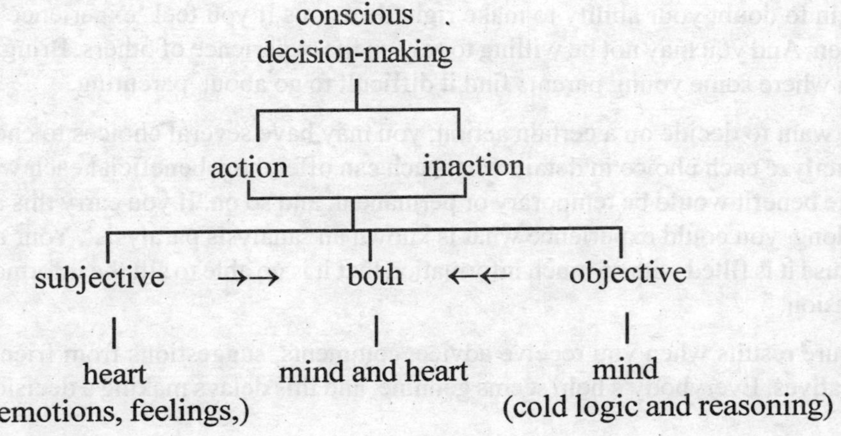

7.3 Delay in decision-making

When you are in the process of decision-making, it's very possible that you'll find it difficult to take a quick decision because you may **delay** or **procrastinate**. There could be any number of 'obstructors' in coming to a decision:

- lack of self-confidence
- too little or too much knowledge
- inexperience
- getting stuck in analysis of a situation
- peer pressure
- prejudices
- images in your mind of:
  others (wrong/inadequate/poor) and
- constraints like cast, status in society, position in hierarchy.

'Can I do it?' is a good question to ask yourself, but if you keep asking for longer than necessary or too often, you'll only be generating self-doubt. Which is not a good thing. It is important, in fact *vital*, for you to believe in yourself and your ability to make decisions without taking too much time. Taking time to think is a positive sign because you want to be sure you make the right decision. But if you decide after a considerable period of time, it's possible that such a delayed decision may do more harm than good. Making decisions without undue delay, moving ahead and making progress are possible only if you have confidence in yourself.

If you feel you don't have sufficient information about a situation or people involved in that situation, you become unsure of what to do. For instance, you fear you'll be conned into buying a useless car if you have little knowledge about cars. Conversely, being an expert on cars can lead to an undue delay resulting in no purchase. Because the mental chart of plusses and minuses of each 'make' you draw up can confuse more than clarify.

You'll begin to doubt your ability to make right decisions if you feel 'experience' is an essential qualification. And you may not be willing to rely on the experience of others. Bringing up children is one area where some young parents find it difficult to go about parenting.

When you want to decide on a certain action, you may have several choices to choose from. You begin to **analyze** each choice in detail, what each can offer, how beneficial each would if chosen, whether the benefit would be temporary or permanent, and so on. If you carry this analysis too far or for too long, you could experience what is known an 'analysis paralysis'. Your mind gets paralyzed because it is filled with so much information that it is no able to sift the information and arrive at a conclusion.

Peer pressure results when you receive advice, comments, suggestions from friends, colleagues, family, relatives. Everybody's help seems genuine, and this delays making a decision.

'Prejudice' is an unreasonable liking or dislike or preference for a person, group, custom etc., especially when it is based on race, religion, sex etc. You'd rather not accept help from someone because you're prejudiced against him/her.

You form negative impressions or opinions, over the years, of people because of some bitter experiences in the past, because they don't belong to your cast or community, because they are lower or higher in status or hierarchy. These can cause delay if you have to deal with them before making a decision.

More often than not, you may know you're unable to come to a decision but you may not know what's causing the delay. If this is true in your case, the above discussion can help you identify the source for delay and deal with it quickly enough to avoid the delay.

William Shakespeare, the master playwright that he is, used 'delay in decision-making' as the running theme and gifted the world with one of its greatest tragedy plays 'Hamlet'. With his 'to be or not to be', Hamlet, the lead character, epitomizes 'procrastination' (delay in making a decision).

7.4 How do you make a decision?

There is no magic formula for decision-making, that is, what steps you should take to arrive at a decision. But you can use these six steps to your advantage:

1. Define in clear terms your goal/problem. Put it in a single sentence.
2. Assess the implications –for you, your family or others who may be affected by it.
3. Explore different perspectives. See your goal/problem from different angles.
4. Be clear in your mind what will/can happen as a result of the decision you are making.
5. Weigh pros and cons of the possible results/effects. Look closely at the advantages and disadvantages of the choices open to you.
6. Decide and act. Commit yourself to a choice or course of action.

7.5 How do you make a right decision?

I'm sure, like everyone else, you also want to make right decisions. To be able to do this, you need to be aware of and avoid certain **pitfalls** arising from the nature of your perception:

- The first choice that occurs to you may be appealing and so you may not think of or look at other available choices.
- Of the available choices, you may like a particular one and so gather facts only in support of it.
- When you face strange situations, you are unwilling to change your pattern of deciding and apply the one you've used before.
- You ignore information that seems to be out of place or to have no direct link.
- You think that a decision you take will work because you want it to work.

- You play it safe by taking a decision that others have taken in the past in similar circumstances.
- You decide to do something because it has been suggested by someone you like.
- You think that you can do damage control later if your present decision leads to complications.

You can avoid these dangers and make a right beginning if you allow yourself to bear in mind the following **simple principles**:

1. *Be open-minded*. Don't allow pre-conceived notions you may have about issues affecting you as an individual or as a member of a group. Otherwise, you're likely to look for information/ ideas/arguments that confirm your notion/belief/philosophy. This is known as 'confirming-evidence trap'.
2. *Don't play it safe*. Don't be over-cautious either. Like several others, you may opt a choice or course of action that seems to be 'safe' or that you know to be 'safe' because you feel other available choices seem to involve an element of 'risk'.
3. *Don't be over-confident*. You may think yourself to be smarter than others, and you may actually be, but it does not always follow that you always make the right decision.
4. *Don't jump at a choice*. Avoid picking a choice just because it appeals to your imagination, aesthetic sense or because it has some immediate benefit, like saving cost.

7.6 Planning a decision-making process

The chances for making the right decisions are bright if you decide on a structured approach, that is, if you make a plan.

There are four benefits to decision-making planning:

1 You have your goal(s), the probable time duration, the probable cost involved, personnel you need, the resources you have and you'll need, the method(s) to employ, written down clearly, precisely.

2. Such planning gives a clear purpose and direction. It can work as your mirror to measure how close (or far) you are from accomplishing your goal. This measure is important because it can show you immediately when you are off the course and need to make adjustments and corrections.

3. Planning is a tool to translate an idea into a specific action or a series of actions. It gives focus and direction.

4. Though planning needs time, it's a time spent well because it will prevent squandering of time during the actual process.

7.7 Decisions affecting a group

The word 'group' can refer to a team as large as a company/firm or as small as a group of, say, three members.

When decisions are to be taken that will affect the working of a group, four decision modes are available:

1. You take the decision (*autonomy*).
2. You delegate the responsibility of the decision to an individual or a group of individuals (*delegation*).
3. You need ideas/inputs from the group (*consultation*).
4. You involve the members in the process (*consensus*).

Choose 'Autonomy' if

you have sufficient expertise and information, you have information that mustn't be shared, time is a constraint, the problem will not significantly affect the relationship between you and the group. Routine rules and regulations and certain policy matters will need autonomous decisions.

Choose 'delegation' if

you are not an expert and an expert is available. 'Specialized' activities like 'market trends', HRD are examples.

Choose 'consultation' if

you feel you need inputs from the members and you think collaborative thinking is preferable.

Choose 'consensus' if

you think active involvement of the group is necessary for acceptance of the decision and for its effective implementation. Involvement of representatives of 'workers' is desirable here.

As a member of a small group

A few employees may form a group for the purpose of deciding on the fate of a specific short-term activity, you <u>initiate</u> the process of decision-making (if you are a leader) or <u>join</u> others in the process of decision-making regarding issues that affect job-related situations involving you and your shareholders, you and your customers, you and provider of jobs/tasks, you and your employees/colleagues. The obvious inference is that <u>you are not alone</u>, and, whether you initiate or join, the process involves others besides you; to that extent, you're governed, controlled, constrained by the thought processes of others. You must learn to be cooperative, to be understanding and to even compromise.

7.8 Decision-making techniques

You'll see below a list of 'techniques'. You're only being introduced to them. For more information, you'll have to either browse the internet or visit a library.

1. Paerto Analysis

- Write down the activity for which a decision is necessary.
- List the choices that come to your mind.
- Apply a score appropriate to the aptness of each choice.
- Choose the one with the highest score.

2. Paired Comparison Analysis

This helps consider the relative importance of different courses of action. It helps you decide on one priority over the others when they all seem equally important.

3. Grid Analysis

- List your options as 'rows' and the factors as 'columns'.
- Award weights to each factor.
- Score each option for each factor using numbers from 0(poor) to 5 (very good).
- Multiply each score by the weight already fixed.
- Add up the total scores for each option.
- Choose the option that has received the highest score.

Say you want to own a house. Your 'options' can be:

buying a plot and constructing a house

buy a built house: single house or a flat

Your 'factors' can be:

cost,
construction quality,
space ('carpet' area and/ or around the house),
proximity to 'facilities' like school, market, hospital,
neighbourhood.

4. PMI

This name stands for 'Plus/Minus/Interesting'.

- Make a table of three columns.
- Use one column each for 'Plus', 'Minus', 'Interesting'.

- List all positive results you can think of under 'plus'.
- List all negative results you can think of under 'Minus'.
- Mention all possible 'implications under 'Interesting'.

Once you've completed listing, you'll probably find that it's easy to decide now.

5. Force Field Analysis

This is a useful technique for weighing pros and cons of an issue. This will help strengthen the forces supporting a decision and reduce the impact of opposition to it.

6. Six Thinking Hats

This technique was developed by Edward deBono. It takes into account diverse thoughts, including emotions of participants. It encourages them to look at a situation from various vantage points or different perspectives/angles. It helps the group to perform a well-balanced act through its approach and analysis.

The six hats of the technique represent six different styles of thinking, and it is thus a comprehensive tool to arrive at a right decision. The different styles allow members to mentally tick off as many perspectives as they need to view the situation from. They do not classify the thinkers but only represent categories of thinking behavior, as members wear particular parts. The purpose of the hats is to direct thinking. It is most likely to inspire creative, inspiring thinking, similar to word association.

What the hats represent

The six hats are named after colours: white, yellow, black, red, green and blue.

- **White** represents *facts and figures*.

  Wearing this hat, you relate the present problem to past trends/experiences from a historical perspective, gather information and data relevant to the problem or situation, present these to the group and maintain a neutral position.

- **Yellow** represents *positives, pluses, values and benefits*.

  Wearing this hat, you look at the problem from a logical and positive point of view.

- **Black** represents *negatives, minuses, losses*.

  Wearing this hat, you look at the problem from a logical and negative point of view. You concentrate on negative aspects—what risks there are and what could go wrong.

- **Red** represents *emotions, gut feelings, intuition*.

  Waring this hat, you react to the problem emotionally or intuitively.

DeBono is quoted as saying, 'Emotions are an essential part of our thinking ability and not just something extra that mucks up our thinking.'

- **Green** represents *creativity.*

  Wearing this hat, you think out of the box and offer original ideas or hypotheses.

- **Blue** represents *control over the thinking, organizing ideas shared, arriving at decision(s).*

  The Chair wears this hat.

  He/She initiates, directs, supervises and controls the decision-making act.

How the hats actually work

The leader can decide who should wear which 'hat' for he/she may know the thinking strengths of each member; or he may invite members to choose the 'hat'. What is important is that they should do full justice to the concept underlying the 'hat' they choose. The leader acquaints the members with the problem or situation, knows who wear which hat, sets a time limit, listens to them, and then takes a decision.

7.9 Mind Mapping

Introduction

Mind Mapping is especially valuable in generating alternatives. The mind remembers structures and pictures much better than it does sentences, words or bullet points. It is a visual tool. It helps show the structure or shape of a topic and the branches as the linkages between the details. If you're making a presentation, it will help your audience understand and appreciate your thinking process. It also allows you to keep track of the raw data or facts.

Mind Mapping can be done as a group, or as a means of individual brainstorming.

How Mapping functions

- Title

  Write down the title of the subject in the center of the page and circle it.
- Branches

  Draw lines as branches to indicate major sub-headings.
- Sub-braches

  For each sub-heading, think of ideas and draw branches.
- Work quickly

  Put down thoughts in single words or brief phrases, without evaluating them.
- Pictures and colours

  Draw relevant pictures if you can. Or simply use different colours for easy reading.
- Reorganization

  Remove repetition, make expressions sharper, briefer, more precise.

Starbusting

This technique is useful when you wish to explore and understand a new idea or a product. You start asking questions with 'who', 'what', 'why', 'where', 'when', 'how'.

Take a paper and draw a star in the middle and put down the idea or product inside. Write each 'wh-' expression inside the star. Now ask as many questions as you can for each 'wh-' expression outside the star. Until you're satisfied you've asked enough questions.

Now you can answer all these questions so that you get a clear picture of what you're thinking about.

Stepladder

Here all members express their thoughts **before** they meet as a group. As such, they can make useful contributions as they will not be overpowered by bullying; they cannot hide themselves behind others' skirts and so will have to take active part.

To make this possible,

1. the task or problem is presented to all members individually,
2. they are given sufficient time to apply their mind to the task,
3. a core group of two members is formed and they discuss their thoughts,
4. a third member is added, he/she presents his/her thoughts before he/she hears their ideas for further discussion,
5. another member is added to the group for similar activity and
6. the members together reach a final decision after an open discussion.

This technique works best with small groups.

The Delphi Method

Like the Stepladder method, this one also encourages active member participation. But it differs in its functioning from the Stepladder:

- it has an objective facilitator or a leader,
- its members will have no idea about one another,
- it's a lengthy process,
- it's used for major decisions requiring inputs from a large number of people.

The following are several other techniques:

1. SWOT— **Strengths, Weaknesses, Opportunities and Threats**
2. PEST Model: Political, Economic, Social and Technology Analysis

3. Cost Benefit Analysis Model
4. Multivoting and Nominal Group Technique

   Multivoting reduces long lists of ideas and identifies important items while Nominal Group Technique generates ideas and prioritizes items.
5. Decision Tree Analysis.

---

8. Creativity

The truly creative person is one who can think crazy; ....The creative person is flexible—he is able to change as the situation changes, to break habits, to face indecision and changes in conditions without undue stress.

Frank Goble

Ideas are the root of creation.

Ernest Dimnet

Creativity is inventing, experimenting, growing, taking risks, breaking rules, making mistakes, and having fun.

Mary Lou Cook

Creativity involves breaking out of established patterns in order to look at things in a different way.

Edward deBono

Creativity requires to let go of certainties.

Erich Fromm

Chance favors the prepared mind.

Pasteur

You need chaos in your soul to give birth to a dancing star.

Nietsche

8.1 Introduction

Creativity is a mental activity, with perception, thinking and imagination going hand in hand. It involves generation of new ideas or concepts, or new associations between or among existing ideas or concepts. To pu it simply, it is the act of making something ***new***.

Creative thinking is also 'divergent thinking' when it considers a variety of thoughts; it is also 'autistic' thinking when it indulges in free association where it can see private meanings which may not occur even to intellectuals.

As a phenomenon, it is simple, but it is in fact quite complex in its nature and function. It is also a rare phenomenon, and naturally experts in different fields of human activity—behavioural psychology, social psychology, psychometrics, cognitive science, artificial intelligence, philosophy, history, economics, design research, business, and management—have studied it with great interest. The studies have covered everyday creativity, exceptional creativity and even artificial creativity. Unlike many phenomena in science, there is no single, authoritative perspective or definition of creativity. And unlike many phenomena in psychology, there is no standardized measurement technique.

Creativity, it's believed, is the result of 'divine intervention', of 'chance'. It's been associated with genius, mental illness and humour. Some say it is a ***trait*** we are born with; others say it can be taught with the application of simple techniques. Creativity has also been viewed as a beneficence of a muse or Muses.

Though people generally associate creativity with 'art' and 'literature', it's also an essential part of '**innovation**' and '**invention**'.

8.2 What is creativity?

It's a process of developing new, uncommon, or unique ideas, using imagination, restructuring and re-evaluating an already existing knowledge.

To put it another way, it's the act of

(i) bringing into existence
(ii) at a given period of 'time'
(iii) an experience
(iv) for the mind, body or both
(v) believed to be unique at that given time.

8.3 Who is a creative thinker?

Creative thinkers may be intellectuals but are definitely ***talented*** in some special way. They desire to be creative, they believe there is a solution, they relentlessly pursue the solution for its own sake, they are highly motivated (intrinsically), are self-directed (no one need prompt them), are self-starting (without external push), are diligent, are independent in their judgements, are self-assertive and do use their talents optimally, do work hard incessantly, consciously and subconsciously. They have such a mind-set that even though they are not mentally busy with the problem, 'chance' seems to hand the solution to them. And they seemed to arrive through accident **insights** or **flashes**.

8.4 Some famous creative thinkers

Archimedes got his 'flash' as he noticed that when he got into the tub exactly the same amount of water flowed over the side as the volume of his body that was in the water.

Sir Jadish Chandra Bose was thought **crazy** when he suggested that plants had a life of their own and were subject to fatigue, recovery, depression and exaltation. He proved this with his 'crescograph'—an instrument that could record the reaction of plants to manures, poisons, that could show that plants are capable of feeling, that they have a sixth sense which tells them of the approach of a stranger.

Alexander Graham Bell's dream of making human voice move from one ear to another without the owners being close to each other was considered 'wild'. He did work hard, kept experimenting, and 'chance' provided him the clue.

Alexander Fleming **chanced** upon *pencillin* when, the unusual scientist that he was, he didn't throw away the contaminated culture but was instead interested in the mouldspore that dropped on the culture plate, and he noted that the 'contamination' was killing germs.

Adi Sankara (Advaitham), Ramanujacharya (Vishishtadvaitham), Buddha (the ten sins), Jesus, Prophet Muhammad, Martin Luther (Protestantism), Sigmund Freud, Karl Marx, Albert Einestein are some other well-known creative thinkers.

8.5 Steps to creative thinking

1. You start with the formulation of a problem or phenomenon and state it clearly.

2. You then gather knowledge, facts, data required from you memory, from external inputs through reading 'literature', your colleagues or databases. You assimilate and process this information, think, associate, sort or align into new categories and contexts, analyze, argue, counter-argue. You work for days, weeks or months in waking and sleeping moments. No solution seems to be in sight. You turn away from your effort either deliberately or involuntarily.

3. Now, whatever confusion there was seems to lose its grip, whatever ideas that were interfering with the solution seem to lose their force or fade. And during the time you may be undergoing an experience, a clue jumps at you out of the blue as it were. But actually you and your main focus have never separated for the subconscious thought process has been at work.

4. Your mind perceives the clue as it strikes you, your conscious mind seizes the opportunity, uses the clue and evolves a solution as it emerges.

5. You now evaluate the worthiness of the apparent solution to check if you do have the solution. It's also possible that the flash turns out to be unsatisfactory, and you are again back to square one, making another attempt.

8.6 Can we produce more creative thinkers than there are?

'You cannot teach a man anything; you can only help him to find it within himself,' says Galileo.

The desire to be creative, the relentless pursuit of a solution for its own sake, the intrinsic motivation are generally innate in a creative thinker. But it is possible to identify or locate such people or those who by their behaviour do indicate a clear 'leaning' towards creativity, and it's equally possible to provide an environment and hope for the best.

Besides, several driving forces like a rapidly expanding marketplace, increasing competitiveness, diverse interests of consumers have driven business houses to plan for and provide an innovation-conducive environment. So that those who have somehow managed to retain their inherent creative talents despite a unhelpful formal education system can be useful to themselves and to the society.

8.7 The environment

This should amply provide an extrinsic atmosphere to nurture and promote the desire to be creative, the relentless pursuit of a solution for its own sake and the intrinsic motivation.

1. It should bring together a band of creative thinkers because 'creativity is contagious.'
2. It should assure them of

   full management support—no interference/restriction in terms of research duration, of budget, of working hours etc.,

   cutting down red tape to the barest minimum.
3. It should announce and implement a system of rewards.
4. It should express appreciation of effort by meeting the expectations.
5. It should ensure non-intervention in the research activity by 'administrative' leaders.
6. It should seriously avoid looking at 'innovation' efforts through 'expenses' spectacles; it's the genuineness of the effort that matters, and if an innovation occurs, it's a bonus.

8.8 Creativity Techniques for short-term job activities

(i) At group level

There are time-bound job activities that can pose problems for which solutions will be needed. When a large number of employees are to be involved for sharing of thoughts freely without fear or favour, seminars and symposiums can be arranged. More importantly, **brainstorming** sessions could be held when a smaller number of people need to come together for engaging their minds. These sessions could be held in an open, free atmosphere when members could air their thoughts without prejudice, without being considered crazy, wild or silly because the intention is to gather as many thoughts as possible before they can seriously consider them for discussion, critical analysis and then arrive at consensus. They can promote cross-fertilization because people working together can think up of new ideas that may not strike them when they work alone. As there are more individuals, these sessions can help them look at all the aspects from as many angles as they are members.

(ii) Thought gathering at individual level

1. Allow your mind to roam freely. If necessary, take a walk, let your mind spin. Have a pen and a writing pad at the ready. As thoughts flow, write them down. Don't worry now about whether they make sense or not.
2. Decide how many ideas will satisfy you before you go to the next step of looking at them in order to analyze them.
3. Once you have the required number, pause for a moment to decide if they are enough or you'd like a few more to crop up. If the latter, go on thinking, who knows, some more thoughts may occur to you.
4. Discuss the problem with someone who is no way connected to the job in hand. Your friend or neighbour may surprise you.
5. Think about the problem just before going to sleep. Tell yourself you're going to dream about a solution to the problem. And before you know what has happened, you may really end up dreaming a way of solving the problem.
6. Think about the problem when your mind is fresh—be it in the morning, be it late in the evening.
7. Think of the problem in visuals. That is, form images in your mind. They help you to see the problem in different perspectives. They give life and colour to your ideas.
8. If you can, put around you objects related to the problem so that they may trigger a thought or an idea even when your mind is on other things.
9. Change your track of thought process. For example, suppose you've been thinking over and over again: 'A, therefore B, therefore C, therefore D, and then you get stuck and ask yourself, 'where can I go from here?' Backtrack, say, to B and see if you can proceed from there.
10. Ask yourself why the problem exists at all. Think about the background to the problem to see if it can throw light upon the problem itself so that you can handle it differently.

Probably there are certain other things you can add to this list and go about solving problems.

8.9 Lateral thinking

You're thinking laterally when you move away from conventional thinking and look for novel solutions. When you think laterally, you produce a solution that no other person can ever think of. The point of lateral thinking is that many problems require a different perspective to solve successfully.

Lateral thinking

- recognizes dominant ideas that polarize the perception of a problem,
- avoids traditional ways of looking for solutions,
- uses imagination to look at a problem differently.

Of course, there's an element of cleverness in lateral thinking.

A few instances

1. Edward de Bono has this anecdote:
   A merchant owed money to a moneylender. He agreed to the moneylender's suggestion that the debt could be settled by selecting one of the two stones the moneylender would put in a bag and that if his daughter picked the white stone, he wouldn't have to pay back the debt but if his daughter picked the black one, the moneylender would take the daughter as his wife. However, the moneylender "fixed" the outcome by putting two black stones in the bag. The daughter saw this. She picked a stone out of the bag, and immediately dropped it onto the path full of other stones. She said that the stone she picked must have been the opposite color of the one remaining in the bag. If the moneylender called her bluff, he would be found to be dishonest, so he left the place without another word. The daughter solved the problem using lateral thinking.

2. In **The Mahabharatha**, The Kauravas and the Pandavas are getting ready for an epic battle at Khurkshethra. Lord Krishna knows that Gandhari wants to pass on her spiritual powers to her son Duryodhana so that he would not be killed in the battle. So when Duryodhana is on his way to meet his mother, Lord Krishna suggests to him that since no grown man should appear before his mother naked, he should cover his loins. Duryodhana acts accordingly and meets his mother. Gandhari removes her blindfold and starts transmitting her powers through her eyes on to the body of Duryodhana as she passes her eyes from head to toe. To her horror, she finds the loins of Duryodhana covered and fails to protect that area. Lord Krishna used his lateral thinking ability to have a portion of Duroyodhana's body unprotected so that Bhima could kill him, striking at the loins.

3. Birbal served at Akbar's court and was known for solving problems in a very unusual manner. Once a rich man approached him and requested his help in finding out who stole a silver plate from his house. He told Birbal that if at all, he suspected only the servants. Birbal went to the rich man's house, called the servants and told them that only one of them could have stolen the silver plate and that a confession would lead to a pardon. When no servant responded, he ordered each one of them to bring to him a stick of the same size. Then Birbal told them to take the sticks home and bring them back to him the next day. He also warned them that the person who returned with his stick grown one inch longer would be the thief.

The thief was so frightened that he could not take the risk of the stick growing one inch longer. So he cut the stick one inch shorter and slept.

When he woke up, he found that the stick had not grown one inch longer.

Naturally!

Birbal thought laterally and identified the thief in a manner no one else could have thought of!

Distinguishing between creativity and innovation

The distincition between the two expressions in one of perspective. Both are novel and appropriate. But creativity provides the concept and innovation realizses the concept. Creativity is of the mind and innovation is of the 'matter'. Creativity is the idea and innovation is its shape.

All the same, creativity is preferred in 'art' disciplines whereas innovation in 'science' and 'business' disciplines.

PART THREE

Retaining the Job

1. Introduction

Getting a good job with a good salary is important. But **retaining** it (continue to work) is more important.

Today you're living in a **highly competitive** world. Especially, if you're working in private organizations. Everyone wants to get to (= reach) the top as quickly as possible. Everyone wants top position, power and prestige. There's nothing wrong with this.

But **position, power, prestige** will not come your way. To get these three, you'll have to work very hard and **show results**. What does "show results" mean? It means that you'll have to

- work extra hours
- innovate
- use all your communicating abilities

to **continually prove** to your Management that they've been gaining from **retaining** you and from **promoting** you.

In the past, working in offices involved mostly deskwork (= dealing with files and papers). Today, people are more important. This means that you must communicate with people. This means that **interpersonal interaction** is very important.

Who are these people you communicate with?

Who are these people with whom you interact interpersonally?

Who are these people you deal with daily or frequently?

- Your Department workers
- Workers in other Departments
- Your superiors and subordinates (= colleagues/coworkers)
- Your customers
- The public
- Members of the other organizations in India and abroad government officials

You meet them in your office, in your organization, in their offices, in their homes, in workshops/seminars/conferences, in exhibitions, in product launching, in sales promotions, in project presentations.

There is constant or frequent exchange of information between you and these people. If this **exchange** has to be **successful**, you should use appropriate relationship while communicating with them. The relationship may be **formal, semiformal, informal**.

formal	:	you're polite and respectful in language and behaviour. Say only what is absolutely essential. Generally, no personal matters.
informal	:	you move freely. Intimacy level is high. Gossip is common. Emotions and feelings are okay.
semiformal	:	partly formal and partly informal

The medium is English, generally speaking. Your success depends on how good you are at using English. If unfortunately, you aren't good, your superiors or your colleagues will have no time to help you. You're reading this book, luckily for you, when you are still in college.

---

2. Communicating in pairs

This takes place between you and another person (**two people**). This occurs most of the time (**frequency**). You can use different **modes**: converse (=speak), write, body language (= gestures); even silence can communicate! But mostly, it is oral. The **medium** may be English, your local language or a language known to both of you. What you say to each other may be personal or official (= **content**). The **relationship** may be informal, semiformal or formal.

Success in pair communication depends on how much you and the other person understand each other. This understanding depends on what you think of yourself (as a person, as an employee, as a coworker, as a friend) and what you think of the other person (as a person, as an employee, as a coworker, as a friend). If you think you are more important to yourself than the other person is to you, there'll be problems in communicating.

The **images** you have about yourself and about the other person will affect communication positively or negatively. These images create **expectations**. You may expect agreement, for instance, but your partner may disagree or may remain silent because he has good reason to but you'll become angry or unhappy because he has gone against your expectation. But your partner may not understand your anger or unhappiness and may be confused or he may think you're being unreasonable. And he may become upset. Like you, he's not patient enough to think with reason.

If the images don't contradict, if the expectations are met , there will be understanding and communicating will be successful. But if they occur a little too often there will be breakdowns in communication and strain in the relations. Both of you will not be able to work together, and this could lead to other problems – your superior's opinion about you, your promotions, even your continuation in that organization.

To have successful pair communication, remember the following and use them:

- The communication must be two way, not one way.
- It must be you-oriented, not I – oriented.
  [Understanding your partner is more important than your partner understanding you.]
- You must show interest in the communication.
- You must use language, tone and voice and body language that will help your partner.
- As a listener, receive the messages and respond properly.

- As a speaker, speak clearly, explain if necessary.
- Respect your partner's strengths.
- Understand his weaknesses (communicating problems).
- Be open - minded.
- Encourage your partner.
- Appreciate his views.
- Be informal or formal to suit your partner.
- Show proper respect to your superior.
- Don't interrupt, give a patient hearing.
- Don't threaten with your status.
- Never make him feel inferior.
- Don't be too brief or don't overelaborate.
- Be intelligible, don't confuse.
- Show warmth, friendship and affection.
- Even go for compromise.
- Success is important, victory is not.
- You are important but your listener is more important.

The first condition to success is two-way (interactive) communication. Let's see what this means:

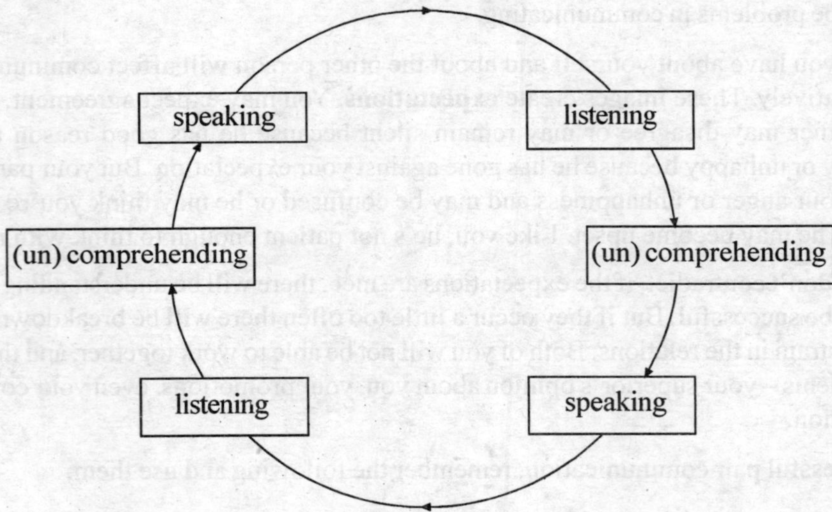

A speaks. B listens. B may or may not understand what A said. So, B speaks, continuing the conversation further or asking for clarification. A listens. He may or may not understand. So he continues his interaction with B either saying more about what he said to B earlier (message one) or adding information (message two). Thus the first condition is fulfilled. This goes on until both decide or one of them decides to stop with or without reason.

3. Communicating in groups (G.D.)

You're already familiar with communicating in a group. You did this as part of job getting process. You've learnt to

- initiate (= begin) a discussion,
- listen to your groupmates.
- continue the discussion intelligently, clearly, precisely,
- summarise upto a point,
- enter the discussion without interrupting,
- conclude the discussion appropriately or properly.

You did all or most of these better than other candidates and went to the interview stage. That is, you scored more points than others.

But when you participate in G.D. in your organisation, your aim to participate becomes different, you're not competing with anybody in this G.D. This G.D. is known as **brainstorming**. This is a

- joint effort
  and
  cooperative effort

for the good of the company you're working for. This is where everyone in the group **shares** ideas, suggestions, solutions, **discusses** them, **analyses** them and their positive and their positive and negative aspects and their impact and **arrives at recommendations** (= choose the best so that your company benefits). In the G.D. for the job, you win over others. But in brainstorming, the company wins (= you, as an individual, don't win).

In brainstorming, you and your colleagues from you Department come together or you and your colleagues from other Departments come together. The purpose is to generate (= produce / think of) ideas and solve problems for your Company.

Content (knowledge + information)

technical

Use what you already know.

Keep in touch with latest developments in your field and other allied fields.

Use this for meaningful discussion.

non technical

Use your world knowledge

= what you know from experience
= what you gather from public services
about govt. policies
stuatutory bodies like ISO
international trade / economics

Note: Use content imaginatively and creatively.

Medium (English and / or local language) + body language

Use right vocabulary and sentence structures.

Be simple, clear, precise in your expressions.

Use right body language:

Have constant eye contact.
Use eyebrows, facial expressions.
Use your hands to support (not negatively).
Put on a smile when necessary.
Nod your head when necessary.
Show you're listening.

Use both mediums to

indicate interest / excitement,
encourage others,
show cooperation / sympathy / understanding.

Activities

- Start discussion.
  [= set the ball rolling]
- Provide information.
- Explain / elaborate / exemplify.
- Ask questions.
- Seek clarifications.
- Clear doubts.
- Analyse objectively.
- Argue for or against.
- Convince / be convinced.
- Think of and discuss concepts (theoretical)
- Evaluate ideas.
- Come to conclusions.
- Allow others to speak.

Behaviour

- Involve yourself totally.
- Involve others.
- Be positive in your approach.
- Don't act superior or inferior.
- Don't be silent.
- Listen carefully and indicate it through your behaviour.
- Don't attack anyone personally. [Attack ideas]
- Don't dominate / let others speak.

- Control emotions (anger / frustration)
- Show respect to age and experience.
- Be frank without hurting others.
- Adjust yourself and go for compromise.
- Prove that the group is important, not you alone.

All these are essential part of your role in brainstorming. Remember that your performance will affect your job career, positively or negatively because your Management will receive reports from your group leaders.

---

4. Oral presentation

Oral presentation means **talking to an audience.**

To a group of people who are

- your top management in their offices,
- foreigners in their offices or in a conference hall,
- the public in exhibitions.
- prospective purchasers in product launching,
- agents in sales promotion,
- officials in their offices or in yours.

What will you be saying ?

To your top management

about production, sales, marketing, profit.

To foreigners

about business arrangements, mergers.

To the public

about your product (s)

To prospective purchasers

about a new product or an improved version.

To agents

about the profit they'll make by selling your product.

To officials

about matters related to

licensing

conforming to regulations

auditing.

Thus, what you'll be saying (= contents) may be very technical, less technical or nontechnical.

How will you say it ?

- Good presentation;
  - convincing introduction
  - appealing body: ideas with elaboration
    explanation
    example
  - productive conclusion
- Good communication :
  - excellent use of language (English)
    words
    sentences
  - appropriate visuals
    (see three pages later)
  - meaningful gestures (body language)

Use all these to convince, to persuade and to succeed.

Oral presentation is very important to you because

- Your performance will determine the growth of your Company, the money it will earn, the respect it will gain and
- Your career growth depends on how well you perform.

---

5. Paper presentation

Before you can present a paper you need to prepare it; that is, you need to write it.

Let's understand first distinctions between and among

essay, assignment, paper, seminar
conference, project work, dissertation, thesis.

Let's understand what the terms in italics actually mean. Essay is a term that can include, in its fold, all the writing forms printed in italics. In other words all these are essays. But the difference between essay and others is in quality: an essay can be of general nature with the author's personal views (that is, subjective) whereas the others are based on study or experimentation and they convey results or conclusions (that is, objective). There is difference in quantity also: essays are generally shorter than others.

There is also difference in intent, though all are academic in content.

1. An *assignment* is (all semesters)

   (i) part of classroom learning which is generally given direction by a syllabus (not intended to be original)

(ii) limited in scope and shorter in length
(iii) for submission for evaluation

2. A *paper* (all semesters)

(i) is based on thinking about a theoretical concept discussing it from a few angles and makes educated guesses or arrives at conclusions or poses a few questions.
(ii) is accompanied by charts, slides or OHP transparencies that highlight specific features, and
(iii) is presented to an audience who can understand and appreciate the pre sentation.

A *seminar* (all semesters)

is usually in a class at college or university where the teacher and the students discuss a given topic in a given discipline.

A *conference* (while in job)

(i) is a gathering of kindred souls (like - minded people, generally speaking) lasting for a few days
(ii) discusses ideas of mutual interest in a given discipline
(iii) makes recommendations.

A *project work* (4), a *dissertation* (5) and a *thesis* (6) are all (as completion of BE, ME, PhD respectively)

(i) much longer than an assignment / a paper and
(ii) original contributions, in varying degrees, to knowledge in a given discipline as the result of studious research.

Activity Verbs

(i) describe: give an account of a process where inter-related activities occur in sequence
(ii) define: specify clearly the meaning of terms (or) mention terms of reference
(iii) discuss: write in detail about various aspects of a topic
(iv) analyse: talk about various parts of a topic in the context of inter- relation ships between / among the parts.
(v) compare: discuss / analyse different characteristics of items to show contrast, similarities or differences
(vi) enumerate: make a list of advantages / disadvantages, weaknesses / strengths, activities etc.
(vii) illustrate : provide examples to explain / support / prove / make clear / disprove a claim / belief / a conclusion / a deduction etc.
(viii) disprove : use logical argument to make your point

(ix) evaluate : look at a problem / question as a critic / judge critically, objectively

(x) summarise : help the listener / reader in the middle or in the end not to lose the thread of continuity by reiterating (repeating) what has already been said or pointed out

6. Paper Presentation (seminars and conferences)

This applies to any presentation you may make.

Business houses conduct conferences frequently. As an employee you may be attending such conferences where you'll be listening to people presenting papers.

What

When you present a paper, you'll be sharing your thinking about a theoretical concept, you'll be making a few educated guesses or you'll be arriving at conclusions. Or you'll be posing a few questions that will make others think. Or you may be showing a new model or an improved version of an existing piece of equipment. You will thus be adding to the knowledge already available in your discipline or field of research.

Why

Such meets and conferences will help you become an *extrovert*. Second, it'll be a new experience, and your learning environment will get enlarged. You'll see new meanings because a concept or a theory is looked at from different angles. You may decide to be an achiever. You may receive recognition, respect and even admiration from learned personalities for your contributions. Paper presentation can thus be a source for growth and success.

Steps to presentation

This involves two major activities and four sub acts:

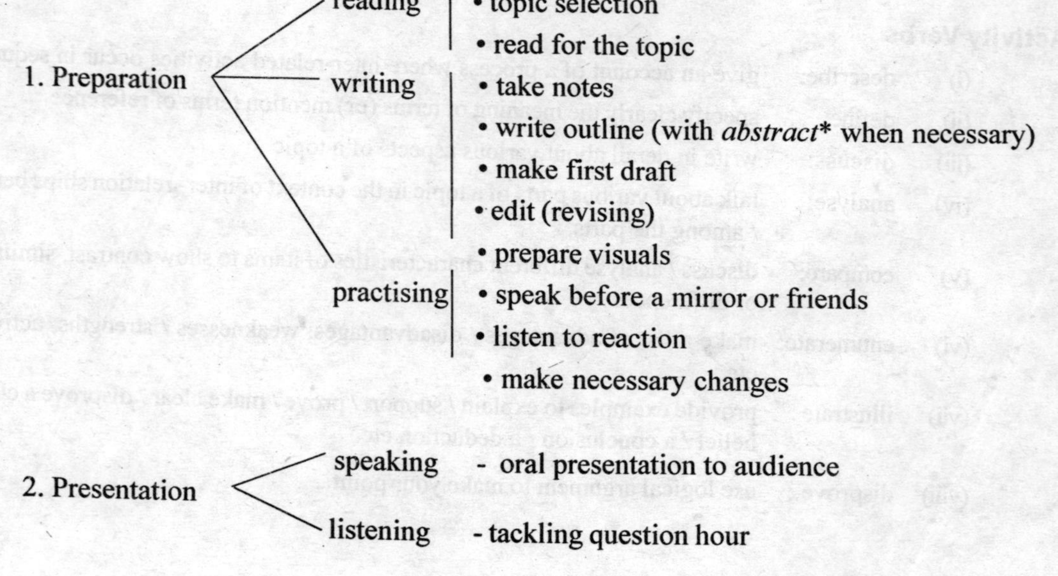

*abstract is a very *brief and clear summary* of your total paper. You may need to send it in order for seminar / conference organisers to decide about the quality of your paper.

Topic selection

As you go through your semester syllabuses, you may develop an interest in a given area in your discipline or in allied disciplines. This will happen through either reading journal articles on researched areas or your faculty suggesting areas for research.

Read for the topic

Once you have decided the topic, your reading begins. With help from faculty, select *books* and *journals*. Use *skimming** and *scanning** skills for this activity. Now your bibliography is ready of course, as you read, you may add those to this list of source materials.

Now you need to *study** these books and journals very carefully to gather information. Information gathering implies *taking notes*. (see Volume 1).

*scanning – looking quickly in order to identify relevant information

*skimming – reading quickly noting only the important points

*studying – devoting time and attention to read widely and deeply to gather information.

When you feel you have sufficient information, write out an *outline* of your paper. This includes *introducing* the topic [the purpose of the paper and placing the topic in the right context (right research area) with appropriate background information related to the topic], *talking at length* about your research and *concluding* your paper. In other words, the outline provides a broad *picture of what goes where*.

Now make the *first draft*. Introducing the topic is crucial to getting the attention of your listeners. It must arouse the *curiosity* of the audience and get them to *think about* the topic. Use these *techniques* or any other:

- Begin with a question and link it to your topic.
- Use a real life situation and relate it to the topic.
- Talk briefly about recent research and connect it to your topic.
- If it's a model or an equipment, talk about one or two expectations of the consumer and say how your model will satisfy the customer.

Make this introduction very brief. Then state what your topic is and how you'll go about presenting it.

Talking at length (in detail) about your research – your theoretical concept or your model – begins. Provide the background with the existing concept or model. Talk in detail about *how different* or *how improved* your research is with *visuals* (see next page). You'll need to explain, elaborate, exemplify by describing, comparing, contrasting, arguing, providing support data with figures, graphs, tables, pictures.

Conclude with findings, solutions, recommendations or with questions / ideas as further research areas.

Editing

Look for weaknesses in your thinking, in your arguments. You may have been very vague, for instance; you can do this by imagining yourself as your listener(s). Ask questions and answer them. Rewrite parts of your paper. Use proper sentence and paragraph connectors. Next, give your paper to your friends and faculty for comments. Use their suggestions to improve your paper.

Prepare visuals

Visuals help listeners comprehend your talk with ease and in comfort. They

- help quick comprehension
- help information retention
- reinforce ideas
- provide variety

Visuals		
Shape	mode	equipment
diagrams		slide projector
graphs	slides	overhead projector
bar charts	transparencies	computer (powerpoint)
pie charts		
flow charts		
cartoons		
drawings		
photographs		
verbals		

Diagrams can depict

1. Different types of an item

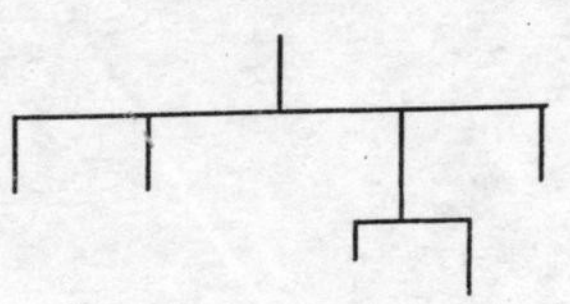

2. different parts of an item

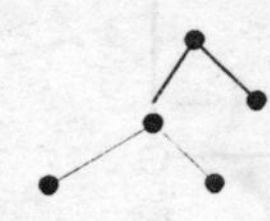

3. interaction between different items

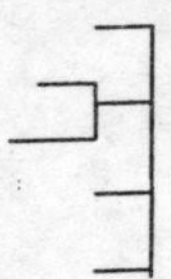

4. sequential process

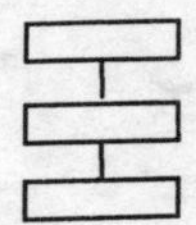

5. cyclic action

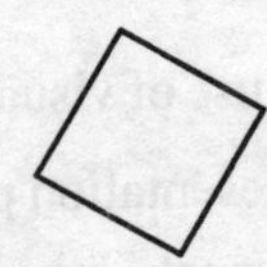

6. comparison / contrast

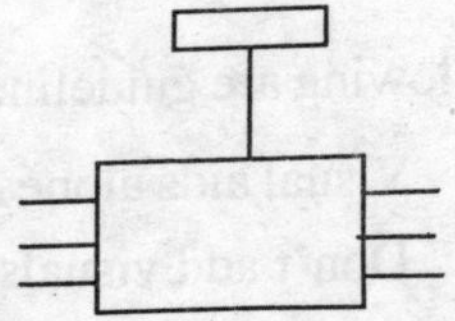

Graphs can talk about *trends* over a period of time:

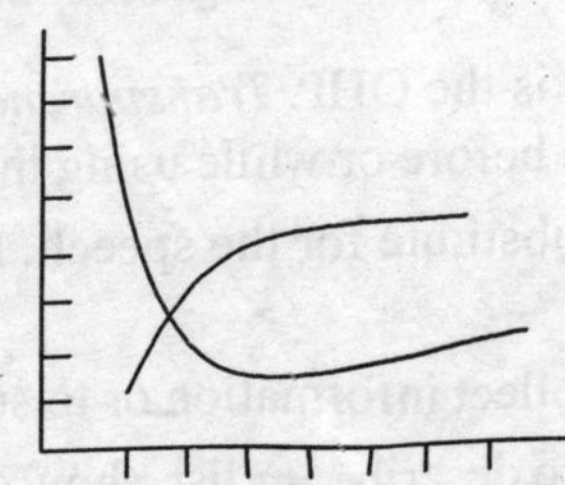

Bar charts express *alternate ways* of displaying (showing) trends:

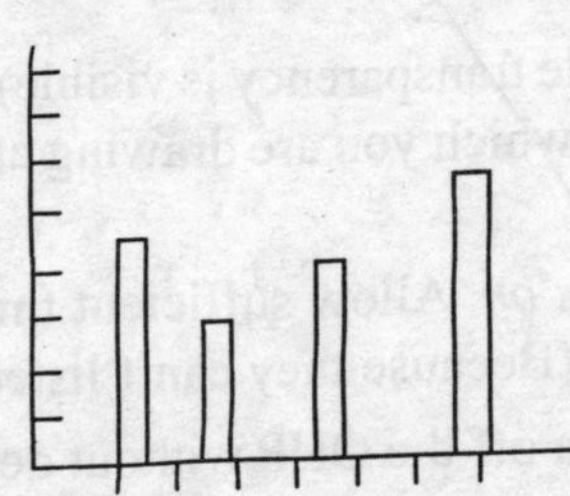

Pie charts can show *proportions*:

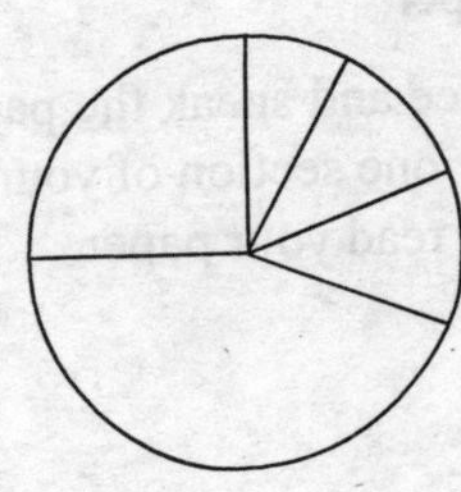

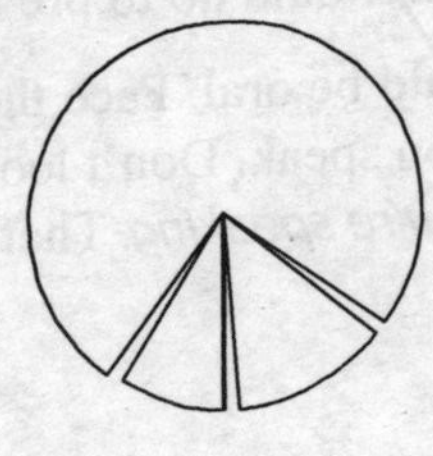

Flow charts describe *various steps* of a process or various divisions and their

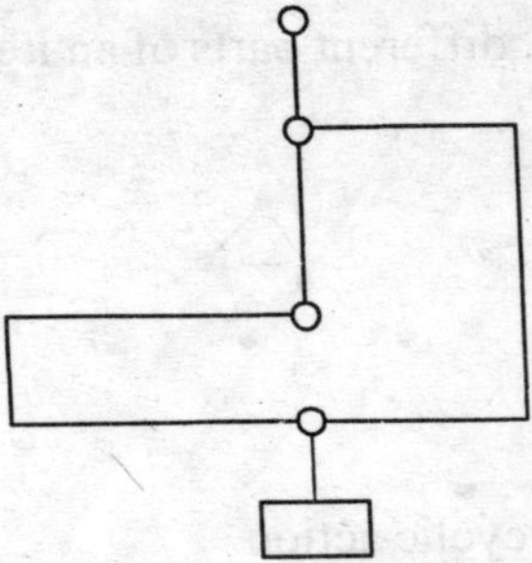

The following are guidelines for the use or nonuse of visuals:

- Visual aids alone do not make your presentation professional.
- Don't add visuals because the other speakers are doing so.
- Visuals should be pictures rather than words to look at.
- Use verbal visuals to summarize. Don't try to get too much information on the visual .

A *popular visual* for paper presentation is the OHP. *Transparencies* are projected on to a wall or screen. Please note the following points before or while using the OHP.

- Don't use transparencies as substitute for the speech. Don't simply read your speech with transparencies.
- Use transparencies only to recollect information or to summarize.
- If you are using transparencies to describe, to list, show only that point that you are talking about; cover the rest with a paper so that the audience are not distracted from listening to you.
- Use a pointer (when the whole transparency is visible) on the transparency itself to point to one word or expression to which you are drawing attention or about which you're speaking.
- *Don't talk while the visual is on.* Allow sufficient time for the audience to absorb the content on the transparency. (Because they can't listen and read the visual.)
- Remove the visual and switch off the OHP without delay.

7. Presentation Act

Let's see now what you should do to present a paper.

Your presentation should be oral. Face the audience and speak the paper. Be in eye contact with your audience while you speak. Don't look at only one section of your listeners. *Look at differe[nt] sections all the time you're speaking.* That is, don't read your paper.

How do you make sure your audience will listen to you?

- Make your introduction interesting.
- Make the audience curious.
- Indicate clearly what you intend to say.
- Use topic sentences. (containing major ideas)
- Provide examples, explanations.
- Make your language simple.
- Use link words.
- Don't fumble in your speech.
  (for this you must be thorough with your ideas)
- Have constant eye contact.
- Give time to your audience to read your visuals.
- Use pauses effectively.
- Don't speak too fast. Speak slowly especially when you have something important to say.
- Don't speak in monotone.
  Let your voice rise and fall as you stress certain syllables of words as you speak them.
- Repeat your important ideas and link them.
- Learn to avoid mannerisms like:-
  moving forward and backward
  swaying from side to side
  walking left to right
  crossing your legs

[Mannerisms distract the audience. Your friends can identify them.]

It's good to practise with your friends as audience. Their comments can be very helpful.

8. Question hour (listening and responding)

Your presentation should affect your audience. In which case, they're likely to ask questions, to clear doubts, to add information. *This question hour is your litmus test.* Your success depends on how well you handle the audience.

- Don't get annoyed.
- Don't be rude.
- Don't be arrogant.
- Don't be condescending.
  (in your looks and tone)
- give a patient hearing.

- Accept an error .
- Be polite.
- Smile and look cheerful.
- Respect your listeners and earn respect.

PART FOUR

Use of English

1. SENTENCE FORMATION

There are seven main clause types : (single main clause)

Type	S(ubject)	V(erb)	O(bject (s))	C(omplement)	A(dverbial)
1. SV(i)	1. He 2. She 3. The clouds 4. The child 5. It	was working. is standing appeared. cried. is raining.			
2. SV(i)C	6. She 7. The soup 8. He 9. They 10. He	is tastes became turned appears	a thief. traitors. foolish.	happy. horrible.	
3. SV(i)A	11. I 12. The teacher 13. She got 14. The meeting	have been shouted is			in the garden. at the top of his voice. into the car. at eight.
4. SV(t)O	15. My wife 16. I 17. The child 18. She 19. He 20. We	enjoys threw is holding has nodded paid	parties. the ball. a knife. a car. his head. the bus driver.		
5. SV(t)OO	21. I 22. We	gave bought	<u>him</u> (d.o) an answer. (i.o) <u>her</u> (d.o) a gift. (i.o)		
6. SV(t)OA	23.I 24. The child	looked up threw	the word the bag		in the dictionary. at him.
7. SV(t)OC	25. He 26. I 27. The revolver 28. She	kept found made called	the car him her me	in the garage. dull. afraid. stupid.	

Note V(i) = intransitive verb (without object)
V(t) = transitive verb (with object)

2. As you can see from the table,

a sentence can have <u>five elements</u> :

S(ubject)

V(erb)

O(bject) — predicate group

C(omplement)

A(adverbial)

in certain combinations as part of its structure.

Generally speaking

The verb
- is the most central element,
- is in middle position,
- is essential for sentence completion,
- and cannot be moved to another position.

The subject
- appears before the verb,
- is what we are talking about,
- and is necessary for sentence completion.

The object
- appears after the verb
- and is necessary for meaning completion in certain structures.
- (see 4, 5, 6 in the previous page.)
- Od – direct object, Oi – indirect object
- (impersonal) (personal)

The complement
- comes after the object (see 7)
- or after the verb (see 2)
- and is necessary for meaning completion.

The adverbial appears
- before the subject
- in the middle
- or at the end of a sentence.

3. Expressions functioning as

Subject

1. *single noun or pronoun*

29. **The street** was empty.
30. **The tree** fell as the lighting struck.
31. **The dog** kept barking.
32. **I** slept late last night.
33. **You**'ll listen to me.
34. **She**'ll see you in the evening.
35. **They** are arriving this afternoon.
    Kamal is with a bank.

2. *plural noun or pronoun*

36. **Jamal, Joseph** and **Jaya** are classmates.
37. **You** and **I** will never part.

3. *gerund*

38. **Seeing** is believing.

4. *adverbial*

39. **Slowly** is exactly how he drives.

5. *phrase*

40. **To Chennai** is not very far.
41. **From here to Tirupathi** is only 150 kms.

6. *clause*

42. **That you did'nt know** is no excuse.
43. **How you'll behave with her** will decide your future.
44. **Whether the book will sell** depends on the sales pitch.
45. **Whoever has done this** will confess.
46. **Watching television** will keep them out of mischief.
47. There's **no mistaking that voice.**
48. **Because she wants to marry him** doesn't mean we would agree to it.

4. Expressions functioning as

Object

1. *single noun/pronoun*

49. He repaired **his car.**
50. She tore **the letter** open.
51. She let **the bird** fly.
52. My Principal likes **me.**
53. I heard **them** talking.
54. He slapped **John** hard.

2. *plural noun/pronoun*

55. I love **my wife and my daughters.**
56. The announcement surprised **all of us.**

3. *gerund*

57. He enjoys **playing the guitar.**

4. *phrase*

58. She likes **to relax.**
59. They want **to go home.**

5. *clause*

60. I notice **that he speaks English without accent.**
61. I don't understand **what you want.**
62. Do you know **where he went ?**
63. He didn't tell me **whether I should wait for him.**
64. She doesn't know **who they are.**
65. No one can say **when they'll reach *here*.**

---

5. Expressions functioning as

Complement

1. *noun*

66. He became **a rich man** overnight (C_s)
67. She was standing, **a picture of innocence.** (C_s)
68. I made my cousin **my P.A.** (C_o)
69. My friends call me **a bull dog.** (C_o)

70. I'm called **a bull dog.** (C_s)

71. Seeing is **believing.** (C_s)

2. *adjective*

72. He died **young.**

73. My class is **empty.**

74. The milk tastes **sour.**

3. *adverb*

75. The pain nearly drove me **mad.**

76. The boy set the bird **free.**

4. *phrase*

77. His threats filled her **with terror.**

78. She likes her desk **to be tidy.**

79. His words prove him **to be a fool.**

80. We are **to be married** soon.

5. *clause*

81. That's **what I wanted to know.**

82. The fact is **that he doesn't really try.**

> ***Note:*** Generally speaking, expressions coming **after** verbs like
> ***be, seen/appear/look, become***
> ***and***
> ***turn, smell, go, come, grow, sound, taste, fall,***
> ***lie, keep, get, wear, like, find***
> are known as **complements.**

Expressions functioning as

6. Adverbials

83. We walked **five miles.**

84. They waited **the whole day.**

85. The baby weighs **nine pounds.**

86. I shall be here **two weeks.**

87. The book costs (is) **two hundred rupees.**

88. She telephoned **last week.**

89. They stayed **in bed the whole day.**

90. My cousin lives **next door.**
91. He disappeared **with the money.**
92. I found the letter **in the kitchen.**
93. She telephoned **after she had seen the ad.**

---

7. A few more examples **SVC** and **SVA:**

SVC

94. I am **a pig.**
95. You are **my friend.**
96. He is **very angry.**
97. All of us are **happy.**
98. I felt **a fool.**
99. I seemed **a fool.**
100. He stayed **a student** all his life.
101. She appeared **a fool.**
102. He proved **a useful friend.**
103. She looks **a great scholar.**
104. He became **famous** suddenly.
105. He turned **a traitor.**
106. She stayed **quiet.**
107. The flower smells **fresh.**
108. The fire burned **low.**
109. He pleaded **innocent.**
110. He went **mad.**
111. She grew **tired.**
112. I am **behind** in my rent.
113. He feels **at home.**
114. I don't feel **upto the task.**
115. This colour suits **you.**
116. This weighs **ten kilos.**
117. He prides **himself** on his appearance.
118. She didn't behave **herself** at the party.
119. He lay **on the seashore.**
120. He sneaked **into the house.**
121. She feels **happy.**
122. She seems **sad.**
123. She appeared **foolish.**
124. She looked **angry.**
125. He sounded **strange.**
126. She remained **silent.**
127. The fruit tastes **raw.**
128. She turned **cold.**
129. I got **ready.**
130. She stood **firm.**
131. I'll go **hungry.**
132. She blushed **red.**
133. They appear **out of breath.**
134. In technology we are **ahead.**
135. Her promise seems **of no importance.**

SVA

136. We're putting up **at a motel.**
137. The drinks are **for the journey.**
138. I stole **into her room.**
139. My office is **in the next building.**
140. The children were running **very fast towards the park.**

141. He lived **happily.**

142. He stepped **into the darkroom.**

143. She lived **in poverty for forty years.**

144. She telephoned **though obviously ill.**

145. They drove **westwards.**

146. She has been enthusiastic **about her work.**

147. Someone was laughing **loudly in the next room.**

148. I've been **in the garden all the time since lunch.**

149. She walked **to the bus stop.**

150. There are **no lectures on Sunday.**

151. Payment is **by cash only.**

152. We got off **the train.**

153. Your scarf is lying **on the floor**.

154. She lives **in a hut.**

155. His grades improved **steadily.**

156. They are **on the continent.**

157. He came in **quietly.**

158. The road is **under construction.**

159. The house faces **towards the sea.**

---

8. A few more examples of **SVOC** and **SVOA:**

SVOC

160. They kept the prisoner **quiet.**
161. She presumed her father **dead.**
162. The music drove me **mad.**
163. I'll hold you **responsible.**
164. The long walk made us all **hungry.**
165. I want my coffee **stronger than this.**
166. The President declared the meeting **open.**
167. He imagined himself **at the point of death.**
168. I found him **in trouble.**
169. The President appointed Mr.Gadgil **his personal secretary.**
170. The Committee has elected you **its Chairman.**
171. We named our daughter **Tharini.**
172. The nation considered him **a genius.**
173. Don't take me **for a fool.**
174. People have mistaken me **for my brother.**
175. They acknowledged her **as the undisputed leader.**
176. He found her **a loyal friend.**

SVOA

177. The teacher assessed her students **wrongly.**
178. The doctor treated the patient **medically.**
179. The engineer tested the instrument **electronically.**
180. Grip the handle **tightly.**
181. I keep a spare bicycle **in the garage.**
182. They put all the toys **upstairs.**
183. You can put the disks **on the table.**
184. She put the money **into her purse.**
185. He defended his client **with vigour.**
186. They're placing the blame **on us.**
187. I shall take my wife **to London for treatment.**
188. They talked me **into it.**
189. The sudden attack caught us **off our guard.**
190. She kissed her mother **on the cheek.**
191. They knew him **to be a spy.**
192. I bribed him **to get the work done.**
193. No one helped me **to reach my goal.**
194. I let her **go.**
195. I saw him **leave.**
196. I saw him **leaving.**
197. I caught my brother **smoking behind the bathroom.**
198. She got the house **painted.**
199. I want the watch **repaired.**
200. Someone must have heard the car **stolen.**

9.

SVOO → d.o + i.o.	**i.o. + d.o.**
1215. I gave **a doll to her.**	1216. I gave **her a doll.**
1217. She provided **an opportunity for me.**	1218. She provided me **an opportunity.**
1219. He told **the secret to me.**	1220. He told **me the secret.**
1221. I ordered **a meal for us.**	1222. I ordered **us a meal.**

SVOO → i.o + prepositional phrase

201. They supply us **with spare parts.**
202. They warned me **of the danger.**
203. She accused us **of cheating her.**

SVOO → i.o + (that) clause

204. He convinced me **(that) I was wrong.**
205. I told her **(that) I was leaving.**
206. I asked her **when the meeting would end.**
207. He would not tell us **why he had resigned.**

SVOO → preposition + i.o. + that clause

208. He wrote **to me that he would repay the debt within a week.**
209. She suggested **to him that he should meet the boss.**

SVOO → i.o + to-infinitive

210. He told **me to leave.**
211. I advised **her to see a doctor.**

---

10. Variations

There are also other types of sentences.

---

11. Sentences with *there* and *here*:

There/Here + verb + subject +complement

212. There're three exceptions.
213. There's no time.
214. There've been too many accidents.
215. There were some books on the shelf.
    [This is preferable to: Some books were on the shelf.]
216. There're many buildings there.
217. Here is a topic you'd like to talk about.

---

12. Exclamatory sentences with here/there

218. There/Here they come!
219. There comes the bus!
220. Here's the one you want!

13. Sentences with *this, these, those* and *that*:

221. This, These, Those, That
222. This is where my wife works.
223. That's my cousin.
224. These are sensitive issues.

---

14. It Sentences

225. It seems (to me) (that) you're not really interested in him.
226. It hardly matters whether we start now or later.
227. It's easy to do that.
228. It's no use your trying to convince me.
229. It's foolish behaving like that.
230. It's a mystery how the burglar got into the house.
231. It's difficult for anyone to be annoyed with her.

---

15. Negative Sentences

- We use **not** or **n't** to form negative sentences.
- We place **not** immediately **after**

    the first auxiliary/helping verb

or

    the only auxiliary/helping verb

232. She'*ll* not come. | after the only auxiliary
233. I'*m* not informed. |

234. She may not have reached home. (1 = may, 2 = have) | after first auxiliary
235. He has not been informed (1 = has, 2 = been) |

- We place **n't** with **the only or the first auxiliary:**

236. She *won't* come.
237. He *hasn't* been informed.

a few more examples

affirmative	negative
238. He works hard.	239. He **does** not/**doesn**'t work hard.
240. He work**ed** hard.	241. He **did** not/**didn**'t work hard.

242. They **go** to church.

243. They **do** not/**don**'t go to church.

244. He **needs to read** the coursebook.

245. He **need not/needn't/doesn't need to read** the coursebook.

246. You **ought to** escape.

247. You **ought not to** escape.

248. You **had better lock** the door.

249. You **had better not lock** the door.

250. He **had to** go.

251. He **did not/didn't have to** go.

252. I **need to** see you. [this is an external obligation]

253. I **need not (n't)/do not (n't) need to** see you.

254. She **dared** to escape.

255. She **dared not** escape.

256. He **used to** smoke.

257. He **usedn't to** smoke.

258. He **used not** to smoke. [Br.E]

259. He **didn't used** to smoke.

260. He **didn't use** to smoke.

261. He **must** come. [this is a positive obligation.]

262. He **mustn't/must not** come. [this is a negative obligation]

263. He/she/It **has to** come. [this is an external obligation]

264. He/She/It **doesn't/does not** have to come. [no obligation]

265. We/You/They **have to** come. [this is an external obligation.]

266. We/You/They **don't/do not** have to come. [There's no obligation.]

267. She **had better lock** the door.

268. She **had better not lock** the door.

269. **I'd rather have** him resign.

270. **I'd rather not have** him resign.

271. He **must be** telling lies. [I think he's.....]

272. He **can't be** telling lies. [I don't think he is.....]

16. Words negative in meaning

seldom, rarely, scarcely, hardly, barely, little, few

273. I *seldom* get sleep. (= almost no)

274. *Hardly anyone* wants this job. (= almost no one)

275. There were *few* people in the street. (= not many)

276. Her throat was so sore she could *barely* speak. (= hardly)

277. He *scarcely* goes out. (= almost never)

17. Only, Just

278. *Only* two of us had previous experience. (= The rest of us didn't)

279. I could *just* see her. (= very little of her)

18. Other negative expressions

280. He *denied* taking bribes.
281. He *forgot* to post the letter.
282. She *avoided* talking to me.
283. **Neither** Sukumar **nor** I believed the story.

un + words = ungrammatical, unbelievable
in +expressions = intolerable, inequality
im + word = immoral
a + word = apolitical, amoral
with + word = withhold
mis + word = misjudge
non + word = nonfiction
mal + word = malpractice
dis + word = disbelief
word + less = meaningless
anti + word = antiseptic
de + word = debug
il + word = illegal
ir + word = irregular

---

2. Questions

We can form questions with

- wh- words
  who/whom/what
  whose/which
  when/where/how/why

284. Who are you? (I'm) A teacher.
285. Who(m) do you want? (I want) The Manager.
286. What's this? (This is) A tractor.
287. What are you doing? (I'm) Painting.
288. Whose book is this? (This book is) Ramu's.
289. Which window was broken? The bedroom window (was broken).
290. When did she arrive? (She arrived) This afternoon.
291. Where did she do her masters? (She did her masters) At Baroda.

292. How was she reading? (She was reading) loudly.
293. Why did you slap him? (I slapped him because) he insulted me.

Note: It's only natural to give short responses to questions with wh-words.

Use *who* for general enquiry and *which* for specific response.

294. Who is your favourite actor? (of the several available)
295. Which is your favourite actor? (Kamal or Rajini)
296. What novels do you like? (non-specific-historical, social, political, spy, etc.)
297. Which novels do you like? (spy novels or murder mysteries)

Yes-No questions

These are formed with the help of

auxiliary/helping verbs			modal verbs	
be	have	do	will	would
am	has	does	shall	should
is		doing		
are	had	did	can	could
was		done	must	
were			have to	had to
being			may	
been				

298. Have they/we/I got the reservation? — Yes, they/we/you have. No, they/we/you haven't.

299. Haven't they/we/I got the reservation? (negative) — Yes, they/we/you have. No, they/we/you haven't.

300. Has he/she/it gone? — Yes, he/she/it has. No, he/she/it hasn't.

301. Hasn't he/she/it gone? (negative) — Yes, he/she/it has. No, he/she/it hasn't.

302. Will I/we/you/he/she/it/they wake up to the situation? — Yes, you/he/she/it/they will. No, you/he/she/it/they won't.

303. Do I/we/you/they pay for this? [**I pay = I do pay**] — Yes, you /we/they do. No, you/we/they don't.

304.	Don't I/we/you/they pay for this? (negative)	Yes, you/we/they do. No, you/we/they don't.
305.	Does he/she/it pay for this? [he pays = he does pay]	Yes, he/she/it does. No, he/she/it doesn't.
306.	Doesn't he/she/it pay for this? (negative)	Yes, he/she/it does. No, he/she/it doesn't.
307.	Did I/we/you/he/she/it/they pay for this? [I pa**id** = **Did** I pay]	Yes, you/we/he/she/it/they did. No, you/we/he/she/it/they didn't.
308.	Didn't I/we/you/he/she/it/they pay for this?	Yes, you/we/he/she/it/they did. No, you/we/he/she/it/they didn't.

Note: When a yes-no question is negative, influenced by our local language logic, we say 'yes' when we mean 'no'. This is wrong. 'Yes' doesn't carry negative meaning in English.

TAG Questions

Tag questions

- are shortened forms of yes-no questions and
- appear at the end of statement sentences.

They are positive if statements are negative and are negative if statements are positive, generally speaking.

309. I/we/you/they *have* come, *haven't* I/we/you/they?
I/we/you/they *have* come, have I/we/you/they not?
310. I/we/you/they have a problem, haven't I/we/you/they? (BrE)
I/we/you/they have a problem, don't I/we/you/they? (AmE)
311. He/she/it eats well, **does**n't he/she/it?
He/she/it eats well, does he/she/it not?
312. I/we/you/he/she/it/they *won't* come, *will* I/we/you/he/she/it/they?
313. I/we/you/they *haven't* eaten, *have* I/we/you/they?
314. He/she/it *hasn't eaten, has* he/she/it?

a few more tags

315. I suppose **you're not** serious, **are** you?
316. It's true, **isn't** it, that you're thinking of resigning.
317. They **used to** write to you, **didn't** they?

318. We **ought to** go now, **oughtn't we/shouldn't we?**

319. **Somebody open** this door, **will you? /will they?**

> **Note:** We in India have a tendency to use **isn't it/is it** as a tag question **to all statements.** This should be avoided and appropriate tag should be used.

More information on tag questions

320. *Let's go* back, *shall we*?

321. *Get* me a glass of water, *will you*?

322. *There's* no problem, *is there?*

323. *This man* is mad, *isn't he?*

324. *It's going* to rain, *isn't it?*

325. *It looks* like it's going to rain, *doesn't it?*

326. *Let's* have a full discussion, *shall we?*

327. *Lock* the door, *will you?*

328. *Close* the window, *will you?*

3. Reported Speech

We use verbs

say			
tell	to report	*statements*	(i)
ask			
want to know	to report	*yes-no questions*	(ii)
wonder		*wh-questions*	(iii)
tell, order			
command, ask	to report	*commands, directives, requests*	(iv)

Statements

329. "The train will arrive on time."

1 4

330. (a) My husband said the train would arrive on time.

1 3 4

(b) My husband said that the train would arrive on time.

1 2 3 4

(c) My husband said to me that the train would arrive on time.

1 2 4

(d) My husband told me the train would arrive on time.

1 2 3 4

(e) My husband told me that the train would arrive on time.

1.	**is the reporting verb.**
2.	**is the object to whom the report is made.**
3.	**'that' connects the reporting verbs with the reported statement.**
4.	**'will' changes to 'would' because the reporting verb is in the past tense.**

331. "I sold my house last Saturday."

1 4 4 4

332. (a) Sushma said she had sold her house last Saturday.

1 3 4 4 4

(b) Sushma said that she had sold her house last Saturday.

1 2 3 4 4 4

(c) Sushma said to her friend that she had sold her house last Saturday.

1 2 4 4 4

(d) Sushma told her friend she had sold her house last Saturday.

1 2 3 4 4 4

(e) Sushma told her friend that she had sold her house last Saturday.

1.	**is the reporting verb.**
2.	**is the object (person) to whom the report is made.**
3.	**'that' connects the reporting verb with the reported speech.**
4.	**'I' changes to 'she' and 'my' to 'her' because the person reporting is a woman.**
	'sold' changes to 'had sold'

329(a)-(e) and 332(a)-(e) clearly indicate the additions and the changes that are made in reported speech.

Additions

1. Reporting verb is used in the past tense, generally speaking.
2. A person with a name or in pronoun form is also used.
3. 'That' is used as a link between the reporting verb and the reported speech.

Changes

4. (i) Changes in the verb occur.

(ii) Changes in the pronoun occur.

Verb changes			Pronoun changes		
present	→	past	I	→	he (she)
present continuous	→	past continuous	me	→	him (her)
present perfect	→	past perfect	my	→	his (her)
past	→	past perfect	mine	→	his (hers)
future	→	future in the past	we	→	they
Shall	→	should	us	→	them
will	→	would	our	→	their
may	→	might	ours	→	theirs
can	→	could	you	→	he (she), they
have to	→	had to	your	→	his (her), their
			yours	→	his (hers), theirs

No changes

1. Verb changes will not occur if the reporting verbs is any one of these:

> says, is/are saying, has/have said, will say
> tells + obj, is/are telling + obj, have/has told + obj, have/has told + obj,
> will tell + obj

333. direct: "I'm not joining the party."

334. (a) She says
335. (b) She is saying
336. (c) She has said
337. (d) She will say
338. (e) She tells me
339. (f) She is telling me
340. (g) She has told me
341. (h) She will tell me

} (that) she isn't joining the party.

2. Verb **changes** will **not occur** if the statement (to be reported) contains a **repeated** or **habitual** action or a universal **truth**:

342. My wife always **drinks** coffee for breakfast.

343(a) Murugan **said** (that) his wife always *drinks* coffee for breakfast.

344. Oil **floats** on water.

345(a) The teacher **said** that oil **floats** on water.

Exercise 52

Change these into reported speech:

1. She said, "I can speak German."

 ____

2. You said to her, "If I had my pen, I would have answered the exercise."

 ____

3. He told me, "I've been trying Ramu's number without success."

 ____

4. They say, "We're leaving for our homes tonight."

 ____

5. I said to them, "I'll take you to my home."

 ____

6. She told me, "I must go to the Post office before it closes."

 ____

7. I'll tell my parents, "I'm not accepting the offer."

 ____

8. He said to the girl, "You can come with me if you like."

 ____

9. He said, "I have to catch an early train every morning."

 ____

10. I said, "I like my new house."

 ____

Yes-no question

346. direct → "Is Murugan your brother?"

indirect

1 2 3 4 4

347. (a) I asked Divya if (whether) Murugan was her brother.

1 3 4 4

348. (b) I wondered if (whether) Murugan was Divya's brother.

1 3 4 4

349. (c) I wanted to know if (whether) Murugan was Divya's brother.

1. is the reporting verb.
2. is the object (person) to whom the question is posed (which is optional)
3. 'if' or 'whether' connects the reporting verb with the reported speech.
4. (i) 'is' becomes 'was' and 'your' becomes 'her' or 'somebody's'
(ii) The question becomes a statement by changing the places of the subject and the verbs.

350. direct → "Will you help me?"
indirect

1 2 3 4 4 4

351. (a) He asked Yamini if she would help him.

352. direct → "Do you know Mr. Prabhakar?"
indirect

1 2 3 4 4

353. (a) She asked me if I knew Mr. Prbhakar.

354. direct → "Did you really talk to your boss?"
indirect

1 3 4 4 4 4

355. (a) I asked whether he had rally talked to his boss.

356. "Has Jamuna agreed to the marriage?"

1 2 4

357. (a) She wanted to know whether Jamuna had agreed to the marriage.

Note : The most usual reporting verb is "ask" with or without the object.

Exercise 53

1. "Are you hungry, Tharini?"

___

2. Prof Narayanan said, "Shall I close the window?"

___

3. Rohini said, "Is your new baby a boy or a girl, Mrs. Sharmila?"

___

4. "Have you had time to look at the object proposal?"

___

5. John said, "Do you think the Congress will win this time?"

___

Wh-questions

358. direct → "What is your name?"
Indirect

1 2 3 4
359. (a) She asked (me) what my name was.

1 3 4
360. (b) She wanted to know what my name was.

1 3 4
361. (c) She wondered what my name was.

> **1. is the reporting verb.**
> **2. is the object which is optional.**
> **3. the question words [What, how, where, when, why, whose] connect the reporting verb with the reported speech.**
> **4. (i) verb changes and pronoun changes occur.**
> **(ii) the question is turned into a statement.**

Exercise 54

1. "What do you want?"

____

2. I said, "How long does it take to get to Madurai?"

____

3. She said to her son, "Where did you put my purse?"

____

4. The stranger said, "Which hotel in Chennai is considered the best?"

____

5. "Why do they go to Bangalore often?"

____

Commands

362. direct → "Play the Veena, please."
Indirect

1 2 3
363. (a) She asked me to play the Veena.

1 2 3
364. (b) She requested her to play the Veena.

365. "Give me a ring as soon as you reach home."

1 2 3 4 4 4

366. (a) Abbas <u>asked</u> <u>Mukilan</u> <u>to</u> give <u>him</u> a ring as soon as <u>he</u> <u>reached</u> home.

367. "Don't open the door."

1 2 3

368. (a) He <u>asked</u> <u>me</u> <u>not to</u> open the door.

369. "Don't play the fool with me."

1 2 3 4

370.(a) He <u>told</u> <u>me</u> <u>not to</u> play the fool with <u>him</u>.

1. is the reporting verb [ask, request, order, tell]
2. is the object (person) to whom the question is posed (which is obligatory).
3. (not) 'to' links the reporting verb with the reported speech.
4. Verb changes and pronoun changes occur.

Exercise 55

1. "Don't listen to John."

2. She said, "Stop listening to John."

3. "Don't all answer at once."

4. The Inspector said to the constable, "Bring the prisoner to me."

5. Teacher said to students, "Write your names at the top of the paper."

Exercise 56

This exercise is on indirect speech. If necessary make changes in the following sentences.

1. He said her why wasn't she listening.
2. He told Raju their boss is coming next week.
3. I told to my father that I am not willing to go abroad.
4. The boss wondered if Seema was really working hard.
5. He asked the stranger if she could help.
6. She asked her brother where was he going.
7. They declared that if their representative was present she would have taken care of the problem.

8. The teacher asked Prema how did she perform in the examination.
9. The teacher said the sun was 92 million miles away.
10. She requested me that to play the piano.
11. The Director warned us not to be late the next day.
12. John wanted to know if Mary wanted lunch ordered.
13. They said this was the book they have been looking for.
14. The hunter asked whether we heard the lion's roar.
15. She said that how did you travel back home.
16. She said whether how you had travelled back home.
17. The officer told for the soldiers to not fire.
18. I promised to her that I won't be late.
19. I replied that I hadn't read the novel yet.
20. She informed us it was time to leave.
21. Renu asked for friend when is she coming to India.
22. The doctor advised to me that not to play for three weeks.
23. I asked Ravi what do you want to become?
24. The applicant wanted to know when will the results be announced.
25. She asked me if she could join me for dinner.

---

4. Concord – Subject-Verb Agreement

For sentences to be acceptable, there should be concord or agreement between words in **number**, **person** and **gender**.

- Number refers to singular and plural forms of nouns and pronouns.
- Person refers to first, second and third person forms of nouns and pronouns.
- Gender refers to male, female and neuter forms of nouns and pronouns.

Agreement exists between subject and verb when both are in the same person and number. Similarly, agreement exists between nouns and pronouns when they are in the same gender.
There are five tables below. The first four show you agreement between subject and verb. The fifth one lists pronouns.

Table 1 forms of the base* verb **BE** in both primary and *auxiliary* functions

person		present	past	-ing	-ed	future
1st	I	am*1/ 'm*1 am not*2/ 'm not*3 (aren't)*3	was*1 was not *2 wasn't *3	being	been	will*1/ 'll*1 / shall*1 will not*2/ 'll not*3/ shall not*2 won't *3
	we	are*1/ 're *1 are not*2/ 're not*3 aren't *3	were *1 were not *2 weren't *3	being	been	will*1/ 'll *1/ shall *1 will not/ 'll not*3/ shall not *2 won't *3
2nd	you	are*1/ 're *1 are not*2/ 're not*3 aren't *3	were *1 were not*2 weren't *3	being	been	will*1/ 'll *1 will not*2/ 'll not *3 won't *3
	you	are*1/ 're *1 are not*2/ 're not*3 aren't *3	were *1 were not *2 weren't *3	being	been	will*1/ 'll *1 will not*2/ 'll not *3 won't *3
3rd	he	is*1/ 's *1 is not*2/ 's not *3 isn't *3	was *1 was not *2 wasn't *3	being	been	will*1/ 'll *1 will not*2/ 'll not *3 won't *3
	she	is*1/ 's *1 is not*2/ 's not *3 isn't *3	was *1 was not *2 wasn't *3	being	been	will*1/ 'll *1 will not*2/ 'll not *3 won't *3
	it	is*1/ 's *1 is not*2/ 's not *3 isn't *3	was *1 was not *2 wasn't *3	being	been	will*1/ 'll *1 will not*2/ 'll not *3 won't *3
	they	are*1/ 're *1 are not*2/ 're not*3 aren't *3	were *1 were not *2 weren't *3	being	been	will*1/ 'll *1 will not*2/ 'll not *3 won't *3

Note: This refers to the Table 1 in the previous page:

* "base" is a lexical item as it appears in a dictionary.

1= nonnegative 2. uncontracted negative 3. contracted negative

"aren't": This is used because there is no "amn't" as a contracted negative for "am not" in British English for use in tag questions. "ain't" is non-standard but is in current use more in American English than in British English. "shan't" as a short form for "shall not" is nonexistent in American English and is becoming rare in British English.

Table 2 forms of the base verb **HAVE** in both <u>primary</u> and <u>*auxiliary*</u> functions

Person		present	past	-ing	-ed
1st	I	have/ ’ve have not/ ’ ve not haven’t	had/ ’d had not/ ’d not hadn’t	having	had
	we	have/ ’ve have not/ ’ve not haven’t	had/ ’d had not/ ’d not hadn’t	having	had
2nd	you	have/ ’ve have not/ ’ve not haven’t	had/ ’d had not/ ’d not hadn’t	having	had
	you	have/ ’ve have not/ ’ve not haven’t	had/ ’d had not/ ’d not hadn’t	having	had
3rd	he	has/ ’s has not/ ’s not hasn’t	had/ ’d had not/ ’d not hadn’t	having	had
	she	has/ ’s has not/ ’s not hasn’t	had/ ’d had not/ ’d not hadn’t	having	had
	it	has/ ’s has not/ ’s not hasn’t	had/ ’d had not/ ’d not hadn’t	having	had
	they	have/ ’ve have not/ ’ve not haven’t	had/ ’d had not/ ’d not hadn’t	having	had

Note: “ **’s**” = ‘is’ and ‘has’. “ **’d**” = ‘had’ and ‘would’.

Table 3 forms of the base verb **DO** in both primary and *auxiliary* functions

Person		present	past	-ing	-ed
1st	I	do do not don't	did did not didn't	doing	done
	we	do do not don't	did did not didn't	doing	done
2nd	you	do do not don't	did did not didn't	doing	done
	you	do do not don't	did did not didn't	doing	done
3rd	he	does does not doesn't	did did not didn't	doing	done
	she	does does not doesn't	did did not didn't	doing	done
	it	does does not doesn't	did did not didn't	doing	done
	they	do do not don't	did did not didn't	doing	done

Table 4 forms of **regular** verbs [that form their past tense with "-ed"]

base	roll	close	fry
-ing form	rolling	closing	frying
-s form	rolls	closes	fries
-ed form	rolled	closed	fried

Table 5 forms of **pronouns**

pronouns					
personal			possessive		reflexive
subjective		objective			
1st	I	me	my	mine	myself
	we	us	our	ours	ourselves
2nd	you	you	your	yours	yourself
	you	you	your	yours	yourself
	He	him	his	his	himself
3rd	she	her	her	hers	herself
	It	it	its	its	itself
	they	them	their	theirs	themselves

Concord of 3rd person number between subject and verb

1. Concord exists between a singular subject and a singular verb:

He speaks several languages.
Stephen walks a mile a day.
Anjali watches movies every evening.
['s' or 'es' is added to the base verb.]

My new car runs well.
That dog never stops barking.

2. Concord exists between a plural subject and a plural verb:

They **speak** several languages.

Hawkers **sell** their wares in the streets.

3. Concord exists between the **head** of a noun phrase and the singular base verb:

A **change** in your attitude is necessary if you wish to succeed.
[head]

A salient **feature** of these proposals is the underlying care for the disabled.
[head]

The **best** of the farewell speeches was made by our mathematics teacher.
[head]

One of the accused has surrendered.
[head]

Even the **best** of the batsmen fails sometimes.
[head]

4. Concord exists between a clause or phrase as a subject and the base verb:

How the book will sell depends on how the readers will receive it.
clause as a subject

To treat them as criminals is going too far.
phrase as a subject

To look after today's children requires immense patience.
phrase as a subject

Whether or not they'll support us depends on how well we convince them.
clause as a subject

Smoking cigarettes is injurious to health.

5. Concord exists between 'wh' clauses or phrases as subject and the base verb:

Whatever he may say is of little consequence.

What *ideas* he puts forward are not his.

6. Concord exists between a subject and the 'be' verb in the past:

He **was** reading a novel.

They **were** waiting for the bus.

7. Concord is not necessary in the case of verbs [other than 'be'] that are in the past:

   The baby slept. The babies slept. The student walked.
   The students walked.

8. The number concord does not apply to modal auxiliaries
   [can, could, may, might, shall, should, will, would, must] :

   You may leave. They may leave. She may leave.
   I may leave. We may leave.

9. The verb is in the singular if we are thinking of a collective noun as a single unit:

   The Committee has sanctioned the money. The public consists of you and me.
   India has lost the match. Our family is a happy one.
   The Management is happy with the contractual terms.
   The Indian team is wondering how they should react to the recent directives from the BCCI.
   [for the use of 'they' see point 20.]

10. The verb is in the plural if we are thinking of the members of a collective noun as individual and not as a group:

   The Committee have sanctioned the money. [not unanimously but by a majority]
   The Committee are divided in approving the plan.
   The public are fed up with the demonstrations.
   [not all people in a given a geographical area but a sizeable number of them]
   The government have ordered an enquiry into the gruesome incident.
   [here, 'government' refers to those officers concerned with public safety.]
   The Management are unhappy with the lukewarm response from the workers to their welfare measures. [some belonging to the management]
   India have won the match.

> Note: This distinction occurs in British English. American English generally treats singular collective nouns as singular.

11. Plural nouns of quantity or measure take a singular verb:

   Ten years **is** a long time to stay away from family.
   Two thirds of the area **is** submerged. Five kilos **is** what I want, not two.
   Fifty thousand rupees **was** a lot of money in the 1950s.

12. The verb is in the plural when two noun phrases joined by 'and' form the subject:[coordination]

   Shyam and I are prepared for every contingency.
   What he says and what he thinks do not seem to match.
   Your problem and mine are not very different.

13. More than one noun phrase as a subject even without 'and' takes a plural verb:

My digital camera, my DVD, my foreign currencies were confiscated by customs officials.

14. The verb is in the singular when two noun phrases are connected by:

with, as well as, rather than, after, as much as [quasi-coordinators]

Sundar, **with his classmates,** was responsible for the wreckage.
The captain, **as well as the other players,** was unhappy with the decision.
One student **after** another has protested against the expulsion.
Devi, **as much as her sisters,** was responsible for the tragedy.
Hemanth, **rather than Srikanth,** has to take the blame.

Separation of subject from the verb by quasicoordinators should be indicated by commas after subject and before verb.

15. The verb is in the plural when we use the following as subjects:

hardly any half some a lot of	of + plural noun

Hardly any of the guests **have** arrived.
Half of the members **disagree.**
Some of the teachers **are** unhappy.
A lot of viewers **have** praised our product.

1. None of the protestors **were** hurt.
2. None of the professors **is** hurt.
3. None of the sisters **is** married.
4. None of my relatives **live** near here.
5. None of my brothers **own** a house.
6. None of the shops **are** open today.

Traditional grammar insists on the verb being in the singular after 'none+of+plural noun as in 2 and 3. But notional concord allows a plural verb as in 1, 4, 5 and 6. Use of the verb in the plural is on the increase and generally accepted even in formal usage.

A number of people have responded to the ad.
A lot of money has been spent.
Some of the sugar is spilled.
Most of these apples have gone sour.
Most of the job is done.
Half of the mangoes are unripe and half are overriped.
Half of the land is covered with thick bush.
She is one of those [the athletes] who have not qualified for the Olympics..

16. Two <u>singular</u> noun phrases joined by "**either....or**" or "**neither....nor**"require a singular verb:

Either the teacher or the student **is** at fault.

Neither he nor she **has** understood the instructions.

But

The teacher or his students **are** to be blamed.

singular plural

The students or the teacher **is** to be blamed.

plural singular

Neither he nor she **have** understood the instructions.

['have' here is acceptable in less formal usage.]

Either
Neither | of them **have** committed the crime.

[Both notional concord and the proximity principle apply here.]

Either your brakes or your eyesight **is** at fault.

Either your eyesight or your breaks **are** at fault.

Such awkwardness can be avoided. Say:
Either your brakes are at fault or your eyesight is.
Either your eyesight is at fault or your brakes are.

17. A reflexive pronoun must agree with the noun phrase it is related to:

I hurt <u>myself</u> as I tripped over a stone.

He injured <u>himself</u> in both legs.

They didn't understand <u>themselves</u>.

she wrote to her brother about himself.

18. Relative pronoun 'who[m]' refers to people and 'which' to things:

He helps those who need help.

Yes, he's the one who[m] I saw picking the pocket.

Here's the screwdriver which I borrowed this morning.

19. Personal and possessive pronouns agree with person they refer to:

She hurt her foot. I've known Sailaja for years. She is a fine person.

Simi knew that she was late.

My parents didn't understand me at all. I felt sorry for them.

The dog wags its tail whenever it sees a friendly face.

20. use of 'they' to refer to a 3rd person singular:

7. Everyone thinks he has a right to decide his future.
8. No one need blame himself for the incident.
9. Nobody in his senses will reject this offer.
10. Has anybody lost his camera?
11. Every parent must provide for his family.
12. The borrower needs two guarantors to support his application.
13. Either he or she will have to change his or her attitude.
14. If a student fails to submit his assignment today he will not be allowed to continue the course.

1. Formal English requires the use of 'he', 'his', 'himself' as pronouns for *everyone, everybody, someone, somebody, anyone, anybody, no one, nobody, every + noun, nouns of common gender, either he or she.*
Such use of male pronouns is today thought of as **sex bias**.

2. To avoid this bias, 'he or she' or 's/he', 'himself/herself', 'his/her' have been tried. However, such use is thought to be awkward, especially when they have to be repeated like in this example:

14. If a student fails to submit his/her assignment today, he or she will not be allowed to continue the course.

3. So, 'they', their', 'themselves' have been used instead:

7. Everybody thinks they have a right to decide their future.
8. No one need blame themselves for the incident.

Such use was initially restricted to informal contexts. But now, it is increasingly accepted even in formal contexts because it is seen to achieve gender impartiality.

Of course, it's possible to avoid the use of 'they':

i. make the subject plural:

If students fail to submit their assignment today, they will not be allowed to continue the course.
We have a right to decide our future.
None of us need blame ourselves for the incident.
None of us in our senses will reject this offer.
Has any of you lost your camera?
All parents must provide for their family.
Borrowers need two guarantors to support their loan application.

ii. rephrase the sentence:

Either he will have to change his attitude or she hers.

21. 'One' is also used as pronoun reference:

One needs to think before one reacts.

[American English may permit the use of 'he', 'him', 'his' in the place of 'one'.]

The exercises that follow contain errors that are similar to the ones you'll find in TOEFL questions.

Exercise 57

Rewrite those sentences that do not show agreement between subject and verb and between subject and pronoun references [you may take the help of the tables in the previous pages and also the twenty-one points in the previous pages]:

1. Where is my spectacles?

   ____

2. Renowned management educators of global repute are leading our programs.

   ____

3. It's I who is to blame.

   ____

4. 'Student satisfaction' is one of the factors that attracts students to this Institution.

   ____

5. A number of books on AIDS is available.

   ____

6. The Disciplinary Committee were divided on the nature of punishment.

   ____

7. The future of Indian business lie in the hands of today's MBAs.

   ____

8. A possible connection between smoking and cancer have been shown by research.

   ____

9. A break-up of various industries that hired our students are as follows: ………

   ____

10. Neither my parents nor my friends have understood my problem.

   ____

11. She watches every step the dance master make and then try it herself.

____

12. Each guest was talking at the top of his voice.

____

13. Several revisions were made before the plan were submitted for approval.

____

14. Our executive MBA program meets the needs of mid-career executives which are preparing for senior management, and they enhances the skills and effectiveness of senior executives.

____

____

15. The Chinese Prime Minister, accompanied by his officials, has come to India on a four-day tour.

____

16. Any community are knit together by some commonly-held beliefs.

____

17. I can't understand how you has misunderstood my letter.

____

18. My father never get angry with me.

____

19. I was willing to go to the market.

____

20. Suresh has never been an ambitious person.

____

21. The present study focus on assessing the relationship between selected maternal factors and birth weight of a newborn.

____

____

22. The birth weight of a normal newborn found to be more in taller women.

____

23. Much of the prenatal women had inadequate knowledge of maternal nutrition.

____

24. The findings of the study indicates that there were significant relationship between maternal factors and the birth weight of a newborn.

____

25. In most parts of India, the mean birth weight are between 2.7 kgs and 2.9 kgs.

____

26. Maternal factors or fetal conditions that adversely affects the vascularity of the placenta will be discussed in this chapter.

____

27. The frequency of previous pregnancies are more likely to influence the low birth weight of the newborns.

____

28. The joy you experience is its own reward.

____

29. Sajan and Surya, behave yourself!

____

30. Some of these genetic maps show the positions of hundreds of genes.

____

31. Such abnormal chromosomes continue to duplicate itself in the new form.

____

32. A number of other traits is inherited in man in the same sex-linked was as color blindness.

____

33. Generally, the pairing of chromosomes is very exact, with the chromosomes lining up against each other gene by gene.

____

34. Reduplications produce various effects, ranging from being lethal to no effect at all.

____

35. Some characters are affected by many more than four genes.

____

36. Although the properties of proteins depend on their amino acid sequence, there are generally more than one sequence that make a protein with about the same properties.

____

____

37. Man probably have at least 10,000 different kinds of proteins most of whom are indispensable.

____

38. Since there are a one-to-one relationship between genes and proteins, the problem of how the genes determine the nature of the organism are essentially the problem of how they specify the amino acid sequences of proteins.

____

39. Women, which are carriers of hemophilia, for example, tend to have slightly lower levels of the blood clotting protein.

____

____

40. Another addition to genome complexity is the "jumping genes," who are able to move from place to place on the same chromosome or onto a different chromosome.

____

____

41. Historians differ on the chronology of this process.

____

42. There was much speculation as to whether the land could support the growing numbers of people except in misery.

____

43. There are hardly any buildings in this part of the town.

____

44. During this period, ventilation of mines were improved.

____

45. I want an hour's permission; I needs to go to the bank.

____

46. Each guest was talking at the top of their voice.

____

47. Each of the girls have won a prize.

48. Each solid object have three principal dimensions in space: width, height and depth.

49. In Fig.2, the terminals has been indicated by the capital letters E for emitter, C for collector and B for base.

50. A baseball is dropped from an altitude h=60m and are found to be travelling at 26 m/s when it strike the ground.

51. Here X stand for the space variables.

52. In principle, the choice of basis to use for the boundary conditions is arbitrary.

53. I don't know when he will come.

54. I'll tell him when he will come.

55. " Will they all come?" " I think they shall."

56. There was a time when "you" was second person plural pronoun.

57. Each of the variables assume importance in this context.

58. In addition to these basic equation solvers, there is four outer groups of programs.

59. When A is symmetric positive-definite, the Cholesky method produce a symmetric factorisation.

60. Integers on the first line define the number of triangles desired in the final triangulation.

[61-100 contain more than one sentence each. Check for concord in all the sentences.]

61. Now Susan were even more doubtful. Encryption algorithms were just mathematical formulas, recipes for scrambling text into code.

____

____

62. "I'm sure you can guess," Strathmore said. "He's not too fond of the NSA." "Well, that narrow it down!" she snapped sarcastically.

____

____

63. "Can we pay Tankado off? I know he hate us, but can't we offer him a few million dollars? Convinces him not to distribute?"

____

____

64. "The EFF doesn't have the first clue about what we does here," Strathmore railed in disgust.

____

65. "At this point, all we have on North Dakota are an anonymous address."

____

66. "Commander, sir. I….I'm sorry to bother you, but the Run-Monitor…..I ran a virus probe and –" " Phil, Phil, Phil," the commander gushed pleasantly as the put a reassuring hand on Chartrukian's shoulder. "Slow down. What seem to be the problem?"

____

67. "Yes, sir. As I'm sure a man of stature is well aware, the Canadian government works hard to protect their countrymen from the indignities……."

____

____

68. He insists that the public need someone to watch over them.

____

69. "They makes a great pair, don't they?" Hale smiled.

____

70. When the E-mail opened, they were a single line. Susan read it. And then she read it again.

____

71. "What do he look like—in his photo? Perhaps I will recognize him."

____

72. "I need to know if a friend of mine made that flight. She was flying standby." The woman frowned. "I'm sorry, sir. There was several standby passengers tonight, but our privacy clause state….."

____

____

73. She gave him a wink. "What's her name?"
"Megan," he replied sadly.
The agent smiled. "Do your lady friend have a last name?"

____

____

74. "I'll erase it before I go," Midge promised. "Unless you and your wife wants it for your private collection."

____

75. Strathmore's voice moved closer. "Let her go."
"No way. You shall kill me."
"I'm not going to kill anyone."

____

____

76. He was surprised to read the news about herself on the front page.

____

77. Susan surprised herself by grabbing the Beretta.

____

78. Becker asked, " Where is his belongings?"

____

79. "And of course there's Christopher Columbus." The officer beamed. "He's buriedin our cathedral."
Becker looked up. " Really? I thought Columbus was buried in the Dominican Republic."
"Hell, no! Who start these rumours? Columbus's body is here in Spain!…."

____

____

80. "Most destructive applications wipes a databank clean," Jabba continued, "but this one is more complex. It delete only those files that falls within certain parameters."

____

____

81. “Cool it!” Fontaine ordered. “What parameters are this worm looking for?…….”

82. David Becker read the inscription, and Jabba typed. When he was done, they double-checked the spelling and omitted all the spaces.

83. Raindrops falls because *everything* falls!

84. The laws of physics are the canvas God laid down on which to paint his masterpiece.

85. Vittoria nodded. “And when my father ran his experiment, sure enough, *two* kinds of matter appeared.”

86. “But there are enormous technological barriers to actually *storing* antimatter.

87. Langdon was intrigued. “So you’re saying that whether you are a Christian or a Muslim simply depends on where you were born?”

88. “Will the little lambs squeal when it dies?”

89. The protection of these holy places have been my sole charge for over two decades.

90. Recharging the batteries is necessary to avoid detonation.

91. Vittoria reached in her shirt pocket and produced her cell phone. “Plenty of tourists carry phones.”

92. The Illuminati altars of science was here in Rome.

93. The guard did not blink. “ I have trained to follow orders. Not debate them.”

94. How he came to be dressed this way and why he was not in conclave remains a mystery.

95. Although MSNBC has yet to confirm a motive for the attack, our sources tells us that responsibility for the murders have been claimed by a group calling themselves the Illuminati.

96. "It appears," the camerlengo said finally, sounding too devastated to be angry, "we have not contained this crisis as well as I was led to believe."

97. I warn you, look around yourselves. The promises of science have not been kept. Promises of efficiency and simplicity have bred nothing but pollution and chaos.

98. We've got a caller here who says he has information that can help us.

99. However much you may try, you shall never find what you're looking for.

100. The only lights on the castle were exterior floods illuminating the façade.

Correction of Errors

You've already practised correcting errors that crop up when we form sentences. Take a look at the Exercises 58 and 59 in the section on 'Subject-Verb Agreement'. Here you can have more practice in correcting a few more errors.

Exercise 58

Rewrite the following sentences only if there is no agreement.

1. The number of failures are high.

2. It's I who is to blame.

3. Our General Manager, accompanied by his family, is lunching with us this afternoon.

____

4. A number of books on Aids is available.

____

5. India support the moves of the American government against Iraq.

____

6. A possible connection between cancer and smoking have been shown by research.

____

7. I want an hour's permission; I needs to go to the bank.

____

8. Babies need constant attention.

____

9. The public consists of you and me.

____

10. The ends of metal is heated to a white heat.

____

11. Everyone was talking at the top of his voice.

____

12. Each of the girls have won a prize.

____

13. Neither the students nor the teacher has understood the new rule.

____

14. Even five thousand rupees were a lot of money in the 1950s.

____

15. Fish and chips are getting very expensive.

____

16. The hammer and the sickle was flying from the flagpole.

____

17. The chapter conclude on a sad note.

____

18. Society are knit together by some commonly held beliefs.

____

19. They has misunderstood my letter.

____

20. A sealing wax is a type of wax that melt quickly.

____

21. Each solid object have three principal dimensions in space: width, height and depth.

22. Each face of the object appear as it is seen from the front, top and side.

23. In Fig.2, the terminals has been indicated by the capital letters E for emitter, C for collector and B for base.

24. The depletion region has been reduced in width.

25. Table 2.1 summarize these relationships for the three passive circuit elements.

26. This chapter place a great emphasis on the idea of language.

27. The polynomial degree m are related to the smoothness of f(x).

28. Find the speed after the ship have gone 1 nautical mile.

29. A baseball is dropped from an altitude h=60m and are found to be traveling at 26 m/s when it strike the ground.

30. A mass system is said to be conservative if it do not lose energy by virtue of internal friction forces that does negative work or by virtue of nonelastic members which dissipates energy upon cycling.

31. We concludes, therefore, that the angular velocity w have no influence on the moment equation about the mass center G.

32. The proof follow the idea used in the 2 by 2 example earlier.

33. Recall that a triangular matrix is singular if and only if one of its diagonal elements are zero.

34. Then there is no linear functionals for 10.2.32 as Lbi =0 for all i.

35. The last example illustrate that there are non-standard methods which can be constructed rather easily.

36. Here X stand for the space variables.

37. In principle, the choice of basis to use for the boundary conditions is arbitrary.

38. Initial conditions is specified for the time dependent problem.

39. The term "image description" have also been used in this case. [50,51]

40. In most cases, the images to be recognized is given in such digitized form.

Exercise 59

Correct the following sentences, where necessary:

1. Arjun never get angry.

2. Suja dresses well.

3. Somu is one of those who has not understood the problem.

4. The shopkeeper was not willing to close the shop.

5. One of the students have rebelled against the English teacher.

6. I heard a noise. Did anyone speak?

7. The principal have not agreed to the proposal.

8. No, Sheela haven't come today. But I think she shall come tomorrow.

9. The street dogs are always barking.

10. The woman at the door appear to be angry.

11. The H.O.D. is annoyed when I told her I couldn't take part in the competition.

12. It was raining the whole night. But we are blissfully sleep.

13. "My principal want parents to attend the meeting. Shall you come?"

14. I haven't attended the meeting yesterday.

15. If you want to know about London, speak to Suganti. She's been to London twice.

16. "Here is the novel. I finished reading it."

17. Buddha's teachings stressed the importance of Karma.

18. I told you the truth. Why aren't you believing me ?

19. I'll tell him when he'll come.

20. "I hear you're constructing a house ?"
"Yes."
"Do you let it out?"
"No. I'm going to move in myself."

21. He said, "Why you don't join us?"

22. He said he was coming, isn't it?

23. He said he was coming, wasn't he ?

24. They have no choice. They shall obey the laws of the land.

25. "Will he come?" "I think he shall".

26. Rajesh, you don't listen to me. Aren't you well?

27. When the speaker sat down, my friend asked me, "For a beginner, she was speaking very well, don't you think?"

28. If you love me you wouldn't be so cruel to me.

29. We've bought the latest machineries.

30. They described in detail about their experiences in Africa.

31. He asked, "When you were married?"

32. The furniture's need repairing, isn't it?

33. They are always discussing about politics. It's disgusting.

34. The speaker emphasized on the need for reform.

____

35. One has to put in a lot of interest in his work.

____

36. It's time we take a holiday.

____

37. We elected Mr. Srivatsan President.

____

38. We have party tonight. Come and enjoy!

____

39. In addition, a range of values are provided for each parameter for guidance in the initial design or analysis of a system.

____

____

40. These surfaces are identified by finish marks, which appear as a small V or script F on all views of the surface, where it appear as a line (edge view).

____

____

____

41. The system of symbols are described in the following sections.

____

42. Each of the variable assume importance in this context.

____

43. In addition to these basic equation solvers, there is four outer groups of programs.

____

____

44. There is a version LEQ of LEQTIF for linear systems whose coefficient matrix do not fit in main memory.

____

____

45. When A is symmetric positive-definite, the Cholesky method produce a symmetric factorization.

____

____

46. In principle, the choice of basis to use for the boundary conditions are arbitrary.

____

____

47. Explicit examples of this form are as follows:

____

48. The last example illustrate that there is nonstandard methods which can be construct rather easily.

____

____

49. Integers on the first line define the number of triangles desired in the final triangulation.

____

____

50. An "unreasonable" distribution of points does not always give large errors.

____

____

Exercise 60

Rewrite these sentences which are not acceptable:

1. The metal was hot that I couldn't touch it.

   ____

2. The thief ran so quickly to catch him.

   ____

3. Will you be patient enough for listening to me?

   ____

4. He's a rude man that you cannot talk to him.

   ____

5. I went to an astrologer in order that I knew my future.

   ____

6. We played the game well that we won it.

   ____

7. We played the game well so that we won it.

   ____

8. I hid myself lest the policeman saw me.

   ____

9. I am used to obeying orders.

   ____

10. The calculator is used to make complex calculations quickly.

    ____

11. She pulled me towards her in order to save me from being run over.

    ____

    ____

12. She came into the bedroom quietly so as to wake the baby.

____

13. We joined the library so as to have plenty to read.

____

14. I'll give you a key so that you got into the house whenever you like.

____

15. She took my shoes so that I left the house.

____

16. There was so much dust that we saw what was happening.

____

17. He didn't dare copy from his neighbour lest he was recognized.

____

18. I stayed indoors lest I should be in the rain.

____

19. My wife learnt German so that she helped me with my work.

____

20. The President's speech went on for so long that the audience did not feel bored.

____

____

21. He told that he had lost his job.

____

22. She said me that she was quitting the job.

____

23. He told to me that he had been thinking of selling his house but decided not to.

____

____

24. He said that he's meeting his boss in the evening.

____

25. I asked to my wife where you went.

____

26. I wanted to know if my father is resigning.

____

27. He ordered me not to accept my resignation.

____

28. My friend told me whether I heard the lion roar.

____

29. She wondered how they will travel back home.

30. He advised her to think before she answered.

Exercise 61

Correct the following sentences where necessary. These errors are to do with **how we use different expressions to convey meanings/thoughts**:

1. It took us two hours to walk across the forest.

2. The young boy swam through the river.

3. According to me, the rent is too high.

4. I've got a headache. I won't be able to make it to the party.

5. The population of Chennai used to be higher than present.

6. She spoke to me very friendly.

7. I'm working too hardly this year.

8. The unemployed are increasing in number every year.

9. Always I make the same mistake.

10. We're tomorrow leaving for Coimbatore.

11. You should have definitely been working this morning.

12. I don't think the repair has properly been done.

13. Come at four o'clock to my office.

14. Give me a ring after you'll have arrived.

____

15. "What's your age?" "I'm thirty five old."

____

16. She has left college three years ago.

____

17. She started working for this company before three years.

____

18. It is not allowed to smoke in the lecture hall.

____

19. "Let me to go," he cried.

____

20. All along the journey she kept complaining.

____

21. "Tilak is unhappy, isn't he?" "May be he didn't get a raise, or alternately may be he's been transferred."

____

____

22. My brother is studying to be doctor.

____

23. The water is made of hydrogen and oxygen.

____

24. The society turns people into criminals and then lock them up.

____

25. She plays Veena extremely well.

____

26. I think there's the letter for you.

____

27. Could I have five rupees stamp?

____

28. "What's that?" "It's a adjustable spanner."

____

29. The men and the women have similar abilities and needs.

____

30. She was elected the President for third time.

____

31. Why do you want to be secretary?

32. Why is she looking at me as though she knows me? I've never seen her before in my life.

33. She's not as intelligent as her sister.

34. Hold it in your left hand, how I told you.

35. She asked for the price of onions.

36. If you ask the time to a policeman, he will always tell you.

37. I couldn't find my pen, so I asked Sam to use his.

38. You have blood in your forehead.

39. I live in 2 Thirumal Nagar Extension I.

40. I live on the third floor.

41. When you'll return the book back to me?

42. I think I'll put the table before the window.

43. Are you born in 1975?

44. Borrow me your comb for a minute, will you?

45. Can I lend your bicycle? I need to go to market.

46. I can to speak with the Manager, if you wish me to.

47. "Will you answer the phone?" "It can be your mother."

48. I'll tell you as soon as I'll know.

____

49. Although I was tired but continued my work.

____

50. If I had a lot of money, I'd do what I'd like.

____

51. He never listens to advice which I give it to him.

____

52. Is it true that your sister divorced last moth?

____

53. Who did see the accident?

____

54. "Who did you meet?" "The Assistant Manager."

____

55. He opened the door but couldn't see nobody.

____

56. My headache's much better. Those tablets are efficient.

____

57. "I don't like sweets." "I also don't."

____

58. Did you enjoy very much at the party last night?

____

59. It's late enough that we can stop work.

____

60. The Manager got very angry; even he told the clerk to resign.

____

61. Have you been to Delhi before in you life?

____

62. I'll wait for you at exactly ten o'clock.

____

63. Please explain me how to fill this application.

____

64. They keep fighting all the time; there's a little understanding between them.

____

____

65. "What do the doctors say?" "There's little hope, they say."

66. His lecture was very technical, a few people understood it.

67. His lecture was very technical; but few understood it.

68. I have known her since a long time.

69. By next March I'll have been here since seven years.

70. I've forgotten my umbrella at home.

71. There's a nice little café in front of our house.

72. I'll have been here for twenty years next May.

73. I live half of a mile from here.

74. "How long have you been waiting?" "one and a half hour."

75. Suddenly I listened a strange noise.

76. If you would have asked me, I would have told you the whole story.

77. I'll come and see you in case, I pass through Hyderabad.

78. She lets her children to stay up very late.

JAWAHARLAL NEHRU TECHNOLOGICAL UNIVERSITY

HYDERABAD

III Year B.Tech EEE II-Sem

T	P	C
0	3	2

ADVANCED ENGLISH COMMUNICATIONS SKILLS LAB

1. Introduction

The introduction of the English Language Lab is considered essential at 3rd year level. At this stage the students need to prepare themselves for their careers which may require them to listen to, read, speak and write in English both for their professional and interpersonal communication in the globalised context.

The proposed course should be an integrated theory and lab course to enable students to use 'good' English and perform the following:

Gather ideas and information, to organise ideas relevantly and coherently.

Engage in debates.

Participate in group discussions.

Face interviews.

Write project/research reports/technical reports.

Make oral presentations.

Write formal letters.

Transfer information from non-verbal to verbal texts and vice versa.

To take part in social and professional communication.

2. Objectives:

This Lab focuses on using computer-aided multimedia instruction for language development to meet the following targets:

To improve the students' fluency in English, through a well-developed vocabulary and enable them to listen to English spoken at normal conversational speed by educated English speakers and respond appropriately in different socio-cultural and professional contexts.

Further, they would be required to communicate their ideas relevantly and coherently in writing.

3. Syllabus:

The following course content is prescribed for the Advanced Communication Skills Lab:

Functional English - starting a conversation – responding appropriately and relevantly – using the right body language – role play in different situations.

Vocabulary building – synonyms and antonyms, word roots, one-word substitutes, prefixes and suffixes, study of word origin, analogy, idioms and phrases.

Group Discussion – dynamics of group discussion , intervention, summarizing, modulation of voice, body language, relevance, fluency and coherence.

Interview Skills – concept and process, pre-interview planning, opening strategies, answering strategies, interview through tele and video-conferencing.

Resume' writing – structure and presentation, planning, defining the career objective, projecting ones strengths and skill-sets, summary, formats and styles, letter-writing.

Reading comprehension – reading for facts, guessing meanings from context, scanning, skimming, inferring meaning, critical reading.

Technical Report writing – Types of formats and styles, subject matter – organization, clarity, coherence and style, planning, data-collection, tools, analysis.

4. Minimum Requirement:

The English Language Lab shall have two parts:

The Computer aided Language Lab for 60 students with 60 systems, one master console, LAN facility and English language software for self- study by learners.

The Communication Skills Lab with movable chairs and audio-visual aids with a P.A System, a T. V., a digital stereo –audio & video system and camcorder etc.

System Requirement (Hardware component):

Computer network with Lan with minimum 60 multimedia systems with the following specifications:

P – IV Processor

Speed – 2.8 GHZ

RAM – 512 MB Minimum

Hard Disk – 80 GB

Headphones of High quality

5. Suggested Software:

The software consisting of the prescribed topics elaborated above should be procured and used. Suggested Software:

Clarity Pronunciation Power – part II

Oxford Advanced Learner's Compass, 7th Edition

DELTA's key to the Next Generation TOEFL Test: Advanced Skill Practice.

Lingua TOEFL CBT Insider, by Dreamtech